Report from a Swedish Village

Sture Källberg

Translated by Angela Gibbs

Introduction by Jan Myrdal

Penguin Books

Penguin Books Ltd, Harmondsworth,
Middlesex, England
Penguin Books Inc., 7110 Ambassador Road,
Baltimore, Maryland 21207, U.S.A.
Penguin Books Australia Ltd, Ringwood,
Victoria, Australia

Rapport fran medels rensk stad. Västerås
First published 1969
This translation first published in the U.S.A. by Pantheon Books 1972
First published in Great Britain by Pelican Books 1972
Copyright © Sture Källberg, 1969
Translation copyright © Pantheon Books, 1972

Made and printed in Great Britain by
Hazell Watson & Viney Ltd,
Aylesbury, Bucks
Set in Monotype Plantin

014 021 4356

T

Pelican Books
Report from a Swedish Village

Sture Källberg is a Swedish freelance journalist and writer. He spent six years at a state school and helped work his parents' farm from an early age. He got his first job at sixteen and has been a factory worker, driver, heavy plater and builder before becoming a writer. For eight years he travelled in east and west European countries, in West Africa and China, North Vietnam and Laos. He now lives outside Stockholm writing essays, short stories and magazine articles, and he is the author of *Rebellion – Budapest 1956*, an account of the Hungarian uprising of 1956, and editor of the *Selected Writings of Ho Chi Minh*.

Contents

Introduction by Jan Myrdal

A Gallery of Swedes

The people in this book are typical. But they are not typical in general. They are individual Swedes; they are not anonymous. The names are their names; they have read what Källberg has written and they have approved of it being printed. This is an important fact about this book. It raises several questions: formal questions – to which I will come back later – and general, social questions.

It is evident that these Swedes were ordinary Swedes, secure in their distrust of people 'above' them. This is not a point which Källberg tries to make; it is a self-evident fact. These Swedes also take it for granted that everybody is suspicious of people 'up there': the decision-makers, the government, the leaders of the organizations. The people Källberg presents are not fictionalized Swedes, they are typical Swedes with individual names.

You will not find them in the official Swedish publications. You will not find them in the publications distributed abroad by the Swedish Institute for Cultural Relations with Foreign Countries. You will not find them in the different publications that in one way or another are subsidized by the Institute or by the Royal Ministry of Foreign Affairs. You will not find them in the publications that are being distributed by the banks, the trade unions, the Party. This is not because these institutions are necessarily lying (even though they of course lie when it is politically important to do so). But they are 'up there', which by definition in Sweden makes it impossible for them to see and hear the people outside their bureaux. Whether these bureaux belong to the trade unions or the Chamber of Commerce or the banks or the Social Democratic Party does not make any great difference. The atmosphere is the same, so is the personnel. Any study of dining among Swedes will show that Swedish labour leaders (once they become leaders) dine with bankers but not with workers. Of course the leaders of the different organizations take care of their members. In Sweden a new word, '*medlemsvård*', has been coined during the last decades to express this function of the bureaux. '*Medlemsvård*' (membership-care) is the term used to designate the activity of taking care of members. In all large organizations several high-salaried posts have been created to deal with this care. (The change of high-level leadership through the actions of members is something we have only read about in history books.)

The fact that ordinary Swedes are suspicious and distrustful does not mean that they are rebellious. Sweden is – I believe – heading towards widespread revolt and rebellion, but these people that Källberg describes are not in a state of rebellion. They are trying to accommodate in a country where they do not trust the decision-makers and where the official ideology functions as an ideology.

Their distrust is thus not that of conscious rebellion but that of suspicious peasants and sharecroppers. Industrialization came late to Sweden. Most Swedes are but a generation from farming and the traditional wariness of poor peasants and sharecroppers still forms much of their thinking. Only a generation ago the proverb said: ' "When I am dining with Abraham, Isaac and Jacob and you are thirsting in Hell – then you will have your reward," said the sharecropper to the Count.' Today the same thought is expressed in less religious terms, but still it is not rebellion.

The people in this book tell of a period of great change. The change from a rural to an urban Sweden, the change to a highly-developed industrialized country. They move from the village to the city, and then the city moves out and takes over their old village. But the pattern has remained the same.

These people are named by their own names. They talk,

they say no more than what they want to say. Thus it would be simple to say that Källberg is a spokesman, that he has performed the role of a secretary to a group of Swedes on the northern shore of Lake Mälar.

In reality the situation is much more complicated. Källberg has acted as their voice. This is often misunderstood. It is as if 'literature' and 'fiction' was the same thing and there was a division only between 'fiction' and 'fact'. Källberg would then be classified as a reporter or as a sociologist. But this book carries on a well-defined tradition in Swedish – and not only Swedish – literature. It is a book in the tradition of the great epic realists like the Swedish writer, Ivar Lo-Johansson. The describers of reality, the tongues of the people. The importance of this book then is not only that it describes a Sweden different from – and to us much more real than – the Sweden of the Swedish Institute for Cultural Relations with Foreign Countries, but also that it is a part of the re-establishment of literature in Swedish letters.

As Sweden slowly changes from distrust and suspicion to revolt, literature is being taken back by the people. Taken away from the aesthetes, the art-loving bankers and bureaucrats, and once more becoming the literary expression of the people. In this general movement Källberg is playing an important role.

Foreword

This is an attempt to portray the everyday life and reality of ordinary people. The ones who don't make a very big stir in the world. None of the names in this report are invented. It took seven months to complete the interviews, and all those involved patiently put up with my practice of taking down all the notes by hand. I did this because written text is easier to take in. Writing is, among other things, a process of clarifying contexts, and in order to do this, you have to have a broad survey. Countless times the people interviewed asked me to read back to them what we had written last Friday or Tuesday and then changed or added something. Gradually the number of pages of notes crept up to 1,200 with almost as many cups of coffee. Thank you all! Throughout the time I spent collecting my material I lived in Västerås. The city's Board of Culture helped with the rent. The money came at a very good time, thank you! Five of the contributors were schoolmates of mine in Kärrbo. We had not seen each other since our schooldays, until now. All twelve people have read and approved the stories they told.

The reason it happened to be these particular twelve out of eight million Swedes is a story by itself. It all began when I went to Västerås. Out of 130 towns in Sweden, I picked Västerås partly because I grew up outside that city and was familiar with the area, and partly because Västerås is the most *Swedish* place I know. It's a rapidly expanding industrial town, rather dull and colourless, with decent, hard-working residents who seldom do any drinking more than once a week and who think Västerås is the best place on earth, or at least in Sweden.

I was thinking of calling the book that I would write *A*

Portrait of Sweden. Then I read the American Marquis Childs's enthusiastic book *Sweden: The Middle Way* (Yale University Press, 1936, 1938, 1947, 1961), praising Swedish politics of the thirties. And I thought that my book should have the name, *Sweden: The Middle Way That Failed.* But the book was still unwritten.

Originally I had planned to do brief interviews with a lot of people and use their stories as bits of a mosaic. In this way I would produce an image of Västerås and Sweden. But the more I thought about the matter, the more questionable the method appeared to be. That picture would be far too random. I hadn't yet had time to begin the mosaic when I rejected the whole idea.

There I stood without even a working plan. The only thing I knew was which people I wanted to write about. I didn't want to write about executives or civil servants, teachers, intellectuals, shopkeepers, or other categories of that sort. These groups make themselves heard all the time in novels and plays, in newspapers and magazines, in radio and T.V. I wanted to write about those who seldom or never are heard from, the ordinary folks who toil away year after year at hard jobs, the many who in the end support the entire society. I've been a worker myself and know what it's like.

One day it struck me that nowadays many of my schoolmates probably lived in Västerås. We'd gone to school in Kärrbo, a farming parish twenty kilometres outside Västerås. Most moved into town after school and took jobs there. Since I still hadn't got anything done on my book I could just as well use the time to look some of them up.

The fellows didn't give me any trouble. They still had their own names and were listed in the telephone directory. Tracking down the girls was considerably more difficult. They had lost their identity and got new names at their wedding. I looked up Zachrisson, Nils, Karlfeldtsgatan 13C, in the directory, tel. 119322.

'Well, God damn it, is it *you*! Where've you been all these years? Come on over so we can talk! I live over by Skallberget. Go out to Salavägen and then take a left at Svärdsliljegaten.'

Through him I found out that Herman Andersson was a construction worker in Västerås and that 'Sessan' Karlsson had got married to somebody named Sjökvist and lived in a little place out on the way to Lövsta across from a taxi-stand.

From then on every day and every evening was spent talking with first one person and then another, and I found out more about what had actually happened to Västerås and its residents during the past twenty-five years than if I'd read ever so many official reports and investigations.

That's how it happened. I found a key and was able to un-lock the city. Suddenly I saw how my book would be written.

Of course, the main thing that's happened in Sweden after the Second World War is that a large part of the population has moved, or rather been forced to move, from the countryside to the cities. Most of them have moved as short a way as possible, to the closest town – from Kärrbo to Västerås.

To put it briefly: Sweden has changed but not the Swedes.

Sture Källberg

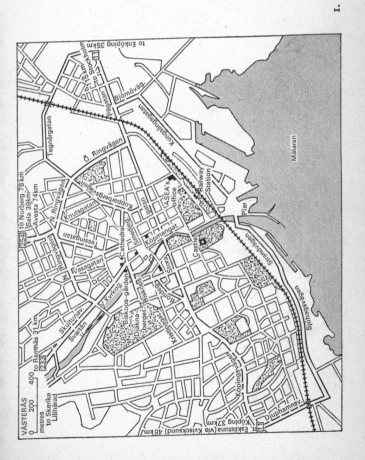

1. The city centre of Västerås

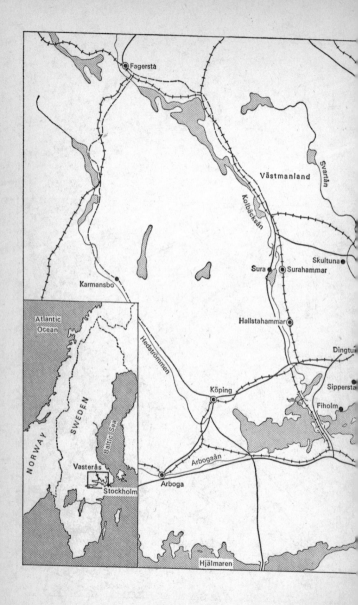

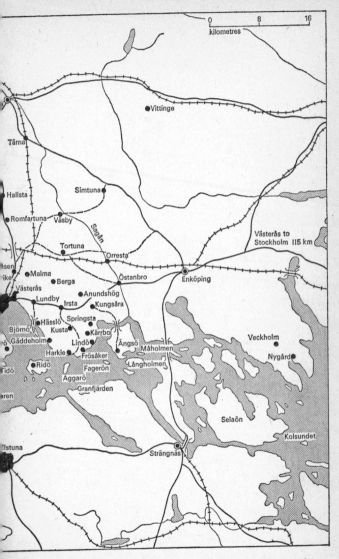

2. Västmanland – the province north of Lake Mälar and west of Stockholm

Population Table for Kärrbo and Västerås

Year	Kärrbo	Västerås
1900	612	15,243
1905	590	18,261
1910	621	22,489
1915	598	28,802
1920	586	30,633
1925	593	29,215
1930	532	30,376
1935	472	32,570
1940	363	38,597
1945	349	48,657
1950	280	59,877
1955	254	68,197
1960	216	77,946
1965	181	89,003

On 1 January 1967, Kärrbo and many other districts were incorporated into Västerås. On 1 January 1970 the population of Västerås was 113,389 people, of whom 157 lived in Kärrbo.

Västerås became a city in the twelfth century. Its name originally was Western Aros (*aros* is an ancient Swedish word which has to do with the mouth of a river). During the Middle Ages Kärrbo was known as Kaever. The oldest preserved building in Kärrbo is the church, which dates from the middle of the thirteenth century.

Table of Equivalents

1 kilogram = 2·2046 pounds
1 hecto = 3·527 ounces = 100 grams
1 litre = 1·0567 U.S. quarts
   (1 U.S. quart = 0·833 imperial quarts)
1 metre = 39·37 inches
1 kilometre = 0·62137 miles = 3280·8 feet
1 krona = 100 öre = $0·27 (1900)
                         0·26 (1930)
                         0·20 (1970)

Part One

Old-Age Pensioners

Nothing Lives Forever

Gösta Lundvall

I've lived in the province of Västmanland my whole life, except when I did my military service. I was born 23 February 1894, in St Ilian, as it was then called – that is, the parish of St Ilian which included the northern part of the city west of the river and the outlying countryside.

I was born not in Västerås itself but in Hedberg's cottage by Skerikevägen – they tore it down long ago. My mother's parents had Heljebo in Skerike parish. When grandfather died the family had to leave the farm. Grandmother moved to the city and opened a dairy store at Hammarbygatan 3.

Her last name was Skoglund. I lived with her and was considered one of her own. My aunts thought I was their youngest brother, which wasn't so strange since the youngest in the family was only ten years my senior.

In 1900 my mother married my stepfather, whose name was Lundvall. He was seven years younger than her. Before that she had worked alternately as a dressmaker and a cook in a canteen at Asea yard which was called the People's House.

It was a common thing for kids to move around, living with different relatives – one extra kid made no difference. If you had a stepfather, you usually got to hear about it from your folks, but I didn't know anything till I'd turned twenty. Then my mother explained that my real father's name was Holmkvist. I've never laid eyes on him.

When my mother got married I moved from Grandma's place to my parents'; they had managed to get hold of a small apartment in the neighbourhood, at Åsgatan 4 in the part of town called Jakobsberg. It gets its name from Jakobsberg Estate, and the same is true for Gideonsberg and Kristiansborg, and so on. When I was a boy there was a big farm called Nygård right back of where the fire station now stands, and the fields stretched right up to the main street and Pilgatan, in what is the central part of the city today.

On Åsgatan we lived upstairs in a 'stove room'. That's what it was called when the stove was located in the room and there was no kitchen. The stove room was quite big and pretty nice in the summer but cold in wintertime. Usually places like this were poorly heated.

We didn't live there for very long – working families moved often, almost more often than the farm-workers in the country. People moved a lot because they were always looking for a better place to live. Our next place was at Hammarbygatan 3, a fine upper-storey apartment, with one room and a kitchen, in the same house where Grandma lived. That's where I started school. In the first two grades my name was Gösta Skoglund and not until the third did it become Lundvall.

Before I went to school I spent all my time with a kid named Erik Ekendahl who was a year younger than me. His mother had her eighteenth child when she was thirty-six years old. He was crazy about playing horses: he would neigh and bolt and kick out and sometimes he would be stubborn and refuse to budge. I was the coachman.

We ran all over town and knew all the streets. Folks sometimes used to ask us the way and we'd go along and show them, and strangers asked us about boarding-houses and hotels. More often than not we'd get a coin for our trouble – an öre or two (if we got five it was a fortune). The money led us to get to know the city even better, but we weren't disappointed even if we didn't get anything – it was fun showing the way anyhow.

I used to wear a square cardinal's cap with tassels on the ends, it was home-made, patterned after a picture in a newspaper. Once a well-dressed gentleman with a hat caught sight of me and Erik in Fiskartorget and he began talking to us and asked if we wanted to earn some change. We were pleased, of course, and went along.

He lived above the Town Hall Buffet, in a room which had fine furniture and a dressing-table with a mirror. I can clearly remember that there was standing on it a grey ornamental donkey of fired clay with panniers. Beside the donkey lay two ten-öre pieces. He told us to keep our gaze on the donkey while he sketched us, for that's what he wanted to do.

Around the walls were a whole lot of drawings of boys and girls, and it looked like some of them had been afraid of him when he was sketching them, even though he was so kind. When he was through we were given our ten-öre pieces and cookies.

Later on I found out that his name was Brandes. He spoke Swedish, though with an accent. He was presumably a younger brother of the Danish critic and author, Georg Brandes.

When I was seven years old I started at Maria School and my teacher was Miss Hallén. The schoolroom had two doors, and on the first day, when she had taken the roll, the teacher went out through the upper door. We started to fool around, naturally, and I was standing on top of a desk when she came in from behind through the lower door. So I was the first to get my ears boxed.

Otherwise I behaved all right. I've always bragged about this to my children – until one day they dug up an old report card of mine in a drawer which showed that I'd got 'B' in deportment once. So much for my bragging.

During the first two grades at school, I went around in a kind of daze, but later on I came to life again. The day began with hymn singing and prayers, then came two hours of lessons and a break between ten and twelve o'clock, and after that two hours for learning our ABCs and writing practice.

There were about forty of us in my class. It was different from country schools where sometimes the schoolmistress could have all six grades at once in the same schoolroom, single-handed. But there were quite a few capable teachers in the country who taught the kids more than they ever could in the city.

Our landlord on Hammarbygatan was a builder by trade and his name was Lundin. He bought bicycles for himself and his wife at the age of seventy-five; she was, I believe, seventy-four. That was in 1903, and a bicycle was considered a sort of speed demon. When the first automobile regulations came some years later, the Town Council decided that in certain parts of town automobiles should not be allowed to do more than six to ten kilometres an hour. The reason given was that otherwise folks would get splashed with mud.

Västerås was an idyll at that time. I remember how we used to play marbles on the pavement outside Wennberg's Bookshop. There weren't any paved sidewalks in town then.

We moved to Rektorsgatan 5 on Kyrkbacken after a while. There we had two rooms and kitchen. My father worked for Asea;* he operated a high-speed lathe, one of the only three existing in the entire country, so people said. He earned twenty-five öre an hour.

In the old days there was an archway going right through the house where we lived – the building was much finer then. Now all that's left are the markings of the porch on the wall. On the south side was an orchard and there was a fence facing the street.

The trouble with the present-day renovated buildings on Kyrkbacken is, among other things, that Flink Cottage isn't there anymore. It stood at the corner of Kyrkbacksgatan and Djäknegatan but was moved to Vallby open-air museum about fifty years ago. And this spoiled the style of one of the oldest parts of the city by Kyrkbacken there.

That's being kind of stuck-up of them too: letting only artists, writers, and other so-called cultural people live in those

*Asea: Allmänna Svenska Elektriska AB, the Swedish General Electric Company.

renovated houses. Why not at least let the inhabitants mix in
with some ordinary folks? But it's a good idea anyway for the
city to put aside some money to preserve Kyrkbacken.

When I lived there as a boy, the two-storey houses, known as
burgher-houses, were painted grey. The small, single-storey
houses were mostly painted red.

Many of the kids who went to the high school lived as
boarders on Kyrkbacken. In the house where we lived, an old
maid named Malin took in lodgers and made her living out of
it.

High-school pupils who lived near enough to town, sons
from estates and manor houses and from some big farmsteads,
rode by coach to and from school every day. Fine horses came
from Tidö, Gäddeholm, Fullerö, Karlberg, Johannisberg and
Fiholm, and there was a coachman behind. At examination
time they came from Tidö in a coach with a team of six
magnificent horses.

I was going to secondary school then and there were sixty-
four boys in my class, including me. Girls and boys went in
separate classes and didn't even share the playground. The
instruction we had was in Swedish language, Luther's catechism, history, nature study, arithmetic, and geography. We
had to know our hymns and catechism by heart, word for word,
before they would pass us.

We found Bible history much simpler, because there we only
had to describe the content of what we'd read. It was a standing
joke, that if the teacher was old and a bit deaf, the boys would
rattle off: 'Up the stairs and down the stairs, up the stairs and
down the stairs . . .' in quiet voices, when we had an oral test in
catechism, and then in a louder voice they'd finish up with
Martin Luther's concluding phrase: 'Verily I say unto you,
that this be true.'

Djäknebergs School, where I went, had been built fairly
recently. The halls were large, and there were parallel bars,
climbing-ropes and other gymnastic gear. We had gymnastics

at least once a week. In the cellar there was even a swimming pool where we were allowed to swim every other week. We couldn't use it more often as there were so many other classes who had to have a turn too.

In the summer vacation we spent most of out time swimming and sun-bathing on a beach down by Svartån. The water was probably just as dirty then as it is now, and sometimes big turds would come floating by. On Sundays quite often Mother and Father and we kids would go sailing in a boat we had to some small islet in Lake Mälar and swim there.

During the school year we had certain days set aside for sports. When the lakes were covered by ice we'd go out skating (nearly everyone owned a pair of skates). The whole class filed down to Old Harbour, and there they donned skates and shot out towards the bay. I remember one time we were out skating and a strong northerly wind suddenly blew up; the lake was covered with glassy ice, and we were swept away from land. One kid blew all the way over to the Sörmland side of the lake – in the next province – where someone picked him up and telephoned to Västerås. Some others came ashore on a group of islets known as the Hästholmarna – Horse Islets. Another boy and I got caught up in the rushes around Björnö – Bear Island. We took ourselves over to the mainland and trudged along the country road back to town.

Kyrkbacken and other parts of the city, when I was a boy, were real garden paradises. Vasagatan at the bottom of Kyrkbacken was cucumber land, tended mostly by old ladies. There was one called Cucumber Johanna and she was a good sort, so we never stole from her. Cucumber Lotta, on the other hand, was a different matter, bad-tempered and a real danger to us boys. We gave her hell.

Whenever a high-school boy with a badge on his cap happened to come up along our streets we gave him a beating, and the same thing happened if one of us went into their area. They came from the nobility, and we couldn't stand each other.

In 1905 there was a big strike in Västerås. Two of my father's younger brothers, who were fifteen and seventeen years old, lived with us. They were members of the trade union and politically organized, and they and my father all picketed during the strike. There were so many discussions ... They were often out in the evenings beating up strike-breakers, and when they came home at the end of the day and had washed and stripped to the waist, they would put in a bit of boxing practice.

When I first started secondary school I was among the top ten in my class, but towards the end of my school days I was among the bottom ten. Our teacher's name was Lindkvist, and his favourite subjects were arithmetic and penmanship. His own handwriting was renowned. He was mean, too, and broke dozens of canes over us, though he never hit us on the head or arms.

In 1907, the same year I finished school, we moved to Gamla Hyttvägen in Hagadal. I began as apprentice to Mr Ohberg, the basket-maker. Both he and his wife were blind. They had a son, Åke, and he could see. Later on he became an actor. Other blind people used to come calling on the family, friends they had made at the Institute for the Blind in Stockholm.

Practically everyone played an instrument or sang, gave recitations or told stories. This was perhaps partly responsible for sparking off a longing for something over and above the grind of work, and thus I found my way to the Workers' Institute on Västgötagatan and started borrowing books from the library there: a library card cost fifty öre, and also entitled you to attend all the lectures for a year. I began with adventure stories, historical novels, and the like. As time went by, I became a member of the Social Democrat Youth League. We wore their emblem in our lapels – the broken rifle. Then I began reading social novels, but also lighter novels for pleasure.

Each week I rode to market with Ohberg's whisks and brooms and his woven basket-work. He also bought chip baskets from Dalecarlia for resale and cheap tin toys from Germany which I had to fetch from the Customs Office. On the first Saturday in the month I went to market in Enköping, the second to Köping, the third to Västerås and the fourth to Sala.

It meant having a gift of the gab and a sense of humour and a quick comeback. But you also had to be stubborn and a bit aggressive if you wanted to sell anything. Folks with peculiar dialects found it easier than we did to capture the public's interest.

On weekdays I often used to go about peddling brushes and whisk brooms around the foundries. Once in Fagersta I completely missed the boat! A new revival preacher had come to town and all the womenfolk were mad about him. These preachers, who were often handsome young men, could be just as big idols as rock singers are nowadays.

One Friday evening the train to Sala was delayed – it was past ten and the city was completely dead. I knocked at the door of the family where I usually stayed, at Ringgatan 15, but nobody woke up; it was the same thing at the hotel. I lay down in a wagon to sleep. It was winter but unusually mild and anyway I was young and hardy and I had a long coat, so I didn't freeze. I slept right through to five o'clock and then – how good a cup of coffee tasted! I remember I had a thin layer of new-fallen snow on me when I got up.

Once at a market in Lindesberg I didn't sleep a wink since the horse-dealers, hefty fellows with great hulking bodies and wallets, sang and shouted, boozing and making a racket all night long. They were real men, those horse-dealers, not any of your jokers, but genuine horse-dealers with fine animals; types who were full of life and didn't waste time sleeping, not when it was market time.

Of course there were rabble and thieves too, and you had to hold on to your things especially at the big markets – like, for example, the Sala winter market. There it was mainly skins that were sold. Folks from the forest came in crowds with their wild animal hides and disposed of them to the buyers. Hides from domestic animals were sold, too.

In Västerås there was a 'Folk Fair' three Saturdays in a row every year before the Feast of St Lars on the tenth of August, with a 'Big Fair' on the second Saturday. Then the boats lay tightly clustered in the Old Harbour and there were trestles, covered with herring and sandwiches and all kinds of things to drink, all the way along Harbour Street, the Fiskartorget and Main Street up to the fairgrounds facing the railroad. People went boating on pleasure trips from other towns around Lake Mälar and even from towns on the Baltic Coast.

Of course, the majority of visitors to the Fair came from the countryside outside Västerås to buy things and have a good time. Farmers hired servant girls and farmhands for the coming November – people bought clothes and knick-knacks, had fun and got drunk.

The biggest day of the year for buying and selling was probably Christmas Eve. There was so much trading then that you never got home from the market place before ten or eleven at night.

My father and nine of his workmates from Asea won the jackpot, 50,000 kronor, from a lottery ticket they had bought in 1910. So he decided to take up agriculture, and bought Hagbo in Kärrbo parish for 7,400 kronor. That marked the end of basketry and marketing for my part, after something like four years with Ohberg.

Kärrbo happens to be close to Västerås, but around that time there were many who became settlers way up in the north of Sweden. They dreamed of a place of their own and imagined they could avoid the risk of unemployment. Though many of them lost their illusions. It was often impossible to make a living in the settlements. Even today there are people who think that having a place of their own will be the solution to their problems when they're out of a job. They don't know how difficult it is to survive on a small farm.

Hagbo consisted of twenty-seven acres for crops and thirty-nine acres of forest. The cottage had one room and a kitchen; previously there had been two stove-rooms, a large one for the farmer's family and a small one for the old folks. We moved there on 14 March 1911 – my mother and father, myself and my younger brothers and sisters Lisa, Ejnar, and Linnea. We took our belongings over by toboggan, on Lake Mälar. The next day my father and I went to the livestock market in Västerås to buy a cow. The cow had to trudge over the country road behind a cart and horse twenty kilometres home.

Next day I got sick. After I'd been in bed five days, my father rode into town to see a doctor. The doctor put in a call to Frösåker, and they sent a message to say I had to get to the hospital. A Flitbo neighbour, Lillberg, took me in by horse. I had peritonitis and was operated on the same evening, 22 March.

The hospital required a security for the period of my stay, and Father got Greijer, the umbrella-maker, to sign the paper. They used to play chess together and knew each other well. As far as I know, my stay in the hospital cost fifty kronor. I was in for two months and came home 23 May. I weighed only 42 kilograms, but I got back to normal during the summer. I had turned seventeen in February.

I can't say I missed the city especially – I liked it there in the country. There was a boat to Västerås that docked at Frösåker every Saturday, and in the late summer I decided to go to the Folk Fair to get a hair-cut. But all the passengers on the boat stared so hard at my long, sun-bleached locks, that I went home again. Later on, John Zackrisson started going around cutting people's hair in Kärrbo.

In October I went into the Good Templar Order and became a member of Lodge No. 2945, the November Flower. The guiding light was a girl in her twenties, Frida Jonsson from Munkbo. The girls represented a majority of the group. We had our meeting place in Karlberg where we rented the big room at Old Lady Solman's cottage.

The Good Templar movement brought up many young people to be organization folks. We learned how to keep the books, how to write up the minutes of a meeting, how to handle the gavel, and how to express ourselves in debates. At that time there was a general discussion within the I.O.G.T. as to whether they should do away with the religious and ritual elements and just have an ordinary governing board, like other organizations, instead of so-called officers: lodge marshals, chaplains and lodge templar (chairman), indoor and outdoor masters-at-arms.

The older members maintained that the old form served as a fine school in which to train good citizens, and drew our attention to the fact that many popular representatives in local, county, and national government had received the fundamentals of their education within the I.O.G.T. Their view was that the fixed procedure of ritual, regalia, solemn initiation ceremonies, and so on gave the whole thing stability.

We young people weren't opposed to the rituals as such, but we wanted to change the content, to put the emphasis on the cultural parts, not the religious ones; we wanted to quote poets, instead of the Bible. Changes were made by and by, though very slowly – even today ritual ceremonies still exist. But nowadays the movement is almost dead.

On Midsummer Day 1914 the Kärrbo Good Templar Lodge held a ball in the elementary school playground, where we sat down to eat at long tables – there was plenty of music and there were speakers from the city. The Minister was against us. Most ministers opposed the temperance movement, which was radical and, according to conservative opinion, spread socialistic ideas.

It's true that the Good Templar movement opened many people's eyes and made them think, got them to lay off the booze and the gambling and to break away from the primitive life led in the servants' quarters and in the farm cottages. At the lodges they learned how to read aloud from the I.O.G.T. ritual, which was quite revolutionary for many of them. Even the lodges out in the country got together small collections of books for people to come and borrow. New ideas struck root and people gradually became aware of another world existing outside the boundaries of their own parish.

I worked at home on the farm until the fall of 1914. In the wintertime Pa drove out in Frösåker Forest while I tended the animals and other jobs around the place. We also cut a whole lot of lumber in Hagbo Woods and sold it in the city. We needed the money to pay off our debts.

In keeping with a very old tradition, the young people held dances in the kitchen in the wintertime. They joined together and invited the kids from other parts of the village in for coffee and soft drinks and cookies and cake. The furniture was cleared away, either into the parlour or out into the yard, in order to make room. The guys used to chip in and buy a bottle of *akvavit* which they'd bring along. There were a number of folks who could play fiddle and accordion and quite often the dancing wasn't over until three on Sunday morning.

The Farmers' Ball, which took place between the third day of Christmas and up to a week afterwards, was another tradition among neighbours. You ate and drank until it was time to go home and milk in the morning, then you slept through the day. The old farmers used to sit in the parlours, smoking and boozing and playing cards. The womenfolk sat in the kitchen talking and drinking home-made wine, while the youngsters lay asleep in the corner.

In summertime there were the barn dances. Boozing was very common in Kärrbo, but it wasn't so common that the young fellows drank themselves silly, which the old farmers often did. Some even fell off the wagon and slept by the road when they'd been to the tavern.

On 28 July 1914 we were cutting barley in Hagbo when the church bells began ringing in the middle of the morning. We had heard and talked about the war that was on its way, and had read in our county newspaper about how the church bells would ring for the mobilization. People came crowding onto the road, either in their wagons or on foot, going to church to read the announcements on the bulletin board.

It turned out to be a false alarm, though, and the bell-ringing was criticized sharply by many newspapers afterwards. It scared folks unnecessarily. The only one from Kärrbo to be drafted was Nyby-Kalle, who was in the Navy and had already got his orders to report in the mail.

In the winter of 1914 I got a job as farmhand in Bälby in Dingtuna, on the other side of town from Kärrbo. In the spring I got my draft papers. I really shouldn't have had to do my military service until the following year, but two years' worth of draftees were called up the same year because of the war.

In July 1915 I was stationed at Vaxholm in the Coast Artillery. I spent eight months of military service in a so-called craftsmen's company, with painters, carpenters, shoemakers, smiths, and others. The first two weeks we spent being drilled in saluting and marching and learning the ranks, as well as rowing and tying knots and a whole lot of other stuff. The funny thing was that we never got to learn anything about how to handle any weapon.

There was a lot of venereal disease going around, and the latrines and other places stank from Lysol. Our military policeman, named Larsson, was a bit loony from being in the army. He used to drill on top of a gun-battery along with his missus and kids and he'd bluster and holler so, you could hear him all over the fortification at Vaxholm.

He got lousy pay. Non-commissioned officers didn't have a much higher salary than day labourers. Officers, on the other hand, had plenty of money to live the way they liked.

The daily allowance for a serviceman was raised from twenty to fifty öre just before we were drafted. That made fifteen kronor a month, the same as I'd had as a farmhand. It reached far enough – I was used to stretching my money.

Several thousand wealthy families from Stockholm came out to the islands of the archipelago as summer visitors, and generally they had three servant girls to a family. So, on Saturday evenings there were often more girls than guys out on the piers and dance floors, a real summer paradise. Not all the girls were completely sober when they went dancing, either.

Every day, looking from the fort at Vaxholm, you could see German freighters loaded with iron ore from Luleå, in the north of Sweden, just like during the Second World War when the iron-ore transports were granted safe conduct through Swedish territorial waters. Swedish capitalists have made a lot of money off the Germans' wars.

After a while I landed up in the supply room, where I sorted and stamped worn-out gear. I remained there the rest of the time until my discharge. Sometimes when I had a Saturday pass I would go and call on relatives in Stockholm. A round-trip ticket on a Vaxholm boat cost seventy-five öre.

A guy called Hjalmar Lundin and I joined up with the I.O.G.T. Lodge in Vaxholm, called Island Flower, and went to a lot of their meetings and functions. The contact with civilians made army life much easier.

We sang a lot, but personally I've never had much of an ear for music and singing and so I was never a good dancer, either. After the lodge meetings we used to go to the Villa Luft Café, which was more like a home than a café, with upholstered sofas and chairs in the rooms. There we went on with our singing and poetry reading.

The evening before we were mustered out we had to turn in our cutlery, mattresses, blankets, uniforms, and everything else. We lifted off cupboard doors to put on our bed-frames instead of mattresses. It was February and we were freezing. The next evening I arrived back in Kärrbo.

After that I started in at the Metal Works in Västerås and I got board and room with Mr and Mrs Lindberg, the same couple my parents had rented an apartment from earlier. There was a sixty-hour work-week, what they called a double shift: you came on and worked the morning, had the afternoon off, worked through the night and were free the following morning and so on – it was like that the rest of the week. We had no break on the morning shift, but naturally we took five minutes off anyhow. In the afternoon we had a short lunch break and at night you were allowed an hour – time to grab some shut-eye.

I earned thirty-five öre an hour, that made twenty-one kronor a week. On rare occasions I managed to get in on some piecework and could earn up to fifty öre an hour, even as much as sixty öre. However, you had to be very careful not to go over the quota in the contract so as not to lower the wages for the next contract period. The contract was good for one year at a time. Nobody felt very pushed.

I remember when the first time-and-motion inspector came to Asea in the early twenties; the workers were all so against him that before long he was under treatment for nervous strain.

On the first of February 1917 we got our rationing cards for bread. Housewives did all their own baking at home in those days. The wholesale price of flour rose. A grocer named Tunholm in Västerås took advantage of the situation and raised the price of wheat flour from twenty-nine to sixty-four öre per kilo; but he was forced to close his shop on Stora gatan for a while since folks knew that he was stocked up with a huge supply of flour he'd bought cheaply before prices rose, and they were so angry over his greed that he didn't dare open his doors. He no doubt would have been more careful if he'd been able to anticipate people's reaction. Tunholm was a big shot in the Swedish Missionary Society and later on when he moved to

Stockholm he became Chairman of the Federation of Retail Merchants.

Sweden had quite a drought during the years of the First World War. People used to talk about how much it rained down there in Europe, and many farmers thought that it was all the shooting at the front which brought about atmospheric disturbance, causing all the rain to be attracted that way.

The food shortage became critical after rationing was introduced, and all the prices rose from week to week. But wages remained as they were before. The cost of board and room went up to twenty-four kronor a week. Since I was only earning twenty-one kronor it was no go, so I had to quit the Metal Works and move home to my parents in Hagbo.

In the spring of 1917 I started work as farmhand again with the Petterssons in Bälby, Dingtuna, where I had been for the winter of 1914–15. It was there I met my wife, Greta. She worked as a maid at a neighbouring farm called Hallsta. It was customary to have two or three farmhands and as many maids, and in the evening you'd go around the various farms paying calls or else you'd go to a dance at one of the barns.

Well, one of the world's most common accidents happened next – by an indiscretion I found myself obliged to enter into the holy estate of matrimony on 6 April 1918. The minister who married us had also baptized and confirmed me. It was pouring rain that day and we were thoroughly fed up, but we consoled ourselves with the thought that rain on your wedding was a sign that you'd eventually get rich. Though I've not noticed it coming true, at least not as far as money is concerned.

Linnea was born on the fourth of July. According to official statistics, recorded at that time, eighty-nine per cent of the people who got married did so because there was a baby on the way. Only eleven per cent had their first child more than nine months after the wedding. The percentage figures are probably still about the same.

Greta had a savings book with 5–600 kronor put away and I

had a book with sixty-four kronor, to give us a start. It was a time of crisis and things were expensive, but you could get hold of cheap furniture at auctions. On 1 May 1918 we moved to Karmansbo in Bergslagen where I became a farm-worker for 600 kronor a year.

The name Karmansbo comes from two brothers whose name was Karman and who settled there in the sixteenth or seventeenth century; the estate included 360 acres of land. There was also a saw-mill and an iron-works. The proprietor's name was von Wernstedt.

Greta and I moved into one room and a kitchen in the farm-workers' quarters called Pine Wood Hill – Tallbacken. Six farm-workers and two cowherds worked the farm, together with a number of boys, half-grown and grown sons of the smiths at the works. I had to do a lot of tractor-driving on the farm.

The smiths were a lively breed and had their own trade union. People discussed unions and politics a great deal in Karmansbo, just as they did in other parts of Sweden at that time. Speakers and agitators would come to Karmansbo to speak in the square. Social Democrats as well as Communists and Syndicalists. The smiths were not committed in any one direction, but were fair in their judgements and considered all speakers good.

I entered the I.O.G.T. Lodge No. 619 called Hedskrona, which had been formed way back in 1883 and had about 170 members and a wide range of activities with a choir, an amateur theatre troupe, study groups, and quite a large library. I was very interested in books and reading and later I was elected librarian.

The smiths were mainly of Walloon stock, with a passion for the outdoor life. They spent all their free time on the lakes and in the forest, and they also sang songs and wrote poetry about the beautiful scenery of the iron-mining district of Bergslagen. Myself, I worked in the forest for over six months of the year and wasn't quite as enthusiastic. But my life became so coloured by the smiths' lyrical turn of mind – their singing and music, poetry and story-telling, as well as their interest in social issues – that my own world of thoughts, my very existence changed completely. At the same time I read a good deal and tried to compare what I found in books with reality.

In 1919, together with about ten other people, I helped organize a Communist youth club in Karmansbo. We laid out a place to dance in a meadow, called Stenhagsbacken, and there we had parties every Saturday with dancing and sometimes we gave amateur performances of plays. There was also an athletics association and we all helped to organize the dances.

A part of the money we made from the parties went to subsidizing subscriptions to the Communist newspaper, the *Folkets dagblad Politiken*. We did this because the big farmers and proprietors gave their employees grants for subscribing to the right-wing newspaper, the *Köpings-Posten*, in order to counteract the spreading of left-wing ideas.

Their campaign was directed primarily against the Social Democratic press which had a much larger circulation than the Communist press. We wanted to prevent the right-wing newspaper – which was subsidized – from being circulated among the works' employees. We got together about thirty subscribers for the *Folkets dagblad Politiken*, a great many, we thought.

Even the wives of the smiths who were Baptists or belonged to the Missionary Society read our newspaper. However, in the long run it turned out to be too expensive for the club, and the newspaper enterprise packed up.

One of the most remarkable speakers in the square was Pastor Spaak who, before he was unfrocked, had written a book entitled '*Can a Social Democrat Be a Christian?*' He got into a feud with the Church fathers when he questioned their attitude towards the common people's living conditions and why it was that the Church always sided with the upper classes and the authorities. What he was calling into question was quite simply the matter of whether they took their Christianity seriously and, since he was well-versed in theology, he came out very well in the debating. That was why they came to hate him, and the Cathedral Chapter sent him warnings and finally removed him from office.

His wife came from an aristocratic family, and when he was left penniless her relations intervened in order to save the family's good name, and signed a personal guarantee for him so he could purchase forty-eight acres of farm land in Simtuna. His wife shared all his ideas enthusiastically and their house became a meeting place for the local Good Templars and Social Democrats. But they spent all their money on these activities, and the relatives finally withdrew the guarantee loan and forced the couple to separate.

After this he moved to Stockholm and became an itinerant agitator for the newly-begun Social-Democratic left-wing party, which later became the Communist Party. He was a very good speaker and at the meeting we arranged in Karmansbo, practically the whole works, about 150 people, came to listen to him. He stayed the night at our house and he spent almost the entire next morning playing and joking with the children out on the slope. Then he grew sad because he missed his own children, so he went and sat in the kitchen and told Greta the story of his life.

Later he wound up poverty-stricken in Stockholm. The Party tried to help him as much as they could with the money they had. Then after another few years, he died.

On another occasion we had Hinke Bergegren, the famous anarchist orator-agitator, as a speaker. The idea was that he would talk about his speciality, sexual matters and the need for the workers to learn family planning so that they could rise up out of their poverty and misery. He was known for expressing himself in drastic terms sometimes. But on the afternoon before the meeting he went around talking to people at the works and realized that it would be better for him to lecture on the works of Ibsen. Nobody minded this, not even those of us who had organized the meeting, for he was a uniquely-gifted orator and teacher.

During the late winter of 1920, I did a lot of agitating at Karmansbo and the surrounding farms with the idea of forming a labour union, and I had called a meeting for one Tuesday evening to meet the representative, Falk, from the Farmworkers' Association. Twenty-four had promised to come.

The proprietor got wind of this, and that Tuesday morning he had the inspector announce that he wanted to see all the farm-workers on Wednesday evening in order to discuss the question of wages, with the promise of a wage increase. I realized then that nobody would bother to come to the Tuesday meeting, so I went down to the store to phone Falk back.

So on that Wednesday evening we were all up at the office where von Wernstedt announced that there would be an increase in our hourly wages of thirty-five to forty-six öre, in order to make all wages in the district uniform, as he put it. The whole show was over in a few minutes; nobody but the proprietor had said anything and everyone trooped out quite happily. They weren't keen to set themselves up against authority by forming a union, and they weren't willing to pay the union dues either.

I stayed behind to talk about union rights with the boss, and we spent the whole night pacing up and down the office and talking till after midnight. He wouldn't even accept the argument that properly organized workers were good for the management too since the union could step in and solve local disagreements.

The outcome of it all was that I was no longer wanted at the farm. So I found my way back home again and at the end of April 1920 we moved to Springsta in Kärrbo where I became a farm-worker. Our household goods were shipped by rail to

Västerås, with a change of trains at Köping, and then were sent the rest of the way by horse and wagon. The furniture got quite beat-up on a trip like that.

At Springsta we got hold of a place to live in Rismattan, one room and a kitchen and masses of bed bugs, which was quite usual. The apartment had just been done over, but the bugs had taken refuge behind the Dutch-tiled stove and when we lit the stove to warm up the room they swarmed out.

I complained to the proprietor, Hallström, and offered to get rid of the bugs with copper vitriol if he paid the costs. He agreed and the result was better than we had expected – all the bugs disappeared.

At Springsta I was paid 900 kronor a year in cash plus the payment in kind, which consisted of three litres of whole milk and three litres of skimmed milk a day, our living quarters, firewood, a potato patch for 200 kilograms of seed potatoes, 600 kilograms of rye, 200 kilograms of wheat, 50 kilograms of peas, and 400 kilograms of mixed seed to grind up for the pigs. We had two pigs, and baked all our bread ourselves.

At that time, during the summer of 1920, many farm-workers' unions were being organized in Central Sweden, and I did my bit by agitating at Springsta. There were fellows there who felt the same way, and others at Lindö and Frösåker. We formed a local branch of the union in Kärrbo, and another was formed at Kusta in Irsta. Naturally the proprietors looked askance at what was going on, but there was nothing they could do about it.

When our union was formed we had a representative down from the Farm-workers' Association to discuss contracts and wage scales with the employers. Negotiations for the whole country were also going on in Västerås. There Ulf, one of the management's representatives, got so angry that he nearly used his cane on one of our representatives.

Westerdahl, the owner of Kusta Estate, who was more of a

diplomat, intervened and explained that such methods wouldn't work any longer. Formerly bosses had been able to beat up rebellious underlings. The law on corporal punishment had just been abolished – this was the old law (governing apprentices and other indentured workers) which said, among other things, that if a man left his post before his yearly contract ran out, he could be brought back to his place of employment by the sheriff.

Negotiations about wage agreements broke down. In early August, just as harvest time began, we went out on strike. It was good timing. The strike lasted eleven days. A couple of scabs came to Springsta – they lived and ate at Farmer Hallström's place. Both were students, and one of them was studying dentistry. There were also three workers on the farm who had not joined the union.

We showed our solidarity with the poorest workers, those who had a lot of kids, by supplying them with rye flour and other things while the conflict lasted. The strike won us a fixed settlement. At Springsta the yearly wage, in cash, was increased from 900 kronor to the 1,150 kronor agreed upon, so our struggle was not in vain.

In October, however, when the harvest had been brought in, everyone in the district who had taken part in the strike was laid off, though at some farms they were rehired. Those who had led the workers in the strike were black-listed, which meant they could not find a job anywhere. I was black-listed too.

Then my brother-in-law, Fritz Hellström, and I began to ride around on our bikes looking for work. He had just married my sister and needed a permanent job instead of the seasonal work he had before at the Frösåker Brickyard. He got a job, since he had not been a farm-worker, nor taken part in the strike, but I didn't.

Things looked very black until one day, quite by chance, I ran into my former employer, von Wernstedt, in Västerås where I had ridden by bike in to the public employment office. We started talking, I told him how things stood, and a couple of days later I received a message from him with an offer of a job. He explained that he had had a lot of trouble with folks who weren't steady workers and who suddenly just took off when they felt like it.

And so we moved back into Karmansbo the same year as we moved away from it. The farm-workers there had still not formed a union, but I made sure that I got a salary that was in accord with the agreement.

I didn't belong to any union during the six years that followed there. Instead I divided my time between the I.O.G.T. and party-political work.

On 28 May 1920 Ingemar was born, just a short time after we had moved to Springsta. Britta was born in Karmansbo on 18 October 1922.

My mother began to get quite sick in the middle of the twenties and because of this my parents decided they didn't want to stay on the farm in Hagbo. We talked it over together and in the fall of 1926 they moved in to Västerås after fifteen years in Kärrbo, and my father began to work again at the Asea factory.

Greta and I took over the tenancy of the farm from him for 500 kronor a year and all the livestock and effects on a contract of sale. This time we moved all our belongings with the help of a truck which belonged to Valle Törngren from Harkie. He had recently started a trucking business in Kärrbo and bought his first truck second-hand from the brewery in Eskilstuna for a little over 700 kronor; it had unusually large rear wheels. He had it for over twenty years.

It wasn't particularly profitable to begin farming just then. In the fall of 1926 my father had got a price of 18 öre per kilo for oats and 24 öre for wheat. Milk brought 14 öre per litre. During the following years prices fell and when things were at their worst the peasants got 7 öre for oats, 17 öre for wheat and

7·9 öre for milk. In the county of Skaraborg the price of milk dropped to 4 öre per litre in 1932.

The year after, a notable piece of 'log-rolling' took place between the Social-Democratic Workers Party and the Agrarian Party. A government agricultural agreement was entered into in order to help raise prices, and increased funds were set aside for relief work for the thousands of unemployed people who were wandering throughout the country looking for jobs.

We took over five cows, one horse and several chickens from my parents, and with us from Karmansbo we had two large pigs and one or two sacks of potatoes. Besides this a blacksmith friend had lent me 400 kronor to use as my basic capital.

In November the price of pork was 1·60 kronor per kilo. I tried to be smart by saving the pigs until after Christmas in the hope that prices would rise after the Christmas slaughter. But in January, when I was forced to sell, the price was only 1·05 kronor per kilo. In February the price of pork fell to 80 öre and in Västerås the buyers were left with railway carloads of pork from Skåne which they couldn't sell.

It was lucky that it was my own father I had bought my animals and equipment from when I took over the tenancy of Hagbo in the fall of 1926. The purchase price, 5,000 kronor, had to be paid off over ten years, but when 1936 came I had not managed to pay even 2,000 kronor. They were lean years. The harvest of 1927 was rotten. My father did not demand any instalments on the loan. Had it been a bank we'd borrowed the money from, we should have been obliged to leave the farm within the first year. In 1928 the harvest was better but prices worse, so the results weren't so hot that time either.

At first Kärrbo struck me as a dreary, backward town, full of nothing but simple-minded clodhoppers. But my opinion changed as time went on. I came to respect most of the farmers in the neighbourhood. They were often very knowledgeable though they didn't get it out of books; their contact with animals and nature had created in many of them an attitude to life which expressed itself in humility and tolerance, and a desire always to see the best in their fellow men and women.

The life of a small farmer was worth living, but you had to stick to it if you wanted to get by. The days were spent doing heavy manual work. I've never been especially strong, but on the other hand I'm pretty stubborn.

At harvest time we'd go on working until about ten at night, Greta and I. Then we'd have to be up at five to do the milking before the milk-truck came. So of course you didn't get much rest. I became so accustomed to getting up early that I still wake up before five in the morning.

We turned in up to a hundred litres of milk a day to the dairy. I concentrated mostly on looking after the livestock, cows, calves, and pigs. The only grain I cultivated to sell was a few acres of wheat, the remainder of the ground being used for growing fodder – grain and hay – for the animals.

It was an everlasting grind to make ends meet. At particularly hard times you really had to get hold of yourself and cut out the worrying over money. It doesn't help to go around sighing, being downhearted – it's better to learn a bit of self-discipline instead.

We were, on the whole, self-supporting. We never were in want of food. Greta was good at baking bread – not only the soft kind but crispbread too. Every fall and spring she set aside several days to bake rye crispbread in the big oven, big disks which were hung up to dry on a bread-rack on the rafters in the kitchen. She also baked rusks in vast quantities, especially in the spring, for us to eat with our coffee in the summer.

When we slaughtered we had sausage and blood bread hanging from the ceiling. The minced sausage was supposed to turn a little sour. This happened during the process of drying and it was the acid taste that made it into a delicacy. If you took down the sausage too early it turned mouldy in the pantry, but otherwise it would keep for months on end.

I also built a smoking-oven out on a slope and smoked pork – just enough for our own needs. It's a method which I'm sure dates from the Stone Age. The best firewood for smoking things is juniper. And then I hunted a bit too, of course, and shot an odd hare and sometimes a grouse, so we didn't lack meat to go with our potatoes.

All our kids went to school. In 1929 Britta began elementary school in Harkie; Ingemar was in the third grade and Linnea in the fifth grade up at the intermediate school by the church. Apart from school they had various jobs to do at home, such as fetching wood, watering the cows, weeding the vegetable patch, and many other things. What they disliked most was washing the dishes. When they were older they came out with us to work in the fields.

In 1930 when I got my planting done and was just finishing up the last field down by Oxhagen, the horse got sick. It was in the morning of 17 May. He was called Pålle, a great big feller, and had had several attacks of colic. I led him home to his stable and called the vet, who realized by my description that the horse wouldn't live much longer. He advised me to leave him alone to die a natural death, otherwise I wouldn't be able to claim the insurance. A slaughtered horse then didn't bring more than twenty-five kronor. I got 225 kronor on the insurance, but if I'd been able to afford it I'd have slaughtered him anyway, to save him the pain he suffered those two hours it took him to die.

After I'd been a farmer a while, I joined various associations. On the hill behind Hagbo was a place to dance, which the Social Democrats had laid out on land my father had let them use. Even before 1920 he and John Elfdal from Dysterdal, a painter by profession, had taken the initiative in forming a local branch of the Social Democratic Party, commonly called the Workers' Commune, in Kärrbo. Many farm-workers and labourers in the brickyard and also the sons and daughters from small farms became members.

The Saturday dance was the main source of income for the Workers' Commune, and sometimes on Sunday afternoons there were lectures and other activities for the Social Democratic Party. I didn't have very much contact with them in the beginning, as I'd been a Communist since Karmansbo and used to ride my bike to Västerås and take part in Communist meetings and parties.

In the summer of 1928 the members of the Workers' Commune built a community centre, the People's House, a short way from where they held their dances. A committee for the community centre was intended to be responsible for the construction of the building, but this didn't begin to function until nearly the spring of 1929. A couple of months before, I had helped with the formation of a new I.O.G.T. lodge in Kärrbo, replacing the old one which had folded around 1915. The new lodge, called No. 4919, Ray of Light, joined the community-centre committee as a shareholder together with the Farm-workers' Labour Union and the Workers' Commune. Elfdal became chairman of the committee and I was treasurer.

The building included one large room with a stage and a dance floor and one small room where refreshments could be served, which also functioned as a study room. The walls were made of rough boards and the places between the beams should have been filled in with sawdust, but this was never done. It was hard to keep heated during the wintertime, even though we stoked the stoves until they glowed. The place was primitive, but it did the job.

We danced to a radio-gramophone which we bought on the instalment plan from Yngve Swenson's radio store in Västerås, and sometimes we had a go at amateur dramatics. We didn't often get further than the rehearsal stage but it did happen . . . I remember once we did a play called *The Family Farm*, a play with a moral in it: it was about a man who drank away his house and lands. We tried writing our own sketches now and then and we also had poetry readings; revue numbers and soldiers' songs were all part of our programme. It was mainly the Good Templar Lodge that organized this kind of thing.

There was no water in the place, but this we fetched from a well belonging to Follin in Lugnet and we chucked the garbage outside the door. In summertime the whole slope smelled sour from our coffee-grounds.

The members of the temperance movement started a small library and we gradually got together a couple of hundred books, which I looked after. I kept them in a cupboard at home, for our house served also as a meeting place to a very great extent. Even one or two of the conservative type of farmers, who were really against the workers' movement, would come to borrow books now and again. The Farm-workers' Labour Union also owned a small library, which Arvid Johansson at Linde was in charge of.

New ideas and efforts at education came into evidence in the countryside, very much thanks to the Farmers' Association's publishing activities and correspondence school. And the history of Sweden, with its nobles, kings, and wars, was shown in a different light when authors like Enoch Ingers, Harry Martinson, Jan Fridegård, Ivar Lo-Johansson, Vilhelm Moberg and others began writing the history of the country-side, describing in their books the life of poor farmers and farm-workers, and their struggle for survival.

I myself was busy reading a lot about fertilizers, feed units, albumen, minerals, and such things that are a part of farming. Though I did get time to read a few novels too and several books by Gandhi and Tagore, in translation. Difficult books like these were easier to read in the mornings when my thoughts were clearest; I used to get up a bit earlier sometimes in order to read a particular passage before it was time to go out to the farmyard.

We started a Workers' Education Association which took over the education side in the beginning of the thirties: there were study circles for mathematics and for Swedish, as well as studies in organized labour and civics. I was elected chairman. We also had a music circle one winter with a teacher from Västerås who travelled out by bus on Saturday afternoons to teach the participants how to play the violin. The circle was to last two seasons but broke up after one winter.

I kept up my contact with the Communist Workers' Commune in Västerås until the mid-thirties. Social Democrats and Communists were having violent discussions at that time about ways and means of solving the question of unemployment insurance. On one occasion a bus-load of Communists came from town to hold a meeting in Hagbo on this subject. Many of them were not sober and I didn't like their behaviour at all.

This was not the first time such an incident occurred. Another time, when they were going to hold an election meeting outside Kärrbo Church and were waiting for the lecturer, some of them began throwing poles and sticks up into the minister's pear trees and snitching the pears that fell to the ground. I told them what was wrong about acting that way. At that point the rowdy element among them began shouting out that all property should belong to everybody. It wasn't actually episodes like that that led me to leave the Party, but they helped.

Well, then I became a member of the Social Democratic Workers' Commune in Kärrbo. By now I've been a member of the Social Dems. for over thirty-five years.

Many Communists in Västerås and throughout the country went over to Social Democracy because of the opposition within the Communist Party after Sillén and the Moscow loyalists had taken over leadership. It was the same then as it is today: one long discussion about how to build a more equitable society, whether one should proceed by violent means with a dictatorship, or democratically with the accent on education.

I remember how my father and his friends used to have a lot of discussions about socialism both before and after the

Russian Revolution in 1917. The focus was on Lenin then, just as it is on Mao now. My father maintained, for example, that if he planted a fruit tree, that fruit tree belonged to him, but there were others who claimed that in actual fact we only have things on loan here on earth and that nobody can own a tree.

But farming in Hagbo went on as usual. There was work to be done from early morning till late at night and we had our financial worries, but seen as a whole, it was also an idyllic life. Our special occasions were not always Sundays or holidays: often enough they might be any ordinary weekday when I was out harrowing or ploughing and Ma and the kids would come out with coffee. We'd settle down in the shade, the horse was fed bread and sugar lumps and there was a slice of sponge cake for us, but that wasn't so often.

My first assignment in local government work came when I was elected to the unemployment committee, at the district meeting in Kärrbo. Säfström, who was the foreman at Frösåker Brickyard, became chairman. He was a Nazi – there were a number who were.

A Swedish-American who lived in Granviken, beyond Saddlemakers Bay – Sadelmakarviken – had his gateposts decorated with swastikas. Some of the farmers were also infected with Nazi ideas. Times were bad, and they believed that Nazism could change things: Säfström propagandized a whole lot for this. They weren't members, but they were influenced. A current of it passed all through Sweden, and it was fairly strong for several years. It was the same in Norway, and in Finland it was much worse than here.

Many people were out of a job in Kärrbo. Frösåker Brickyard was operating only intermittently and when it finally stopped altogether, unemployment of course grew worse. My brother Ejnar worked at the brickyard and was without a job for long periods. In 1927 he borrowed a couple of hundred kronor from Ville Holm, whose daughter he kept company with, and he bought a ticket to Canada. He paid

back the money, but he remained there in Canada until he
died in 1954. He left behind a wife and four teenage kids. He
never was able to afford the fare home to come back and visit.

The Unemployment Committee for Kärrbo was awarded
state funds to rebuild the road over Gryta Hill and twelve to
fifteen men got work there for nearly three years. Everything
was done by hand and the pay was 32 öre per hour. On the open
market roadwork was paid about 1·05 kronor an hour.

Säfström was foreman for the relief work and looked after
the chequing account at the post office. When the jobs were
done in the spring of 1931 or 1932, I don't remember which,
he gave a report on the accounts. They were in order and about
2,000 kronor were left in the postal chequing account. But in
those days a statement on such accounts wasn't issued more
than once a year. When it arrived the following New Year it
showed the balance to be only a few kronor instead of 2,000 –
Säfström had withdrawn the rest.

The members of the District Council then reasoned among
themselves that if there was to be a trial, a high-priced lawyer
would have to be called in, and that was money the Council
would have to fork out since it was uncertain whether or not
Säfström could cover the costs of a trial.

He had taken out fifty kronor a week from the account after
the work on the road was completed. At that time he was out of
a job and had used the money in order to live. In a way he had
a good reason for embezzling. His family needed food. But he
was slightly addicted to buying lottery tickets also.

It was decided that Ral from Frösåker, who was the chairman at the rural district meeting, together with old Törngren,
would go to Vittinge where Säfström had moved, and talk to
him, instead of reporting the matter to the police. They also
talked to his father, and it was cleared up. The money was
paid back.

Later on I had a lot of other business to do for the parish
and was elected to the Rural District Council which also

functioned as a public health board and poor relief board, and which at the same time served as the child welfare and pensions committee and the local authority on fires and forest fires.

No fees were paid except to the chairman of some of the committees, when he might receive fifty or a hundred kronor a year for all his work. The rest were honorary offices.

There was never any question of paying travel expenses, either. You rode your bicycle to and from your assignments and it didn't cost anything. If anyone ever demanded payment for something, the demand generally got voted down as unnecessary, since everybody was agreed that local taxes had to be kept down. They were high enough as it was.

All of us looked upon the community and its business as common property you felt responsible for – beyond party lines. Everyone wanted to co-operate. It didn't matter very much that I held left-wing views and that others were right-wing. We discussed the problems and for the most part we came to a satisfactory agreement anyway. It was really only a matter of doing things that had to be done and that everyone had a shared interest in.

During the thirties the farmers' co-operative movement snowballed throughout the country and we Kärrbo farmers made our contribution to it. Althén, the tenant at the vicarage, and I agitated for a local Rural Credit Society. It was formed in August 1933 and served the parishes of Kärrbo, Irsta, Kungsåra, and Ängsö. I became chairman. Althén was cashier and Nyby-Kalle representative from Kärrbo. Besides him there were representatives from Irsta and Ängsö.

The shares cost five kronor each and every new member had to put his name down for at least one share. And this is how it worked: if you borrowed money you had to buy a new share for every 200 kronor you borrowed, which meant you put in twenty-five kronor for each 1,000 kronor borrowed. We never decided about paying interest on the shares.

From each share 1·50 kronor went into the reserve fund and the remaining 3·50 kronor was collected by anyone who left the Credit Union. If anyone died, for example, the shares invested were paid out. The money for the loans came from the central credit union in Örebro which had been formed several years before and which functioned as the mother organization for all local credit unions in the Mälar Valley.

It was a successful start. In Kärrbo the first to borrow money was Erik Andersson from Rosendal, who needed it to replace a cow that had died. Since we knew the guarantors and what kind of people they were, he could get his money within two or three days. If he had borrowed the money from a bank in Västerås, it would have taken a long time before the guarantors' credit rating had been checked, and if the bank had not found their credit good enough, then he would not have been granted a loan at all. We, on the other hand, could base our judgement on the personal integrity of borrower and guarantor just as much as on their economic assets.

The aim of the Rural Credit Society was in the first instance to help the small farmers organize their finances. Customarily they bought tools and fertilizer and seed and other requirements with bills of exchange, and their exchange transactions were often so muddled that a large share of their normal working time went to driving in to the city banks and going around the countryside looking for new guarantors.

In order to clean up a farmer's finances, the union gave him a larger loan which he used to redeem his bills of exchange and to pay off his small loans. He then paid interest and an instalment to the union on 15 June and 15 December. The commercial banks made a lot of money from the high rate of interest on bills of exchange. So naturally they were very much against the farmers' credit union movement, which was growing fast.

Sometimes the banks took advantage of some of the farmers, who were proud to be financially independent. The farmer in Kärrbo called Vallatorparn was one of these, and he must have lost a whole lot of money through co-signing for various people borrowing money. He was proud that the banks accepted him as a guarantor.

Vallatorparn always had money. When he bought a car and the salesman began talking about instalment terms, he took his wallet out of the pocket of his filthy, patched trousers and paid in cash. After that the car stayed home there in Vallatorp for four years, unused, until his son Georg got his driver's licence.

There were many stories about old 'Vallatorparn'. He did business with Valle Törngren and once on his way to the city by bus he started kidding Valle, who was driving. 'Look here', said Valle, 'this is *my* bus.' 'Yes', replied the farmer, 'but it's my horses that are pulling it!'

The Rural Credit Society had a lot of work to do, what with accounts and records and reports and keeping office hours for the members, but not one of the board members ever asked for a fee or got one, with the exception of Althén, who received a hundred-kronor note a year. He provided the union with office space in his apartment, and since he was cashier, he had most to do.

On the first and fifteenth of every month we had our board meetings and these were pleasant affairs. Everyone was enthusiastic and afterwards Rosa Althén served us coffee and something to go with it. She was an uncommonly cheerful and friendly woman. Both she and her husband were very hospitable.

He kept a tiny bit of cognac in a bottle – never more than that – and would invite us to a nip each. I myself was a teetotaller, but I've never in the least been disturbed by other people taking a drop so long as they have been happy and managed their own affairs.

At about the same time we started the local credit union, the co-op slaughter-house for Västmanland was formed. Likewise the co-operative dairy had come into existence a few years before. In Kärrbo it was Ral from Lindö who agitated for the co-op slaughter-house and got the farmers to sign up for shares. Everyone became members.

A short time before the co-op slaughter-house was formed, I sold two cows to a private butcher and received a total of 200 kronor for them. If I'd been able to wait until the co-op was formed, I would have got over 400 kronor. The difference was that great. We became members because we benefited by it. The private wholesale butchers were able to offer shamefully low prices because the farmers needed cash and so were forced to sell.

Being a member of the co-operative slaughter-house meant that you had to deliver to them. But the private butchers didn't give up, they raised their prices and often bought up the best slaughtering animals to breed. The farmer who sold the animal received a receipt saying that he had sold livestock – which was permissible according to the co-operative's statutes – whereupon the animal was immediately slaughtered. Loyalty towards the jointly owned slaughter-house was only so-so.

However, eventually nearly all private butchers were absorbed by the co-op, which took over their functions and at the same time gave some of them employment, for otherwise they would have started over of course. Jäder from Dingtuna, a butcher, was hired as foreman at the co-operative slaughter-house, and Skiljebo-Lasse was employed as a buyer of livestock when the co-op began having auctions of dairy cows and other animals.

Towards the mid thirties farming conditions became better. The farmers' co-operative associations caused prices to be much more stable. I was even able to get a bank book for the Rural Credit Society.

Each member had all his accounts from the slaughter-house and dairy put into a chequing account in the Credit Society. The banks' propaganda against us claimed that the farmers weren't mature enough to handle cheques, and they tried to oppose the producers' co-operative movement by refusing to accept cheques from the farmers' credit union.

No doubt this was partially an attempt at revenge, because the credit union had begun to take over the mortgage loans the farmers had in the banks. But as time went by, they had to give in and start co-operating. Of course members occasionally took out more than their chequing accounts were credited with, but the majority of them were trustworthy farmers, so matters were usually quickly settled.

One form of credit that was very useful was the harvest loan. Before, the farmers usually bought seed and fertilizer with bills of exchange in the springtime, which had to be paid on 1 October. Since so much grain had to be sold in the fall in order to pay off the bills of exchange, the grain buyers were overloaded. Their storage space was insufficient, so naturally the mills took advantage of the situation to force down the prices.

Because of this, an arrangement was made whereby the farmers could get a loan from the credit union on harvested grain, which they stacked into the barns and didn't need to thresh and sell until the early spring, when grain prices rose. The state provided a certain guarantee for these harvest loans.

Farmers who received such loans had an obligation to notify the union before threshing and selling. Sometimes they sold without any notification and spent a large part of the money instead of repaying their harvest loans. Those of us who sat on the board naturally didn't want to play the role of police and go snooping into their barns, so instead we sometimes had to help such members get other loans in order to pay off the harvest loan.

It certainly caused us a lot of headaches. But you soon knew the shape of their finances like the back of your hand, and you also knew what kind of character they had.

At home in Hagbo we managed very well. The kids had finished school and we all worked together on the land and with the animals, and seldom bought anything for ourselves. The girls never spent a lot of money on stylish clothes; they did all their own sewing at home. We all had the same attitude and we lived frugally – partly because we had to, of course.

Generally, there was a lot of good will between neighbours. They all borrowed things from each other, household goods, tools, and even horses. I borrowed the Källsved horse and he borrowed mine in the fall, when you needed two horses for ploughing. There was never any question of money when you borrowed a horse.

We also used to help each other with repairs. Thunell from Solbacken used to help me thatch the roof on the barn – it was made of rye-straw and had to be changed every other year. We and the Thunells were together a lot; the kids were pals at school and some summers we would go down to Solbacken every day and swim. On Sundays we used to visit each other and drink coffee.

It was really beautiful there with the cottage on the slope and the meadows stretching down to the lake. The party who'd lived there before had done a lot of work planting and grafting fruit trees. There were a couple of hundred. At home in Hagbo we had one of our fruit trees grafted onto a rowanberry bush. The result was large streaky apples, very lovely to look at but sour to taste.

In 1937 a co-operative grain and feed store was formed, located in Västerås and christened Arosbygden. It was included in the Farmers' Central Union and it was the small farmers from the surrounding districts and the Swedish Farmers' Purchasing and Marketing Association who took the initiative in this. The big grain store, Forss, was bought up by the Union and served as a base of the operation. The owner was part of the deal, so to speak, and was given a job in the office. The smaller grain dealers were put out of business one by one as the Arosbygden grew bigger and became completely dominant.

But there were private grain dealers who survived in other parts of the country. Disloyal members sold their best grain to these and the poorer grain to Arosbygden, which was bound to accept all deliveries according to the statutes. They certainly got sneered at for their behaviour sometimes, but since it was mostly big farmers who were disloyal, it wasn't so easy for the smallholders to say anything.

The union branch in Kärrbo came into existence the following year. The National Farmers' Union originated, I think, in Norrland and had already existed for about ten years. The organization concentrated on the cities and was to look after the interests of all the country folks. It was intended that gardeners, as well as day-labourers, fishermen, farm-workers, and others would be members, but it turned out to be farmers almost exclusively.

In several places in Norrland there was dire poverty. You read in the papers of children falling down on their way to school, as a result of malnutrition and vitamin deficiencies. Towards the end of the thirties the union took up collections, and the farmers of Kärrbo donated a sack or two of grain or potatoes each as well as cash. All in all, the relief shipments, which were sent north by rail, were quite large.

The system of having free meals at school was introduced in these needy areas. The state covered eighty per cent of the cost of the meals and also transportation for kids who had a long way to school. Nowadays, of course, everybody gets free meals at school.

On 7 January 1937 my mother died. The year before, when the ten-year lease was up, we bought Hagbo for 9,000 kronor. Almost a giveaway, you might say. I paid 300 kronor in cash and the rest I got a loan for. Besides this there were 3,000 kronor left to pay for the animals and equipment we took over in 1926, but since the worst farm crisis was over, we figured we'd make a go of it. My share of what we inherited from Mother went to repay that debt.

At the end of the same year our youngest daughter, Stina, was born. This was a bit of a sensation since our next youngest had been born fifteen years before. You see, Ma was built rather broad in the beam and weighed nearly a hundred kilograms to my sixty kilograms, so nobody in the district had been able to see that she was expecting.

The following year, from spring to late fall, barges from Bohus County unloaded paving stones at Frösåker Pier for the highway construction between Västerås and Enköping. The traffic was very heavy, the trucks drove by in one long stream, and Kärrbo Road was almost ruined. The highway construction kept a lot of people busy, and many people from Kärrbo got jobs too.

The girls from the district were very fond of riding their bikes down to the pier in the evenings to meet the seamen and one of them got pregnant; the others were lucky. Maybe there were married women who went along, too.

The outbreak of war in 1939 didn't cause such a panic as in 1914. Everyone had known for a long time that there would be war. The nation entered into a state of emergency, but in Kärrbo you didn't notice much difference. Later on in the fall the Russo-Finnish Winter War broke out, and in April 1940 the Germans occupied Denmark and Norway. At that point many Swedes were called up and sent to the Norwegian border and up to Norrland.

In Gäddeholm, on the opposite side of the forest from Kärrbo, there was a military encampment and the emergency troops (i.e., older guys between thirty-five and forty-five) drove their horses and supply wagons and exercised and did manoeuvres in the woods all over the place. There were many divorces during those years. The reservists were good-natured and happy, and the women were lonely with their husbands away in military camps in other parts of the country.

It was time for my boy Ingemar to do his military service in 1941 and he was stationed with the armoured troops in

Strängnäs. He rode home on his bike almost every Saturday and back again on Sunday evening, a hundred kilometres there and back. In the fall he was allowed a two-weeks' 'harvest leave' and brought home a buddy of his. They hauled the manure out onto the fields that were lying fallow. And they dynamited rock for foundation stones for the new barn at Hagbo which Hedberg later built. Ingemar was the sort of person who always had to be busy doing things – he couldn't stand to hang around waiting.

When he was home again for Christmas he got a pain in his back and at New Year's went along to see the doctor. He was sent straight to the hospital in Västerås for a cyst on the lung. We figured he must have contracted the illness when he lay in a tent soaked through in freezing weather on a manoeuvre before Christmas.

At Whitsuntide, after an illness of more than four months, he was discharged from the hospital and came home. But on the eighth of June he had to visit the doctor again. He felt numb and couldn't piss properly. The doctor didn't do anything for it, he just sent him home. That night we had to drive him in to the hospital, and he never did get well again. He was later sent to Seraphim Hospital in Stockholm and they found out that there was an injury to the spinal marrow and that Ingemar would never recover from his paralysis.

The first wheel-chair he had was one with control levers. In it he drove sometimes from the nursing home in Västerås out to us in Hagbo for a visit. He had to take a detour, by way of Vreta barn, altogether nearly twenty-five kilometres – the hills were too steep for him the other way. Luckily, his arms were strong. We used to bike down to Frösåker and help him up the hills at Larsbo and Skyttebo.

After the war he bought a wheel-chair from a man named Nordin who worked at Asea and had made it himself. Ingemar had a small motor-scooter engine attached to it and he still rides around in it, sometimes all the way to Arboga and Sala.

He has also been up north to Hälsingland and south to Småland to vacation homes owned by the National Association of the Handicapped. Of course he took the train to these places.

I myself was past forty-five when the war broke out, and was therefore exempt from military service. The only difference it made to us in Hagbo was the rationing it brought, but that presented no problem since we grew all our own food at home. The meat coupons more than covered the licences for the pigs we slaughtered at home, and we farmers used the mill licences for flour-grinding twice. It was slightly illegal, but if the miller was given ten kronor for taking the risk, we could manage an extra grinding on the same licence. The food situation was actually better than before the war, since we had more money.

Farming throughout the country became divided up into different working-blocs. Hagbo belonged to the Harkie bloc. The idea was that in the event of war, the bloc leader would take command of all division of labour within the bloc, among old people as well as the young. It was designed to function like in North Vietnam now and like the N.L.F. in South Vietnam. We see pictures from there in newspapers, how everyone is working out in the fields to bring in the harvest.

If there was war I was to be in charge of accommodations for Kärrbo and would also be responsible for food supplies to people who landed up there. I was given a batch of blank cheques for making payments and also received instructions that I was entitled to expropriate from farmers and stores, if they refused to sell. I was also to be in charge of the evacuation of the entire population if the district were bombed, as a result of its proximity to Västerås, with its industries. The maps and armbands that I was given are still lying up in the attic.

Blankets and mattresses from the Red Cross were stored here and there at different farms. Food and ammunition shelters were blasted out of the rocky hillsides. They even laid cement runways for airplanes in the forests; they were covered up with earth and trees were planted there. Cement runways like this can quickly be cleared off when they're needed.

At the beginning of the war the state rented the big building in Täby for the Polish families who had received assistance in their escape to Sweden. They were mainly wives and children of Polish officers. Among ourselves we discussed the fact that there wasn't a single working-class or farm wife among them, only well-to-do, upper-class hags in furs. When they rode on the Kärrbo bus to the city, they wouldn't move over to make room for as many as possible – no, they spread out over the seats with their bags and baskets and acted rude to common folks. They lived in Täby for several months before they were placed in various cities.

A while before the Polish women arrived, Swedish-speaking families from the islands off Estonia came to Sweden. Some settled in Kärrbo. They were working people, small farmers and fishermen. Towards the end of the war Estonian refugees, as well as a few Latvians, were quartered in Täby.

They had escaped in small boats over the Baltic Sea. They were educated people, teachers, lawyers and doctors, and assorted others. At that time there was a stipulation in Swedish law which said that foreigners who took refuge in this country could have jobs only in agriculture or forestry.

The Estonians in Täby didn't want to take the lumber-jack jobs that were offered to them. It seemed like they looked down upon manual labour and folks who did that kind of work. They wanted to get away from the country and its farm people and would rather go without working while they waited for the chance at a job in the city. By and by they disappeared from Kärrbo.

They were long and hard, those winters during the war, and it was so dry the summer of 1942 that I only managed twelve loads of hay whereas normally I'd get forty or forty-five loads. The farmers had to buy cellulose as emergency fodder, chips of wood treated with lye to take away the turpentine and make them edible. All the old straw-stacks were used up during those years.

Farmers who had plenty of forest sold great loads of wood in the city and earned a lot of money. The demand for it was great, since wood was used as fuel all the time. The forest was precious and the state issued directives to all districts requiring them to organize voluntary fire departments. The one we had in Kärrbo used to have drills in putting out forest fires.

The Civil-Defence people also practised a lot, as well as the women's auxiliary and the Home Guard. I wasn't in on this because I had so much else to do with my civic duties and other jobs. I was also the administrator of slaughtering and went around each month to all the farms and counted their animals to make sure that they weren't slaughtering them for the black market. It was an annoying job but I didn't work at it too seriously.

In Kärrbo we didn't bother about what the farmers slaughtered and ate themselves, even if they sometimes slaughtered without a licence. On the other hand, what we did tell everyone was that they shouldn't sell on the black market, not even to relatives or friends, since people find it so hard to keep quiet. Actually, there was never any trouble in our district, but from other parishes so much pork and meat was sold on the black market in the city that there was talk of replacing their own slaughter officials with state ones.

For a while it was also forbidden to sell eggs, when they started rationing them. I remember that well, because the head of Civil Defence asked if he could buy two dozen eggs from me once, when he was out inspecting. 'We can pack them down into the potato sack,' he said. It wasn't forbidden to buy potatoes and he had bought a sack from me.

We felt the effects of war, rationing, and regulations for quite some time, even when the war was over. Though on the whole, of course, we weren't badly off here in Sweden. I had stopped fattening calves and pigs, since just then they brought such low prices that it was more profitable to sell them right away as sucklings and send the milk to the dairy. Which made less work, too.

The years immediately following the war were pretty good harvest years. I bought quite a lot of fertilizer, mostly super-phosphates and potash – nitrogen being supplied mainly by cow dung.

Beside one of the fields stood a big oak. It sucked up all the nitrogen from the ground around it in a large semicircle reaching as far as the roots went out into the field. When I had cut it down, very fine wheat began to grow where once there had only been thin, dry wheat. You'll no doubt find that many a small farmer with a strip of plough land in the forests has been fertilizing the trees more than his crops.

On many occasions before the war we discussed the fact that the community needed a better meeting place than the com-munity centre made of boards on the slope of Hagbo. In 1937 the state started to allot funds for building projects and the question came up for consideration at the Rural District Meeting in Kärrbo. And then the war came along and it wasn't until it was over that the question was really considered seriously. Then the schoolhouse in Harkie was sold. The district received 8,000 kronor for it and this amount served as a nest egg for the building.

After this we applied for a state grant for a sauna-bath and got 2,000 kronor on the condition that once a week the sauna should be open to the general public. It was to be situated in the cellar of the community centre which the Rural District was planning to build in the neighbourhood of the church. The state contribution to the building costs for a rural community centre was as much as fifty per cent, yet this plus the 10,000 kronor we already had was still not enough.

Then the problem got solved, for the people of the parish volunteered to help according to their means and ability. It was unanimously agreed that the building should get built, since it was something that everybody could use and enjoy. Lists were sent around and people put their names down for voluntary work.

The Rural District owned the Municipal Forest where you could take all the timber you needed. The men from Ekevi felled the trees. Farmers with horses did the dragging. Nyby's tractor supplied the power to drive the saw. Tractors from other farms moved away rocks when the foundation was being dug. Gravel was driven to the site free of charge by Valle's and Lindö's trucks.

The foundation was dug in the evenings and so were the ditches for water and drainage. The menfolk in the community took turns working and sometimes there were so many of them that there was hardly enough room for them all. The cellar floor and the foundations, of hollow concrete stones, were laid entirely by volunteers. It was like the old days when they built meeting places. The men worked half the night and the women brought them coffee and sandwiches, and there was merry-making on the hillside almost every evening.

In the fall of 1946 the foundation was ready, and the following spring the necessary timber was sawed up. The actual wood-construction work was given to a professional builder to take care of. Towards the fall of 1947 then, the community centre was ready and the dedication was quite a solemn occasion, for everyone had been in on the project and contributed to it. The sewing circle and several individuals had donated curtains and linen, and Erik Idar, the painter, had donated a painting of a seascape, which was one of the finest pictures he has painted, I believe; it was the view from his summer cottage in Solbacken, looking out over the bay towards Rid Island – Ridö.

The picture is hanging in the library. We combined the W.E.A. and I.O.G.T. libraries with the Rural District's public library to make one whole library, as soon as the community centre was ready. I was librarian to begin with. There were many fine books there.

The main hall in the centre has room for a couple of hundred people, and it was there that various associations had their parties and functions, and the parish folk used it for their fiftieth-anniversary parties and for funerals. Weddings, on the other hand, were fairly rare occasions since the population of the parish began to decrease quickly after the war, and the young people moved into the city, leaving mostly old people behind.

When the final accounts were ready for the building of the centre, it was found that we needed to levy a five per cent increase on local taxes during a year, and then everything, including furniture, would be paid for. This was not such a burden, at least not for those who lived on the larger farms, who for the most part managed to pay the lowest taxes.

I used to help some of the folks in the parish with their paper-work, like filling in their income tax returns, and writing out inventories when somebody died, and so on. One of the people I helped with his tax return was the new farmer in Källsved. He was from the south of Sweden, from the province of Småland, and said 'milk-jaw-er' instead of milk-can: a can was a jar and so he was always called 'Jaw-er'.

He was deaf and strong as an ox. He had three brothers who resembled him and they always got into a fight when they met. A fourth brother was completely different. Their father was called the Herring Strangler and Jaw-er and his brothers were known as the Herring Strangler's boys. No doubt they all got his name because they were brought up on herring.

Jaw-er could read people's lips. He was far from stupid. He himself shouted loudly when he said something, and he had a sharp temper, especially where his missus and kids were concerned.

Another real character was 'Stamper' who got her name from the fact that she never stood still, but always stamped her feet on the ground when she was talking. She used to leave the house about five or five-thirty a.m. and go around the farms chatting and gossiping. Two of her daughters used to go with her.

Her old man was the cowhand in Harkie and he was a little short on grey matter too. But both he and Stamper were diligent workers, though their household budget was a bit doubtful. He was forced to lock up the bread and other food in the bureau in order to have anything to eat. When they had slaughtered a pig Stamper would go around to the cottages offering everyone a taste, so the pork ran out after three weeks. The kids probably didn't get the food they should have had, either.

In their old age they lived in the tenant cottage at Skämsta for a while but then, when the district authorities got into the act, they were moved into a cottage at Karlberg. One morning the old man went to the privy and was away a long time. So Stamper went out to take a look. When she opened the door the old boy fell out – he'd gone and died sitting on the john.

Feeder-Kalle was another: he got his name from the work he did – feeding mud and sand into the mixer at Lindö Brickyard. When it was closed down, he took to digging drainage ditches, a job he was good at. But that job also folded, so he began trading in rags and scrap and empty bottles instead.

Eventually he was put on welfare by the parish, for there were five or six kids in the family. Then he began to brag that since now they were getting supported, he could afford to have more. And that's what he did – they had four or five more kids before his missus conked out.

There were a lot of other odd types in Kärrbo, Råstock-Sven, Lappa, and 'Clockwork', for example. I suppose I was also considered a character.

I gave up the farming at Hagbo in 1950. With one boy an invalid, three gals wanting to leave home and the old woman beginning to wear out, there was no point in going on. And I myself didn't have the energy I had before.

When I sold Hagbo I figured we ought to have 25,000 kronor left after the debts had been paid off – a mortage loan of 2,700 kronor – and we did. If instead I had leased the farm and sold it now to some real estate company that builds summer cottages, we might have got 200,000 kronor for it.

One of the reasons why I didn't do this was because of a new law which had recently been passed specifying that tenants could demand repairs to their residence. It could have cost more than I could comfortably pay, for the cottage in Hagbo was in bad shape, and so was the barn. Because of the new law, the Count of Ängsö gave all his tenant farmers notice and drew up new contracts, formulated so that they couldn't take advantage of the law and demand repairs.

On 2 March 1950 we auctioned off lock, stock, and barrel in Hagbo – machines, tools, and animals. A lot of people came; the auction went well and we cleared 12,000 kronor on the sales, after the auctioneers had taken their cut. The animals brought in the most money; the rest of the stuff wasn't worth much. I had two horses, but I sent one of them to the slaughter-house. I didn't want anyone else to have him.

From Hagbo we moved here to Anundshög. The name comes from the burial ground here behind the grove. Many generations have lived and worked in these parts since King Bröt-Anund died and was provided his burial mound in the seventh century. Though no one knows for sure whether it's he or some other Anund lying there. It must have been an important person anyway, since the mound is about 200 metres in circumference and fourteen metres high. There are also some smaller mounds beside the 'ship formations' below.

We bought the house here for 20,000 kronor, and it's situated conveniently close to Västerås. We've got water and drains and central heating and a lavatory in the cellar. The ground covers 5,510 square metres.

When I came here I started work at the nursery up by Malma Farm. It's owned by the Forestry Board. But I wasn't very happy there. In the summer the work was heavy and in the winter there wasn't a thing to do.

I became a sort of foreman for school kids and housewives who did a bit of part-time work weeding and planting and packing. Some of the youngsters from the city were very good at it, but others had to be watched over like wilful calves.

The pay was what an ordinary farmworker got. Since it was only seasonal work, I thought the pay was too low. There was no chance of organizing a union for school kids and housewives who were not willing to fight for their rights. So I started looking around for something else.

During the first few years we lived here we kept chickens, and I used to buy chicken-feed at Arosbygden's store on Sturegatan. The man who looked after the store was getting on in years, and one day I went up to the office and asked if I could take over his job.

In time I was given the job and became store manager with a monthly salary. I was now a white-collar worker and transferred to the commercial employees' trade union. The salary wasn't so hot, about 1,000 kronor a month. The job was fun, but there was a lot to keep track of, over 500 different kinds of items and prices. One had to be really careful with charge accounts. Customers who were black-listed for failing to pay were not allowed to buy anything unless they paid in cash.

I had a good friend in the store named Sigurd Nysell. He was a fantastically good worker when the customers were standing in line, especially on Saturdays when the farmers came to town and the whole parking lot and the street outside were full of automobiles. They came for bran and grain, and seeds and weed-killer, preparations to control bugs and medicines for their pigs, and everything else.

It was quieter all the other days, though we had the trucks

coming instead with new stocks of goods, and then we had to carry in the sacks, which was a lot of drudgery. But it was a friendly business. If I didn't know the farmers around Västerås before, I certainly got to know them then. In the springtime some of them would race in here, their hair standing on end in their nervous state, asking for insecticides. Then they were in a hurry. For example, on a sunny day, fleas on the rape seed will hatch from eggs lying in the earth. They can eat up an entire field of rape plants. On other occasions, when there wasn't any hurry, the customers might stand around for hours, just talking.

To begin with I rode my bike to my job, as it was only eight kilometres. Of course the weather was bad sometimes, still you never noticed it. You just put on your rain-clothes. In wintertime I usually took the bus. Then I didn't need to start work at seven a.m., quarter to eight was good enough.

In 1954 I began taking driving lessons. I had Erik Åhs as my instructor. He was nice and calm. I was sixty years old and altogether it took me sixty half-hour lessons in order to pass the test for my driver's licence.

One day in August Erik suggested that we go down to Bergfeldts and look at automobiles. The outcome was that I bought a new Fiat 1100, the first and only motor vehicle I have ever owned. That car has been running without any trouble for over sixteen years now. But I haven't driven very much, only 67,000 kilometres all in all.

I had the car parked until I took my driving test in November. And then I started taking it to work every day. That worked all right. I was glad I had learned such a lot at driving school. The fact is that you need a thorough training in order to drive safely in traffic.

On 3 May 1958 I quit at Arosbygden. I had three years to go before I got my old-age pension, but Ma and I figured we'd get by with what we grew at home, potatoes and vegetables and raspberries and strawberries, which we took to market and sold. We didn't have the same kind of income as when I had a permanent job, but it was enough for us to manage on.

On the side I did some day-work now and again on the farms round-about in the summer, and once or twice in the forests during the winter. And we had a little money put aside in the bank. The produce from our garden plot gives us enough to buy the things we need for the house. For the most part we're self-supporting and grow all our own food.

A person doesn't need many clothes, either. Four years ago I bought a suit and I've only worn it once – the rest of the time it's been hanging up in the attic. I feel more at home in my work clothes. When I've been to the city, I'm no sooner home than I change back into my dungarees. There's always something to fiddle with here around the house, some job to be done.

One summer, after I'd quit at Arosbygden, we took our first vacation in an automobile. We drove down to see Ingemar who had contracted T.B. in a lesion on his hip and was being treated at Apelviken Sanatorium outside Varberg. He had his wheel-chair with him and he was busy doing a lot of photography. He took a bunch of pictures of us and I wrote a verse about one of them in the photo album:

> The old gal sits there, plump and chubby,
> With sponge cake and buns around,
> Me, I'm so spindly I risk blowing off the ground,
> So there sure is a difference 'tween wife and hubby.

We were away for a week. Britta and her husband were here to pick strawberries and tend to things while we were gone. At night we slept in the car, and in the daytime we swam or sat and talked. We got permission to drive in to Apelviken's grounds and park down by the sea. There were only flat rocks all over there and fine sand in the coves. The sun was shining all the time and we had the whole place to ourselves. The only outing we made was to Varberg Castle; apart from that we just relaxed and spent the time with Ingemar.

The sanatorium's graveyard is located nearby. In the old days when the country was poorer, patients were buried there. The majority of crosses were for children from up in Norrland. It probably was too far away and too expensive, I think, to send the coffins home.

The first few years we lived here in Anundshög we were quite active in the Good Templar Lodge, No. 4888, Anund, the old gal and I, but now that she has a harder time walking, we don't get out to the lodge meetings quite so often. I've been a teetotaller since 1911. The thing with alcohol is that it can have a positive effect on reserved people. Though it depends on how intelligent they are. Most people get silly from drinking alcohol and the negative effects outweigh the positive ones, if there are any.

In the beginning I looked after the I.O.G.T.'s books but since they could only be taken out at the members' meetings, not so many books were loaned out. Myself, I borrowed quite a few books from the library in Västerås for a while. Nowadays it's not that often. I read novels and a book by Gandhi, *Experiment With Truth*. He really was a very broad-minded man – that's why he was murdered.

People talk a lot these days about how short the average life expectancy is in India and in many other countries. In England during the 1830's only nine out of every 1,000 industrial workers lived to the age of forty and only one out of 1,000 lived till they were fifty. You can read this in *The Century of Social Democracy* by Hjalmar Branting.

I personally am still an active Social Democrat and agent for the party's magazine *Aktuellt*. We have about twenty subscribers within the Badelunda workers' district. But people are so strange, they complain about having so much else to read, or that they don't have any time.

The study circles aren't working out very well, either. Many members get tired of going or they don't give a damn whether they learn anything or not. A few of us have kept a circle going for a time on ideas for a future society, but it all seemed hazy. These days the leaders of the workers' movement don't know what it is they want to achieve.

It sure is encouraging that there are so many young people with political consciousness who are protesting. Even if sometimes they get a bit too excited and stir up a big fuss, it's obvious that the young ones know better than the old just what's got to be done. There's a wave of rebellion passing through all countries now, and we may well need it, the way the world looks today, with all its injustices.

I read as much as I have time for.

I spend most of my time in the summer working in the garden. I can't stand weeds, I cut them down with the rotary plough. Though I will admit that even flowering weeds can be very pretty.

Greta became a diabetic three years ago and that's why I specially grow a lot of vegetables like cabbage, lettuce, spinach, carrots, onions, marrowfat peas, and other things. Greta was forced to slim down and she's taken off nearly thirty kilograms since we stopped eating potatoes, coffee-breads, and so on. I keep to the same diet as she has. It was a bit monotonous to start with, but if I sit there eating something else, she's tempted to do the same, to eat a whole lot of meat, for instance. I've never been fussy about my food; so long as you keep active, working, you can eat anything at all. If you're hungry enough, you'll eat, O.K.

The first thing I do every morning is to go up to the highway and get the newspaper. I subscribe to the Social-Democratic paper, *Folket*. Then I listen to the six-thirty news on the radio and make tea and sandwiches which I take in to Ma in bed. She gets pains in her legs and doesn't get up so early any more.

We go to bed early in the evenings. I think the Swedish people are getting to be nervous wrecks from sitting up late every night watching T.V. – you just don't get enough sleep that way.

The first hour in the morning I sit at the kitchen table

reading *Folket*. Then I go out and do some work in the garden. We eat around ten a.m. She fixes the food and washes the dishes, and I go on working outside right after we've finished our meal. At twelve-thirty we listen to the news, drink coffee and chat a while. Then I'm out again pottering around until the meal is ready at five p.m. Afterwards I help dry the dishes.

Ma is very fond of playing Old Maid, and we do often, but in the evenings I like to sit and read or write a little. There are so many books unread. In the summertime, in bad weather I usually sit indoors at my writing-desk.

Sometimes we have errands to do in the city, to arrange different things or to visit children and grandchildren. Once a month we go to the co-op supermarket and get our main supplies.

The winter goes by and you don't really get anything done. Quite often I go down into the cellar and mess around with one thing or another. One winter I renovated a chest of drawers, but I really haven't any proper tools for that kind of thing.

For the most part, I sit indoors reading, then I copy out various passages and compare books; I do this when it's cold outside and the snow is whipping at the windows. In the attic I have a pile of back numbers of *The Study Companion* which I get down sometimes and look through. There's a series of articles from the thirties about how Nazism was fought – much of this is timely again now in the case of South Africa and Rhodesia. And in east Africa, the Indian minority, and in south-east Asia, the Chinese minority are parallels to the Jews in Europe.

I copy out what I think is worth saving and now I have seven black notebooks filled with pieces of prose and verse. Some of the poems I've made up myself, but most of them are copies of other people's poems. Underneath I make a note of the name of the publisher and date of publication, name of translator and any other point of interest.

Sometimes there are fine little poems by lesser-known talents to be found in *Folket*, and I copy them off. In the magazine *We*, which is the consumers' co-operative society's magazine, on the teenagers' page there are often fantastic poems sent in by kids between the ages of fifteen and nineteen. Young people are much more outspoken today than before and certainly this is a result of improved schooling. Otherwise it's mostly poetry of more well-known writers that I collect: Ekelöf, Pasternak, Theodorakis, Vreeswijk, Rilke, Alvaros, Strindberg, and many more. When I was young, people used to say that when Strindberg was writing at full speed he ate as much as two manual labourers.

In the summer we usually drive out and visit friends and relations in Bergslagen. Actually we've been leading a pretty lazy life the last few years. The house really needs a coat of paint and repairs made on it, but I'm not so happy about climbing up high any more.

We have talked about selling and moving into an apartment in the city. Ma has a harder and harder time walking as the years go by. And the toilet is down in the cellar and we have no bathroom. Usually we heat water on the stove and bathe in a large tub on the kitchen floor. It's O.K. but it certainly would be lovely to have a shower.

In the city you could exchange garden work for sitting at the library, at least as long as your eyesight and your mind are still working. Though we're not that eager to sell now when the value of property is rising so fast.

I am not afraid of death, I don't believe any old person is. Of course I hope to avoid being bedridden for years, that would be miserable. But since the brain's activity diminishes at the same time, maybe you wouldn't mind it that much, lying there.

When you're young, you think you're going to live forever. But it's the same with people as it is in nature: nothing lasts. The old ones disappear and are resurrected in new generations. Nothing lives forever. Everything's renewed.

Life's Lonesome without a Cow

Milda Åhs

Skämsta is located in the far end of Kärrbo. I was born there in 1898. My grandfather, on my father's side, owned the farm there. Dad stayed home and worked for him. Mom came from a working-class family in Skultuna. She worked as a maid at Skämsta before she married Dad.

Signe is the eldest of us children and has always been called Sissan. I was born a year after her and then came Märta, Herbert, and Ejvor, who is fifteen years younger than me.

We grew up in a good home. In those days parents were stricter with their children than they are now, but Dad wasn't as mean as a lot of other fathers were then, though he was strict of course. He only had to look at us to make us obey. Mom was kind to us, too. Otherwise it was quite common for youngsters to suffer, and to get beaten a lot. Kids weren't fresh like they are now – nowadays, practically, it's the parents who obey the children. We would never have dared to go against our parents.

In 1905 Dad rented Tibble Farm in Dingtuna and we lived there for five years. We moved all our belongings there by horse and wagon. Dad's cows followed along by themselves behind the load the whole way from Skämsta to Tibble, more than thirty kilometres, and even through Västerås. They weren't used to being led, and instead had to be driven. The same thing happened when we moved back to Skämsta again, though we had even more cattle at that time.

The building we lived in at Tibble had three rooms and a large kitchen on the ground floor and two rooms upstairs which two old maids rented. The servant girls had a small room inside the house. The farmhands lived in a room in a separate cottage.

We ate in the kitchen. First the men, then the womenfolk and us kids. We ate a lot of our own pork, which was so heavily salted that it was almost green. Calves were sold for cash; we couldn't afford to eat these. We never had eggs except at Easter and on the last day of April, when there was a great feast. Herring was our staple diet, fried herring and potatoes in the morning and porridge. We had butter on holidays and sometimes on Sundays. Most of the butter Mom churned was sold in the city the same as the eggs. We ate margarine instead, since it was cheaper.

Pancakes and lingonberries was a common evening meal. We girls were allowed to help pick berries, mostly lingonberries and blueberries. This was great fun. Tibble lay in the middle of the big fields in Dingtuna with very little forest, so we went to Sippersta Woods to do our berry-picking.

We had a tree of Bergamot pears in our garden and an apple tree, which I remember clearly having great big rosy apples on it. The fruit was used to make soup and dessert sauces but sometimes we children were allowed to eat fresh apples and pears.

I began school in Kärrbo. In those days the school year began on the fifteenth of February, and we moved to Tibble before the fourteenth of March, so I was only there a month. Next I went to school in Dingtuna. We had examinations at Christmas time and the end of term was just before Midsummer.

What military discipline there was in schools back then! In Dingtuna the schoolmaster had the sixth grade and the boys from the fifth grade on the ground floor, and the schoolmarm had the fourth grade and the girls from the fifth grade upstairs. We filed in and out in a line. One of us had to stand guard on the staircase and report anyone who talked going up or down. Anyone who made the slightest peep had to stay after school.

Our teacher had no singing voice. The last lesson on Fridays downstairs was singing and the ones who couldn't sing were sent upstairs to read *The Wonderful Adventures of Nils*. The teacher we had for handwork on Saturday mornings was not so strict as the rest of them. We knitted stockings and sewed pinafores and other easy things. But we weren't allowed to make the nicer things like tablecloths, or bobbin-made or crocheted lace. The material was provided by the school. The boys had woodwork.

There were a huge number of children at the school. Most of them were poor: children of farm-workers, tenant farmers and children from the day-labourers' shacks. The clothes many of them wore were pretty bad – hand-me-downs from older brothers and sisters or things made over from grown-ups' clothes. The poorest ones got shoes from the parish.

The rich farmers and the minister were the big shots in the parishes. Even the teachers were a couple of notches above ordinary folks. The difference in social ranks was great. The ones with money made the decisions; the great majority of people had no say. Nowadays there's a little more equality.

At home we weren't too well-off and it was a bit of a struggle. Dad had started out empty-handed and I believe he had borrowed money to get going. We had two farmhands, two servant girls, a married farm-worker and a married cowman. Mom had to work very hard. There were six grown-ups and three children in the household.

In March 1910 Dad took over Skämsta. We lived downstairs and Grandpa upstairs. He was a churchwarden. Grandma died in 1904. Aunt Amanda, Dad's sister, did the housekeeping for him, and they ate alone upstairs. Mom had enough to do anyway, poor thing, what with four farmhands to feed and my brother Herbert, who was born two months after we came home to Skämsta. She had two servant girls helping her, but they were supposed to do the milking and help out with other work outside all the summer.

In the sixth grade I went to school in Kärrbo. We started at eight-thirty a.m.; it was three kilometres to school and I remember how cold the wind blew sometimes over Vreta plain. We had catechism and stories from the Bible, arithmetic, and theme writing. They were very particular about penmanship. We had Swedish history and geography and we also read about Asia and Africa. By the time we finished school we had by and large forgotten everything.

In the fall of 1911 I started going to confirmation classes. It was a year too early, I was only twelve, but Dad had been to see the minister and asked if I could go along with my older sister Sissan. This was so I'd be considered a big girl sooner.

Åhrén, the rector, led the confirmation lessons. There were sixteen of us. Nobody was scared of him, he was so nice. The lessons were held in the community room at the other end of the elementary school.

It was there the council meeting was held and community affairs decided. No women took part. Of the men, it was only the big shots who went to the meeting, the ones who controlled local council business.

Before the confirmation ceremony, we asked if we might serve coffee in the community room. We were granted permission, so we served coffee to the minister and to our teacher. We bought the coffee at the grocer's in Norbo, right nearby on the other side of the road, cater-corner from the present rural community centre, where there used to be stores.

The store burned down in 1914. It was the grocer himself who set fire to it, because he couldn't make a living out of it. He had probably been hoping to claim the fire insurance, but he didn't succeed. After that he disappeared from Kärrbo. There was a store in Valla too, you know, and quite a number of customers, since the brickyards were operating both in Lindö and in Frösåker. But there wasn't enough business for two stores.

We were allowed to decorate the church all by ourselves before Confirmation Day. It was in April, and we'd kept young birch branches indoors so that the leaves would be out in time.

We spent the whole Friday before confirmation decorating the church, and then we girls invited everyone to coffee twice. We managed to borrow flowering potted plants from the gardener in Frösåker, and we took them back on Monday when we took down the decorations in church. Then it was the boys' turn to serve coffee, but we didn't get any, they let us down.

When you were confirmed you were grown up. I had turned thirteen. Then came work. We didn't have any servant girls any more, so Sissan and I had to take over the milking and all the other jobs done by the womenfolk outside. The first job we had to help with that spring was hauling manure.

We had a cowhand but he wouldn't have anything to do with milking. That was women's work. He would stand leaning on his manure shovel and talk to us while we milked.

Dad was handy. When he came home to Skämsta he had a whole lot of rebuilding to do: the barn and wagon-shed, wood-shed and washhouse. In 1911 he bought a baling machine. The farmhands said that he'd never make a go of it, that he'd go bankrupt. But he didn't and managed to get along.

The baler saved us women a lot of work; for before, you know, it was always the women who had walked the fields every day in the fall, bent almost double as they bound up the sheaves.

In winter we threshed. It was cold and there was a lot of dust. The dust lay in grey layers over our faces and clothes and a cloud of it billowed like thick smoke out through the barn doors. We had a farm labourer who always threw up more sheaves than I could take care of and once I let him load the board I was standing on full up, and then I tipped them all down to him again. Just then Dad came along and of course it was me he got mad at.

On Saturday evenings there was usually a dance on at one of the farms. We had to ask permission to go until we were almost twenty. Once there was a dance at Lindö Brickyard and we went anyway; Dad wasn't at home and Mom didn't say very much. The room the dance was held in was so dusty that our white dresses were completely filthy when we came home in the morning just in time for milking. The dances usually lasted all night.

The following Sunday night Sissan and I were dead tired, but we had to sit in the stable and keep an eye on a mare who was about to foal. If we had enough energy for dancing all night, we certainly had energy to work as well, said Dad. That was our punishment. If we had boys come home with us, we had to creep in quietly so Dad didn't see us.

During the war two brothers bought up neighbouring Springsta and cut down the forest. Their name was Lundgren and they came from Skultuna; they hired a whole gang of lumber-jacks. Wood brought high prices. After the trees on several hundred acres had been cut up into lumber, the lumber-jacks threw a party in the big building at Springsta where nobody lived yet.

Dad said that Sissan and I couldn't go unless an aunt who had come to visit us went along with us, but she didn't want to go. She didn't have any dancing shoes. But we nagged her into borrowing a pair. They were too tight and her toes hurt her all night long.

The lumber-jacks didn't drink too terribly much and there was no trouble. When we went home over Oxle to Skämsta, we each had a lumber-jack with us, Sissan and me and our aunt. The boy who took me home was from Liljeholmen in Stockholm. Sissan's partner came from the province of Värmland, from Sunne.

One Twelfth Night we had a dance at home in Skämsta which lasted until six-thirty a.m. Then we rushed out to the cowshed to milk the cows. It wouldn't do to be tired then, let me tell you. Axel Johannson from Råstock played for us and we danced in the upstairs room. He got a bit dizzy towards the small hours and he stood halfway up the stairs with his accordion and played for the people sitting downstairs and for us who were dancing upstairs at the same time.

So sometimes we did have a bit of fun all right. Life was not all work. It seldom, if ever, happened that young girls got pregnant. Well, of course there were some girls who were fast. But usually girls didn't get in the family way until they were over twenty. And when it happened, they got married. That's how it was for both me and my sister.

We didn't pay much attention to the First World War. There was a lot about it in our local newspaper, but it was really only Dad who read it a little. Mom wasn't much for reading, and she didn't have time either.

The outbreak of war was scary. The church bells rang and everyone thought that Sweden would be at war too. I remember how Nyström, the schoolteacher, who came to Kärrbo in 1913, had to stand guard for a time by Ängsö Bridge. Whatever that was supposed to accomplish.

Before the newspaper started coming out every day, a man named Eriksson, from Kungsåra, delivered it in Kärrbo by horse and wagon on Tuesdays, Thursdays, and Saturdays. We had to go to Skysta to fetch it and often had to wait in the kitchen for the 'paper-wagon' to come.

The only connection with the outside world, apart from walking or going by horse, was the boat between Ängsö and Västerås; it was called *The Pole Star* and lay to at Springsta Pier on Wednesdays and Saturdays. The workers who didn't have a horse and wagon used the boat. We were never able to ride by boat since it cost money, so we always rode by horse and wagon.

We seldom went to town, except for the Folk Fair in August. Then all we kids were allowed to go along. When we were older we biked in and stayed overnight with relatives.

Birger Andersson's father sold bicycles. He was the engineer at Frösåker Brickyard. When Birger became caretaker up at the church he repaired and traded bicycles.

The farm-workers had a rotten life: small wages and large families with no family allowances or any financial help at all. Old people weren't much better off either. At Skämsta there lived a widow who made her living mainly from going around doing other people's washing, mostly at the rectory and the larger farms. She also used to help out at the many parties they gave. She didn't earn much from the work, but she had only her solitary self to keep alive.

All of my brothers and sisters and I worked at home practically our whole childhood and adolescence. We certainly weren't very demanding when it came to clothes and money for entertainment – the little money our family did have got spent first on upkeep of the farm. Dad looked after the finances and managed to make ends meet. Mom knew what the situation was, but it was Dad who handled the money matters.

Sissan went to domestic science school in Katrineholm one summer, and my younger sister, Märta, to summer school to a folk high school at Tärna. One winter Herbert went to Svalöv in Skåne to study agriculture. He didn't like it at all down there and was glad to come home again. My youngest sister Ejvor took a summer course at Tärna and after that she tried her luck as housemaid at Haga Palace outside Enköping for a couple of years.

I was also away for a year, beginning in November 1918, working as housemaid at Lycksta in Romfartuna. It was a large manor house with a kitchen-maid and a cook and a nurse-maid. The owner's name was Grevesmühl and he was called 'The Engineer', since he had an engineer's degree, I believe. The lady of the house didn't do anything, she just sat around looking beautiful.

The housemaid's job consisted of, among other things, setting the table and serving at all meals. The kitchen-maid and I did the cleaning and made the beds, and in winter we had to light the glazed-tile stoves. There was never any dry wood, so it was hard to get the stoves lit. The working day began at six a.m. The house had to be warmed up by eight a.m., when the master and mistress ate their breakfast. Oatmeal was their standard breakfast but they often ate herring too in the mornings.

The Engineer ate lunch at twelve noon. His wife and we others just drank coffee. Dinner was at four-thirty p.m. I was always very hungry by then since, you know, I was used to eating dinner in the middle of the day at home. We maid-servants ate in the kitchen. The master and mistress always stayed upstairs. The Engineer could behave naturally and would sometimes come into the kitchen and talk to us. But the mistress was a bit stuck-up and didn't talk to servants unless she needed to.

The master and his wife often gave big dinners for other proprietors, who came in horse-drawn carriages, sometimes from long distances. The old Westerdahl couple must have had a two-hour carriage ride from Kusta. The coachmen waited together in a room in a separate wing of the house at Lycksta, until it was time to drive home again.

The first time I waited table at one of these dinners, I was very nervous about how it would go. I had to provide my own black dress. I got twenty-five kronor a month, but after half a year, the mistress raised me to thirty kronor. She had shown me what I was to do, from which side I should serve various dishes to the guests, which plates should be taken away and which should be set out.

I felt very shaky, but afterwards, the mistress came down and thanked me and said she thought it had all gone very well. That was a great encouragement. I also had to help take the guests' wraps when they arrived and help them on with them when they left. Sometimes you got a tip, maybe fifty öre or sometimes even a whole krona.

In summertime the parties were held in the garden. It was a long way to go and tiring to carry out food and dishes. There were never any late-night parties, they all ended fairly early in the evening. The guests were served wine but hardly ever liquor and nobody was ever drunk when they left.

My usual working hours were from six in the morning to about six at night. All that was left to do then was to bring coffee up to the drawing-room at eight o'clock. On Sundays we had a free hour or two during the day, which could be spent in your room or going out for a walk. I worked on Sundays as well as weekdays and had one week's vacation in the summer. Then I would ride my bicycle home to Skämsta and help out there.

Before I took the job at Lycksta I had started going steady with Valentin. One Saturday he came from Törnby in Kärrbo to call on me. How long it took him to walk nearly thirty kilometres, I don't know – he *was* a big fellow with long legs. It was a summer evening and I knew he was going to come, so I went a little way down the road to meet him. He went home again on Sunday morning.

We continued seeing each other for a while, but to tell the truth, it was really over between us before I moved home to Skämsta. A year later we took up again, and in the fall of 1920, we were forced to start thinking of marriage. The thing was, I was expecting a baby.

Then I started thinking about all the things I wanted to do when I was married, sewing and weaving and other handwork that I'd never had time for. But it didn't work out as I planned. There wasn't much time left over for things like that.

We got married in May 1921, and settled down in Berga in Kungsåra. Ellen was born in July. Valentin and his younger brother, Gunnar, rented Berga Farm on a crop-exchange deal for the summer, but they didn't get on so well. I didn't have to help with the work outside, the men looked after that.

We stayed on at Berga until March when a new owner came and took over. We had nowhere to go, farms were scarce. So my Dad asked Engineer Ral at Lindö if he would allow us temporarily to rent a little land from him and move into the cottage at Vrederbo.

It was a soldier's cottage named after a man called Vreder. He was still alive when I was in school – a nasty old man. At Christmas-time he would go around the farms in Kärrbo collecting food in a bag. One Christmas he was given turnips at Lindö and he thought they were too small, so he stuck them in the snow in the garden there and wrote in big letters on the crust of the snow, so everybody could see: STILL GROWING – RIPE NEXT YEAR.

Engineer Ral was kind and accommodating and he let us rent about thirty acres of ground. Later on the acreage increased to forty-eight. No contract was ever drawn up. Neither side considered it necessary. Of course, we didn't intend to live there very long.

But farms continued to be scarce in the twenties and we couldn't get hold of one. At last we got so settled there at Vrederbo that we gave up trying to find a farm of our own. We continued to rent from Lindö and lived in the cottage for twenty-three years.

It's situated very nicely on a southern slope, the same as nearly all little cottages like this. Surely the spot must have been inhabited long before Vreder built on it. If the cottage had been bigger and in better repair I'd certainly have liked to live in it the rest of my life.

The kitchen was fairly big, but there was only one other solitary little room. It was rather draughty and cold inside, the windows weren't sealed against the weather and neither was the door. We were happy there anyway, and it took less than ten minutes for me to bicycle home to Skämsta on a visit.

During our first summer in Vrederbo I was outside the whole time helping stack hay and sheaves of grain and hauling in the hay and grain. Ellen was only a year old, and I had her out with me on a blanket while I worked in the fields.

We didn't have much money to live on, since prices for farm produce were low. To begin with Valentin had just one cow, which my Dad gave him. Little by little, as we reared the calves, the numbers grew. Eventually there were five or six milk cows, and heifers besides. Valentin borrowed some capital to start out with from Gunnar, who was more thrifty. He bought a second-hand seeder, a harrow and plough, and other tools at auctions.

We got up at five a.m. the whole year round, on Sundays as well as weekdays. I guess I worked harder than he did. It was common at that time for the women to have longer working days than the men, and it's still the same in many homes where the women go out to work.

The first thing I did in the morning was to light the stove and make coffee. Then when I'd fed the chickens and pigs I hurried to do the milking. You had to be ready when the wagon came to pick up the milk. Valentin fed the cows and horses and cleared the manure out of the barn. Milking took about an hour. He sometimes gave me a hand, but mostly he used to prepare for the rest of the day's work.

After milking, I made breakfast: usually oatmeal – that was the simplest. When the kids were little I gave them gruel in a bottle, and many times I gave them the bottle to drink by themselves, as I didn't have time to sit still and feed them. In time there were five of them: Ellen, Sven, Erik, Berit, and Bo.

After we'd eaten breakfast I had the milking equipment to wash in the barn and dishes to wash in the kitchen, the beds to make, and the rooms to clean out. If there was any free time left over I did a little weaving or sewing. The loom stood in the kitchen, where really it took up too much space, but there was nowhere else we could have it.

I wove mats and towels and sheets. It was cheaper than buying them. We were very short of money. Once I even wove some mats and sold them – to the Anderssons at Rosendal. When I look back now, I don't know where I got time to do it all, but you have a lot of energy when you're young.

At nine-thirty we drank our morning coffee. Then Valentin

used to come home, as long as he wasn't off in the fields way over by Vreta. When he went over there he used to take coffee with him in a rucksack.

There was always something to be patched or darned or washed. And of course there was the cooking. We ate dinner at twelve noon. The men usually rested a while after dinner but never the women. They had the dishes to wash and other chores.

You worked out in the fields until about seven in the evening, with a coffee break at three-thirty p.m. I managed to get the milking done between five and six p.m. After this there was food to fix. At seven o'clock we ate supper and that was the end of work so far as the fellows were concerned. The women had dishes to wash and other little jobs.

We didn't have any water installed, so all the water had to be fetched in a bucket. It was about fifty metres, I'd say, to the well. Beside it we had a wooden trough for the animals to go and drink out of twice a day. Up in the hen-house we kept three or four heifers who had to have water brought to them – they were so wild and crazy that it was impossible either to round them up or to lead them.

During the first year at Vrederbo, Valentin started a little slaughtering business on the side. He rode his bicycle around to the farms in Kärrbo parish, and at Christmas-time he would be completely exhausted in the evenings after he had slaughtered at many places on the same day.

He also traded slaughtered animals. The first calf he'd bought and slaughtered, he tied onto the carrier of his bike and rode in to Västerås, where he sold the meat. Gradually he began buying up calves on a regular basis and slaughtering and dressing them. Then he drove all around Kärrbo in a horse and wagon selling meat.

The sales went very well. Since times were bad ordinary farmers couldn't afford to slaughter and keep a whole calf at home for themselves – instead they sold it and bought back a bit of it. A little later I started grinding up scraps and innards to make sausages which Valentin took with him to sell.

My sausages were much in demand and of course it meant that I had even more to do. Anna Andersson gave me some help with them; at that time her husband was the farm-worker at Skämsta, and later they bought Flitbo. We ground all the sausage mixture by hand in an ordinary meat-grinder which we took turns in cranking. We used entrails, heart, and lungs, and we even cleaned and ground up the stomachs from cows, plus the udders, shanks, and skulls. The mixture had to be seasoned, blended, and kneaded well, a tough job.

We made sausages two days running every two weeks. Some-times it was every week. You had to try all kinds of things to make money. I remember how Lundvall used to drive around in a horse and wagon in the fall selling cabbages for twenty öre a kilogram, and that certainly wasn't much money for all the trouble he had had in growing them.

In 1929 Valentin built a slaughter-house with the help of Hedberg, the carpenter. Valentin laid the brick walls; he knew a little about masonry. He spoke to Ral first about the building, since of course it was Ral who owned the land. There were no papers signed that time either.

When the slaughter-house was ready, Valentin was able to buy full-grown animals to slaughter and then drive in to the inspector's office in Västerås, which was the wholesale purchas-ing depot for the meat markets. It went quite well, but there were expenses too. He rode in by horse-cart on Fridays and even on Tuesdays sometimes. It took up a lot of time but he managed all right anyway, since the farming wasn't such a big operation he couldn't handle it too.

Later on he got hold of an old truck and drove that – it was a little one. But in the thirties when the co-operative slaughter-house was formed, the private butchers went downhill. The farmers received higher and more uniform prices in the co-operative.

In 1933 my Dad received only forty kronor for a fine cow which had udder inflammation and had to be slaughtered. He was forced to accept that price because he needed the cash. The following year, after Dad died and Herbert had taken over Skämsta, they had another cow that had to be slaughtered for the same reason. At that time the co-op slaughter-house had been organized and the payment for that cow was 200 kronor.

The co-op put an end to the butchers. Valentin quit. His brother Gunnar was also a butcher and he kept on going a little longer. For a while he drove meat to Hedemora up in Dalarna and sold it there. But this stopped too. The organizing of the co-op slaughter-house presented no great problem for Valentin, since he was mainly a farmer. At the same time he stopped drinking completely and didn't touch a drop for over ten years. It was at this time that Ral agreed to lease out more land. Our farm grew to forty-eight acres.

Of course, Valentin was a very big, thick-set, strong man who could easily handle a lot of work. He weighed a good deal more than a hundred kilograms without being fat. We kept working away, but the results were not spectacular. The prices of farm produce were still very low. The rent, I must admit, was also very low. We paid 375 kronor a year, if I remember rightly.

Henry was born in October 1925, but he died five months later of pneumonia. He's buried in Kärrbo churchyard. In 1929 Erik was born and then came Berit in 1931 and Bo in 1935. It was a very busy and strenuous time. One year I had a girl named Rut Holm from Springsta helping me. She spent the nights at home with her parents in the cottage in Berga beside Hellstigen. Rut was fourteen years old and got fifteen kronor a month plus her food.

Some years later, when Bo was born, Rut worked for me a while too. Then my eldest girl Ellen grew up and could help out at home and Sven started to help Valentin out in the fields.

In wintertime Valentin cut wood in the forest at Lindö and

sometimes he hauled pulp-wood and timber by horse. We had two horses. Wood for our own use was included in the lease; we chopped off the large branches and the tops left behind after cutting and carted them home.

I never went to any meetings except for the sewing circle. The sewing circle, which used to meet once a month, had about fifteen members. It was fun and you got to meet folks. The different wives from the small farms and at the parsonage took turns being hostess.

The minister was always with us and read aloud for us while we sewed. There were different stories – I've forgotton what they were about. The sewing circle meetings were coffee *klatsches* with cake and cookies and lots of chatting. I myself could never invite them home – there simply wasn't room in our crowded cottage.

For Christmas each year the sewing circle held an auction in the elementary school. The money from this went to charity, mission work and so on. Getting rid of the things was no problem since the whole of the parish flocked to the sewing circle auctions. These were the only public entertainments in Kärrbo.

Old Törngren was in control of the gavel. He was fond of joking and fun to listen to when he called out mittens and woollen ski socks and towels and spreads and other things that we'd made. After his death Ral from Frösåker became auctioneer.

During the break, coffee was served and home-baked pastry and cookies which the wives had donated. There was always a door prize as well and it was something nice, like sheets and pillow-slips, for example. Folks didn't go to the sewing circle's auctions because they were religious or anything like that, but because they thought it was fun and perhaps in order to help some poor folks who were hard up somewhere and who were worse off than they were themselves.

There weren't many who went to church. I myself didn't go

very often as it was difficult to get away in the middle of the day. Valentin went sometimes. He was interested in the church, and joined the choral society for a while and sang in the choir at the early services on Christmas morning.

That was probably the only day of the year when the church was packed full. The Christmas service began at six a.m. In our family, only one of us could go, either me or Valentin, since we had the milking to do. The kids loved to go along too, those who were old enough. It was so beautiful and solemn there in the church on Christmas morning with all the candles lit and all the people singing.

We celebrated Christmas in the traditional way with a Christmas tree and special Christmas tablecloths on the tables: there was ham, stockfish that had been specially prepared by soaking in lye, rice pudding, sausage, and slices of bread to dip in the gravy left over from cooking the ham. Our Christmas presents were mainly useful things, but there were also a few toys for the children.

At Easter we didn't decorate so much, we just had a few Easter chicks. We ate boiled eggs on the night before Easter. I'd really like to know where the tradition of eggs and Easter chickens comes from exactly. On Walpurgis Night (30 April) we ate boiled eggs too. Why, I don't know. We always had a bonfire in the evening of the last day of April.

We didn't celebrate Midsummer in any special way. We had no maypole. But it's a festive occasion anyway. You're so happy that summer has finally come, with all the beauties of nature. In the old days, young and old people danced together. Even the folks who sat home all the rest of the year were up and around on Midsummer's Eve. In Kärrbo they celebrated Midsummer down at Frösåker Pier but I was never down there.

We set great store by holidays since they gave us a break from the daily routine. Otherwise life went along just as usual. One year was the same as the next. The youngsters grew up and started to help out as they got bigger.

Ellen was first to leave home. At that time she was seventeen years old. It was 1938 and she got a job as a baker at the Margareta school of home economics in Västerås. I was all alone with the housework when she went away. Berit was only seven years old.

We heard something on the radio and read a little in the newspaper about what was happening outside of Sweden during those years. But we didn't pay too much attention to it. None of us was political. Of course people were saying that there would be war and naturally we were afraid that it would come. Though in fact there weren't many people who believed that Sweden would be drawn into it.

The outbreak of war in 1939 hardly changed anything in Kärrbo. Life went on as usual. Later in the fall, during the Russo-Finnish war, people took up collections and held sewing circle auctions, and the proceeds went to Finland. I remember how the kids in school went around selling little Finnish paper flags for ten öre each. There probably wasn't a single family who didn't buy a few flags – at least not in Kärrbo.

In the spring of 1940 everybody thought that the war was suddenly getting much closer when the Germans took Norway and Denmark. It was at that time that we started having ration cards for almost everything, and you had to scrimp on a lot of things so there'd be enough to go around.

Even in the beginning the coffee ration was small. I roasted bran – nearly everyone did. Some people parched peas to use as a substitute. To me that tasted bitter, though bran, on the other hand, was not bad at all. There was also a tobacco shortage and some folks dried cherry leaves to add to the tobacco.

I think it was in the fall of 1940 that Valentin was called up for military service in Malmköping. But he applied for exemption so he could come back and manage the farm, and it was only a week or so until he was home again. Then things became quieter in Sweden and hardly anyone thought anymore that Sweden would be drawn into the war. And we weren't, as luck would have it.

Before Christmas of 1944 we moved to Törnby, on the other side of the hill from Vrederbo. Valentin bought the farm for 15,000 kronor from a man called Svensson. He came from the city and didn't know a thing about farming. He had been there only a few months during the summer and then he gave up.

After twenty-three years, we had our own place at last. The price was very reasonable, considering that both the house and outbuildings were in good condition. The house was practically newly renovated. In 1940 a furniture dealer in Västerås had bought the farm as a summer place and rebuilt the house.

I was very happy to have another, much better place to live in. There were two rooms and a kitchen downstairs and two rooms upstairs. The other members of the family were also glad that we got so much space. When Erik moved away from home there were five of us living in four rooms and a kitchen in Törnby as against seven at the most in one room and a kitchen in Vrederbo.

Erik was fifteen years old when he suddenly announced one day that he was going to go out and earn money. It was at the end of the war and he had read an advertisement in the newspaper that they were hiring people on an excavation site at Hässlö airfield. He rode his bike out there but didn't get a job, so he went on into town where he'd read another newspaper ad about a job at Johansson's tyre repair shop. He got a job there, and I remember how glad he was when he came home and told us about it.

He lived at home for a while and rode his bike sixteen kilometres morning and evening and was dripping with sweat when he came home. I felt sorry for him but he wasn't tired, oh no. He would have a bite to eat, change his clothes, and then he'd take off in the evenings to play ball or go to a dance.

Törnby consisted of only twenty-two acres of ground and that's why Valentin wanted to go on renting the forty eight acres at Lindö from Ral. Ral wanted everything back, but agreed to rent out eighteen acres of land to us. In other words, our farmland was thus all in all about forty acres and that was really too little, since Sven was also working at home. He was twenty-one years old and full-grown. But we had quite a number of cows and they were his job, so there was enough for him to do, all right.

The work became much easier for me after we'd moved to Törnby. Valentin installed water the first year we were there though there was no drainage system.

On Saturdays I used to ride in with my eggs to the market in the square. I rode my bike to Väsby Wood and took the bus to town, which cost one krona there and back. It was fun standing there in the square, and it put a little variety into your everyday life. I had a lot of chickens in Vrederbo and later in Törnby and I used to take along ten score of eggs with me, for which I got three kronor a score.

The egg money was generally considered the farm-wife's own income. Money she decided herself how to spend. My egg money went mainly to clothes for me and the family. Sometimes I also sold dressed chickens. There was a big demand for them, especially during the war. The foreigners who came to Sweden were very eager to get hold of fowl, and in the market square in Västerås there were often Poles asking for 'checkens'.

Now and again over the years we had family parties, but mostly it was the kids' birthdays and name-days we celebrated. Of course, we didn't have very much time to go out, it was so hard to get away. Only the nearest relatives came to kids' parties, Grandma and aunts.

I remember when I had my thirtieth birthday. Oh, lord, what a crowd there was in the cottage at Vrederbo. I made my way through that mob, serving them all food. Then the men-folks sat around playing cards. We women sat together in a corner and talked. The kids fell asleep in the beds and on the floor before the night had set in and it was time to go home.

We never once went to the movies. The only movie-houses were in Västerås. There was one open on Sunday evenings in Östanbro, though only young folks went. Our last few years in Törnby the youngsters sometimes went to the movies at the Kärrbo rural community centre, but I myself never went.

Bosse, our youngest boy, lived at home until he was fifteen years old, when he started out working at different places. Berit was already engaged by the time she was seventeen, and married when she was nineteen. That was in 1950, at the same time Bosse started working. She was a lively one, she was.

The years just after the war were lean ones, farm produce brought such low prices. Then little by little they began to get better. It was in 1954, I think, that Valentin got rid of the animals. He was going to try growing rape, that's what everybody was doing at that time. The price for oil-plants was high and they didn't take much seed.

I thought to myself that it was silly to get rid of the cows, but we didn't discuss the matter. Valentin was the one who made the decisions on farming. Whenever I thought that something was wrong he wouldn't listen. I worried much more than he did about economy, often unnecessarily, of course. It was the same for most of the small farmers – the men looked after things outdoors and the women took charge of the household.

Growing rape took a lot of trouble. The plants had to be sprayed with insecticide and they had to be weeded and hoed several times. There was a lot of work with that sort of crops. In rainy years it was hard to get the oil-plants to ripen properly. In the beginning, at least, prices were high, but then, when everybody began cultivating rape, prices fell.

It got lonely on the farm without animals. I liked cows, they've always been part of my life. Cows are calm and contented animals – most of them anyway. Another reason we sold the cows was because of the artificial insemination station and the artificial insemination association that was formed. We used to have bulls before, and other small farmers would come with their cows to have them serviced. This brought in a little money too.

In the early spring of 1958 Valentin fell sick and after he'd been feeling bad for some time, he went to the doctor. He was told he was suffering from the after-effects of pneumonia, but it was really a tumour he had on his lung. They knew this at the hospital the whole time, but didn't tell us till there was no hope left.

He was admitted to the sanatorium in Västerås the last day of June, where he soon picked up and put on a lot of weight in a short space of time. But then he got worse again, and after that he went steadily downhill until he died on the twenty-fourth of September. Erik and I sat with him the night he died, but he was lying there in a coma and didn't see us.

After the funeral Sven and I were left alone. We kept the farm and things didn't go too badly. The following spring I got the notion of buying a cow and some calves. My brother, Herbert, came with me to buy them at the co-op slaughter-house livestock auction.

I was glad to have a cow again. She was a beauty. I fattened the three calves for slaughtering. Once in the fall, September 1959 it was, I had ridden my bike out to put flowers on Valentin's grave and on the way home, I took the cow along from the meadow. I rode up in front.

When I turned around to look I saw that she had her rump in the air and her horns pointing to the ground right in back of the bike. It struck me that she must be angry and I got so scared I pedalled as fast as I could down the stony path. I crashed and hit my head on a rock.

I was unconscious and they had to come and get me in the ambulance, and I had to stay in the hospital for six weeks. A nerve in my left eye was injured and ever since I've seen double. There's nothing that can be done about it.

After that unpleasant experience I had no desire to go on farming. Sven wasn't particularly interested, and wasn't very strong, either. He had been sick on several occasions. Berit and her husband moved out with Sven while I was away, so she could take care of the house for him. When I came home we simply decided to swap. Berit and Rune settled into Törnby, and Sven and I took over their apartment in the city.

And so as it happened I became a city-dweller in my old age. The question was whether or not Sven would get work at Asea, the Swedish General Electric Company. This was necessary since the apartment belongs to Asea, and only their employees are allowed to live there. But Rune, who works at the electrical office, which also belongs to Asea, went along and helped Sven get a job lacquering wires at Asea, to begin with.

Rune drives his car to work. He and Berit like it best out in the country and their three children wouldn't hear of moving back into the city. They farm their twenty-two acres in their spare time. The land we rented has gone back to Lindö.

Sven thinks it's much better in the city. He never had this much free time before. Now he works a five-day week. I myself got along very nicely at first. I had never had modern conveniences before. In this apartment we have hot running water, indoor toilet, and bathroom. It's easy to keep clean, and close to the stores. And there's only myself and Sven to look after.

By now a good number of years have already gone by since we moved in here, and I can't say that I like it as much as I did in the beginning. It gets boring being alone all day long, especially in summertime. That's when I really wish I were back in the country again. But later as the fall and damp weather come, then it's nice to be in a warm, cosy apartment.

Things will probably just have to be this way now, as long as I'm alive. It's a good thing I've got so many children anyway. We keep in touch. They visit me now and then, and on Mother's Day they all bring flowers, every single year, and on my birthday as well.

They often drive out and pick up Sven and me in the car, so

we can visit them. Last Whitsun, for example, we were at Ellen's on Whit Saturday, and at Berit's out in Törnby on Whit Sunday, and at Erik's in Hallstahammar on Whit Monday. The family ties are still strong; we stick close together. That way you get out a little too.

They come here most often in the winter. In the summer it's difficult to get them to come in to the city. They'd rather stay out in the hills then, so they come and pick up Sven and me when we get together.

Ellen and her husband Kalle have their summer cottage out in Törnby. They began building it themselves in 1953 and they've lived there every summer since then. As soon as it gets warm at the beginning of June they move out, and they stay right up to the end of October – they have electric heating in the cottage.

Bosse and his family lived in a city apartment a couple of years but they couldn't stand it, so they moved out to the country for good. They rent a place in Kusta, not far from Törnby. Bosse said he'd go crazy if he had to live in town. He never wants to live there again if he can help it. Berit and her husband say the same thing and their kids do too. Besides, it's cheaper to live in the country. Here in the city they build such expensive apartments that both husband and wife have to work in order to pay the rent.

I also meet my sisters sometimes; we visit each other now and then. My sister Sissan is a widow like me and she lives here in Västerås. I even keep in touch with my cousins – mostly by telephone, though. It means a lot to me, and nowadays I wouldn't dream of being without a telephone. Every day someone rings me and some days I have several calls, so I can keep up on everything that happens to my children and their families. I often call them up myself, many times when I don't really need to, but, well, a person likes somebody to talk to.

I did a lot of handiwork in the beginning when I came to the city. I didn't have anything else to do and I had to be working at something. So I embroidered towels and knitted and sometimes knotted rya rugs from morning to night. I may have been too eager and strained my eyes so it affected my sight, but I don't know, maybe it would have turned out that way anyhow.

My eyesight has been failing for a couple of years now. It may be due to diabetes, which I've had since 1953. Sugar diabetes is so common now that it's really a national disease. I don't know why people get it and I don't think the doctors know, either.

I can't read newspapers and magazines without a magnifying glass. It's really a pity. I don't watch T.V. either, but I do listen to the radio on station three, they play a lot of music and there are different kinds of quizzes that are fun to listen to. It's good company.

It certainly is much better for old people nowadays than it used to be, and for the youngsters, too, of course. Folks can afford to buy things to make their homes attractive and they have many more clothes, though they've almost gone *too* far with clothes.

There's not such a big division between rich and poor any more. In the old days most people were poor, and now there isn't anyone who's actually poor, not even families with lots of kids. They get family allowances from the state and the parents can keep them in proper food and clothing, and shoes, too.

No old person needs to be poor either, not like before, when there wasn't any old-age pension at all. I don't know how they managed to survive. In fact many people died of malnutrition.

Everybody – not just rich people – can go to school much longer than before and can learn a lot. But they don't seem to be doing too well on discipline. It sure can't be easy to be a teacher. A lot of kids must get pretty fed-up, going to school so many years. Why not let those who want to learn go on, and those who don't want to, finish a little earlier? But then there aren't any jobs for them, either.

Still, all in all, when I look back on my life, I have to admit, conditions certainly have improved. Here in Sweden, at least.

Part Two

In the Midst of Life

Sense at Last

Nils Zachrisson

We lived in the house in Ekensberg. There were four families living there. One room and a kitchen. The apartment was about thirty square metres. My God, when you think of it, the way people had to live!

There were beds everywhere. Ma had seven kids between 1918 and 1929, plus miscarriages. I was born in 1926.

Four of us slept in a double bed. The two eldest boys slept in the kitchen. Ma and Pa had a foldaway bed with high ends. Counting the youngest in the cradle, there were seven of us in that room, and it was much smaller than the kitchen.

One of our neighbours was named Säfström and they called him 'Hitler'. He was the parish Nazi. When my grandfather died, Säfström raised the Nazi flag, he was so glad a 'bastard Social Dem.' had died. He did the same thing at the funeral.

There was constant war between us. Oh, my Pa was a Social Democrat through and through. During the summer a couple of us boys lived in a shed in the garden. There was a cat-hole in the door. Once when one of Säfström's brats was peeking through the hole we threw piss on his face from a bottle. What a commotion that caused.

Another time Säfström stood outside with his shot-gun threatening to shoot Ma and Pa through the window. He was never reported. It wasn't usually done in those days. If we'd told the cops about it, we'd only have got mixed up in a lot of odd interrogations and they'd probably have talked us out of it.

There's no real justice, of course. In everything you'll find it's the money that matters – to some extent, anyway. A common ordinary taxpayer who got into a squabble with an embezzler, for example, wouldn't have a chance because the other fellow would have the money on his side. Judges pay attention to name and position. It's just stupid to think you can get any justice without money.

Pa worked as a brickmaker at Frösåker Brickyard. Säfström was foreman, he took over after my grandfather. There were about fifteen men working there before the works was closed down. Lindö works was closed down earlier.

The place was swarming with kids running in and out and playing and making all kinds of mischief. One of our most popular hang-outs was in the brick sheds where the bricks were laid on shelves to dry in the air; there was lots of room there. My brother Ingemar and I just about set fire to the whole business one time when we were playing with matches and wood shavings.

The clay pit was another place where we often hung out. And the kilns. The horse that drew the wagon-loads of clay was called the 'Old Dark Gal'. Dozens of tramps used to come and warm themselves in the glow from the brick kilns. That's where Pa worked. They worked on shift in the furnaces.

All the hobos had lice. They cooked their grub over fires and shat into the 'bells', as the kilns were called. Sometimes we kids got the blame for shitting on the bricks.

There were all sorts of tramps, but most were common folks who were out of work. Some of them could do magic and showed us small fry some of their tricks, while we stood staring, open-mouthed.

Never a day went by that we weren't up to some new prank down in the brickyard. That's where I got my crooked nose. I was lifting a brick from the chute and it fell on me and cracked the bridge of my nose.

During several summers I played down by the colony, where the workers' kids from Västerås were turned out to pasture. They used to kid us, but since you were small and defenceless you just had to turn the other cheek. You didn't know what it was all about. Though later on we Frösåker kids formed a real gang and sat on the rocks by the turn of the road waiting for the colony kids when they came to pick up their mail. After that they weren't so cocky any more. It went so far that they had to take a grown-up along with them.

On the first of May we used to hold a demonstration. We filed from Kärrbo church to Hagbo. We youngsters went along too. Säfström hoisted his swastika flag. The marchers used to stop down by the bend in Frösåker Avenue, and look off in the direction of Ekensberg at the flag. Then we marched on.

It was Säfström who was in charge of the unemployment insurance fund. He hadn't been elected but just seemed to take charge of it. Nobody opposed him. He was such a gruff character.

At times it was impossible to sell the bricks so the brickyard came to a standstill. Pa was out of work and we were even worse off than usual at home. On one of these occasions he was offered farm-work at Frösåker, but he turned it down. Between times the yard was in full swing, and I remember once when he had been unloading for several days and nights in a row, he came home with fifty kronor, which was a fantastic lot of money in those days.

Pa was seldom at home in the evenings. Ma never left the house, he was the one who went on errands. He was involved in a lot of activities, in the labour union, politics, and local council work. Luckily he was a teetotaller. Ma came from a family of Baptists, and when he married her they made him promise that he wouldn't drink. So we were spared the misery of having a father who came home drunk.

I went to the elementary school in Harkie. We had a long way to go to school. First you took the path through the forest to Sköttbo. The snow wasn't ploughed away in the winter. I was on good terms with the teacher because I sang well. She used to give me milk. I nearly always had a belly-ache and sometimes she let me lie down there at school and she'd take care of me. Sometimes my brother would come and pick me up on his bike. I sat on the crossbar. The bicycle leaped over the tree roots on the path through the forest. He pedalled like a madman with no thought for the fact that I was in pain.

You were never lonely. There were always a lot of other kids to play and have fun with. Remember the spring, when we got to walk around in our sneakers, and the fall, when you got new rubber boots. What a beautiful feeling! So much happened on the way to school. We picked flowers and studied all different kinds of insects. When you come to think of it, we were quite happy in many ways.

When they closed down the brickyard we moved to Eriksberg in the forest, a little north of Täby, by Gäddeholm Road. There we had one room and a kitchen downstairs, and one room upstairs where we boys lived. There was no electricity, we used kerosene lamps instead. In fact, the cottage was vacant because the old man who had lived there had gone and hanged himself. It's been a long time since it tumbled down; the place no longer exists.

Pa had various jobs up around the church and was a kind of municipal worker. Sometimes he went around to the small farmers to help dig their ditches, and in the winter he chopped wood in the forest. So we managed all right.

Myself, I continued hanging out down in Frösåker, playing and romping through the forest across Munkbo and Karsbo to Rian. What we liked to do best of all was to hang around a stall on a summer's evening and watch our chance for a horse to ride bareback on to the meadow. They had ten pairs of horses at Frösåker then.

When the fall was coming on I used to be frightened of the dark on my way home through the forest. You would walk along and look up in the clearing above the path and recognize different trees and know that this is a stump and there's a rock here. In the dim light I could be scared stiff of juniper bushes which looked like people or elks.

You didn't learn very much at secondary school. What I hated most of all was learning about ancient kings and that kind of crap. A little arithmetic was drilled into us. Geography was fun, but we never got further than the Nordic countries. We were happiest when Nyström, the schoolmaster, was hung over and we could go home. He sometimes did a lot of celebrating with Valle.

We had wood-working in the room above. He couldn't give us real instruction there either. We made wooden cutting boards: we'd saw off a piece of board plane it, and bore a hole in one end. Or clumsy clothes-hangers. That was called sloid.

For lunch I took with me to school half a disk of crispbread with margarine. Sometimes when I hadn't eaten all my sandwich I slung it in a ditch on my way home – you weren't supposed to bring it back with you.

We kept chickens at home but we never got a fried egg sandwich. The eggs were to make pancakes, I suppose. Once when one of the hens was broody I sent for some turkey eggs from an ad. in our local newspaper. The hen hatched out four or five turkey chicks, which gradually got big and mean and used to chase us and give us quite a scare. Ma sold them as poultry in the fall and got a good price for them, but not an öre came my way.

We had pigs, of course, and smoked ham. I used to have to sit for three days lighting the smoke-fire with juniper branches. In the evenings we each took a piece of crispbread and crept out into the shed where the ham was hanging in a sack, and carved ourselves off a slice.

We didn't play only during recesses at school, we sometimes played hooky from entire lessons, when we'd rush out onto the hills and tear around. Nyström didn't say a word. He must have been glad to get rid of us now and then. One recess when we were playing hide and seek around the schoolhouse I ran into Gudrun Karlsson at one of the corners of the playground. She banged her head into my temple and gave me a concussion, so that I temporarily lost my eyesight. Nyström took me to the hospital in Västerås, and the rest of the kids were allowed to go home.

When the bell tower was moved to make room to widen the road, we climbed up it on the struts right up to the ridge-pole. We were scared of course and shook like leaves as we lay on top of the joists. But you just *had* to climb up to prove you were brave. To think that the old codgers didn't try to stop us! But not in those days. It was none of their business if we did stupid things.

One of our most pleasant pastimes was fishing in Ångsjön. The water was hardly more than half a metre deep but the bottom of the lake was extremely dangerous. You could disappear right down through the mud. The steam that rose from the lake in the fall gave out a foul stench. Foxes used to roam around the shore of the lake, howling.

We caught bucketsful of carp and trudged home with them to Ma. We went out a little way from shore on a board and caught them with our hands. The carp moved slowly and couldn't get away. They may have tasted a little muddy, but there was lots of meat on them. We ate them cold, jellied.

In wintertime we played bandy down there – a game something like hockey. As soon as the lake had frozen over we were out skating on the soft ice. It swayed and creaked but we egged each other on to skate out again and again. If we'd gone through the ice there wasn't a chance that we would have come up from the mud at the bottom – we just didn't have any sense.

On dark evenings we went and 'threw straw men'. I've no idea where the custom came from. We'd build a straw man with arms and legs about a half metre long and take it a considerable distance, then we'd choose a cottage and creep quietly up to it, tiptoe into the hallway, fling open the kitchen door and throw in the straw man. And then you had to run for all you were worth.

Anyone who was chased and caught by one of the cottagers

was shamed. Then they were taken into the cottage and given coffee. I threw a straw man into Hagbo one evening when Lundvall's boy Ingemar happened to be sitting on a chair right near the door. He could run like nobody else and so I hid in the hall when he came running out, but he realized that there was something funny about my disappearing like that, so he came back, found me, and led me into the kitchen.

Later on he became an invalid. It happened when he was home on leave from military service and went running in the forest. He jumped over a fence and broke some bone in his back, I think, and was paralysed. Since then he's ridden around in a wheel-chair. I sometimes meet him here in town at bandy and soccer matches. It certainly is strange that such an outdoor man and nature lover has been able to adjust to a wheelchair.

Of course we all smoked. I had a whole can of cigarette butts that I picked up all over the place; I got hold of a pipe and really felt grown-up. One day I suddenly ran into Pa but I didn't get a beating. He didn't say a word, he just looked at me sort of disapprovingly. Nobody at home smoked. They used snuff in those days.

At school we smoked during recesses. We sat around back underneath the cellar roof and took deep drags. Eventually it was forbidden to buy cigarettes down in Valla grocery without a note saying that you were buying for a grown-up. Though it was pretty easy to find someone who would write a note for you. But when I finished school, I stopped smoking too, since it wasn't exciting any more.

School books were free. You could also get hold of shoes. Money for the shoes came from grants and foundations. A committee composed of some of the parish's top men decided which kids were most needy. It was like a lottery every fall to get school shoes.

Every single desk lid in the secondary school was scratched up with names carved into them from several generations of school kids. Once Nyström came up to me just as I was carving a big Z in the lid, but he didn't make too much fuss about it. I had worse luck when I put my hand up the skirt of a girl who was sitting on the window-sill. She recoiled so violently that her behind went through the glass. I had to pay for the damage. The pane of glass cost a couple of kronor. Pa was livid. Two kronor was a lot of money in our house.

A good deal of the fuss and mischief was a result of the fact that we were so restricted. A whole gang of boys, both young and older ones, used to go down by the church in the evening and make such a commotion that folks hardly dared walk past them. After a dance or a prayer meeting or some other gathering, we'd get a notion to steal apples at the parsonage and we would sometimes tear down whole branches from the trees. We caused damage, vandalized, and behaved stupidly. The big guys were the worst.

There was really nothing outside of Kärrbo. The world we lived in was pretty small. The only thing we could possibly imagine was getting a job somewhere as soon as we'd finished school. Everyone we knew worked in Kärrbo. We were almost afraid of the city, so it wasn't any wonder that the city kids talked about dumb farm kids.

My first job was tending the sheep at Frösåker. We lived in Tistebo then, so I didn't have very far to go. I got 1·50 kronor a day. In the fall there was fruit-picking down there.

During the same fall I joined the I.O.G.T. lodge. There wasn't anything else you could join. We didn't take that business of the sobriety oath too seriously. We brewed a home-made concoction of yeast, sugar, and juice. In winter we dug a hole in an ant-hill and let the keg lie there for a month in the warmth until it was time to take a swig.

We met down at the hall in Hagbo. That's where I had my first girl. Though I wasn't too proud of it. She was older than me and a real number. It was late in the evening and she positively dragged me in and lay down on a high bench while

I stood on the floor hardly able to reach her. I was only thirteen then and really didn't know what I was doing. She was at least a couple of years older.

The following winter we tried a little amateur dramatics in Hagbo. Without bragging, I can say that I was something of a star in that gang. We didn't have a proper leader. It was the Lundvall girls, Britta and Linnea, who kept the whole show afloat.

My classmates went to read with the preacher when they had finished school, but not me. I'm neither baptized nor confirmed, a heathen, really! None of my brothers or sisters was baptized or confirmed. One of my sisters got baptized when she was grown up. Probably the main reason we weren't confirmed was that we couldn't afford to buy confirmation clothes.

In the summer when I was fourteen I worked for Tree-Per at Lindö. All gardeners were called Tree-Per. It was a hard job hauling soil into the hot-houses in a barrow, with a grown-up who didn't give a thought to how heavy it was. I got some kind of rheumatism and couldn't lift one of my arms in the mornings. But you couldn't expect any sympathy at home, nobody had time for that. It didn't pay to feel sorry for yourself.

I had just bought my first bike when the gardener wanted me to ride to Springsta one Saturday with three baskets of flowers. For once I stood my ground and at last he let me take his old bike. I was so afraid of spoiling the paint on my new one. His old lady remarked that in any case the tyres wouldn't get scratched. They were both religious – real hypocrites.

In August I left the farm country and went to work at Asea in Västerås. That was 1940. The gatekeeper was in charge of employing people, without any formalities. There was a shortage of people, and they took whoever they could get hold of. You stood shuffling your feet outside Mimer Gate until he came out and pointed at the crowd: 'You there, you, you, and you can have a job here,' he said. I didn't want to let on that I came from the countryside, so I gave my sister's address in the city when he took down my name.

The next morning I was given a locker for my clothes and a time-card. The foreman took me to a winder and said, 'Here's a new hand.' And that was all. There was no mention of getting any help in the beginning, you just had to start in as best you could soldering coils of copper and taping the connections. We wound electric motors.

To me the halls of the shop were enormous. The overhead travelling cranes looked like monsters. But you soon got used to it all and it was nice to have a warm factory to come to for the winter. The winder I was helping said to me, 'Wait until you've been here ten or fifteen years, then you'll see how nice it is.'

Since you were new and green, everyone made fun of you. A lot of young boys were sent on an errand to fetch the 'site angle' or to the elevator man to borrow the 'ring tongs'. His last name was Tångring, and he would get mad as hell.

Earnings were small; the most I earned was thirty kronor a week. Everybody who worked there at Sotebo was in debt. It's the same now, I guess. When you had put your name down for the credit union you could buy clothes and shoes and radios and anything else on credit. Then it was deducted from your pay-check. It was the same with the rent for those who lived in Asea Town. Everything was done through Asea. People got tied down. It was a real feudal system.

For the first months I stayed in Kärrbo and rode my bike back and forth morning and evening, but towards winter my brother Tore and I rented an attic in the city, in a house behind Djäkneberget. The landlord was a retired cop. The room was cold and primitive. We had to wash at work. We couldn't afford to eat out, so we cooked our own food on an old hot-plate. It was usually nothing but blood pudding.

Nobody cared about you, either at work or away from it.

There wasn't a soul to guide you; not even relatives bothered themselves about how you lived. I just don't know how we got by. You felt like a poor, skinny little bastard, thin and small, poorly clothed and scared of being laughed at.

I was too inexperienced for city life. I wanted to play soccer but never got around to joining any club. You hardly dared ask, you were afraid of being branded a ploughboy. So all that was left was *akvavit*.

When spring came you felt suffocated inside Sotebo. On sunny days I just let everything go and stayed away from work. Which didn't precisely improve my budget any. I finished at Asea and took a job in a market-garden. But that wasn't much good either. After a while I was back at Sotebo again.

Gradually you got a little older and earned more money, but you were constantly broke anyway, you just couldn't hang on to your money. The same story every week, pay on Thursday, paint the town red over the weekend, and be broke by Monday morning. Then you had to live on the verge of starvation till the next pay-day. Many times we ate potatoes and gravy with nothing else to go with it at the co-op store. And felt ashamed of being so poor.

I didn't belong to the labour union. It cost money and we earned very little. At work the older union men went around nagging at us young guys, but when it came to piece-work negotiations, they thought of themselves first and didn't give a damn about us.

My brother Ingemar and I, and Rune, one of my brother-in-law's brothers, found a room on Smedjegatan and rented it together. Some drinking went on there, all right. Ingemar worked for a brewery delivering beer, so we borrowed the money from his cashbox on Saturdays and had a struggle scraping together the money for him to present his accounts on Mondays.

We lived for the day without a thought for the future. We

didn't give a damn about the war going on outside Sweden. At the beginning of the week you thought about where you'd go on Saturday night. In the summer there was open-air dancing in Klinta, in Skyttebacken by Panko, Gottsta hills, Ångsö Sound, and many other places. We were often so drunk that we had no idea afterwards what we had said or done.

I remember one Saturday evening when we'd been to a dance and came home to find that there wasn't anything to drink. My brother had a key, so we were able to get into the brewery and take some mash. We were only going to take a few swigs, but of course we got thirsty and ended up by dragging away a five-litre keg. It was in June, on a bright summer's night, and when someone came along on the street we had to stand in a circle and hide the keg in the middle.

We soon got tired of drinking that brew, but our landlord drank it up, every drop. He was a drunk. Once we started drinking on Friday evening, continued all through Saturday and were completely done in when we woke up on Sunday afternoon. Then in came the landlord with a new bottle. I was in such a bad way that the very smell of *akvavit* made me want to vomit, but I managed to get down a couple more glasses anyway.

Well, then we perked up again and went on boozing the rest of Sunday. On Monday we played hooky from work. Then I got the feeling that I better get hold of myself and lay off and cool it a bit, I didn't want to wind up an alcoholic. Several friends my age from those days have gone astray completely and become drunks and bums around town here. Luckily, Ingemar stopped working at that blasted brewery and became a heavy sheet-metal worker at Arvid Svensson's.

I was with the Communists one winter, in their youth league. A lot of farm boys like myself collected there, and Norrlanders who had moved down, clodhoppers and lower-class folks, so to speak. There were quite a few gals there too who caught our interest, mostly country hicks. At our meetings we had discussions and then refreshments; though nobody really knew anything at all. I was struck off the list later because I failed to pay my dues.

The Communists had their own demonstration from the market square on the first of May, but I wasn't interested. The Party had a bad reputation.

In 1942 I got into the Rapid Boxing Club. A friend from home managed to get me in. Before long I came to be considered a talent. The training matches were a cinch. For me, it was practically child's play – I could beat guys who were both bigger and heavier. But when it came to serious matches, I wasn't so good – I got so confounded nervous.

No doubt the reason was not just mental but also physical: I ate too little. In spite of everything I took part in several matches, in Hallsta, Sura, Eskiltuna, and Enköping. The trainer could take out up to fifty kronor for various expenses. Then he handed me a five-kronor note and dribbled away the rest.

The newspapers began writing blurbs about me. One evening when I had a match on at the Sports Hall in Västerås, the speaker presented me as an up-and-coming champ in the city. That finished me. My opponent was twenty-seven years old, full-grown and heavier – I was only sixteen.

If I'd had the guts I usually had, it would have been O.K., since he had quite a bad boxing technique. But when I entered the ring and saw the hall jam-packed with spectators, I got such stage fright that I could only see him as a shadow. He punched me right away and I fell to the canvas, and that decided the match.

Nobody would believe me afterwards when I told what had happened. Instead they all thought I was a fraud. Jesus, what an idiot I felt in front of my buddies. At work I kept my mouth shut when they razzed me. I must have suffered some kind of a nervous breakdown. Nowadays it doesn't sound quite as silly to say that. I've often thought how terribly dangerous everything actually was. I could have been injured for life. Who would have looked after me if I'd become an invalid? We weren't even insured.

But in the gang I was a king. At dances I could stand up to guys who were much bigger than I was. And most of them were big – myself, I was 'fly-weight' in those days. The biggest advantage with boxing, of course, was that you were popular with the girls. But maybe it was mainly because I was born with the gift of the gab and knew how to talk my way into their hearts.

In the room on Smedjegatan there was a wash-stand with a basin. There was no point in buying bread or other food to take home since somebody else always ate it up. In any case there weren't any cupboards to keep anything in – we just had one bureau drawer each.

We ate at the co-op cafeteria farther down the street. In the mornings you'd be down like a trotting horse to be first in line for a bowl of porridge. There was rationing on, and a dinner of meat dumplings, with one miserable lump of meat inside, took three coupons. There were always lines, both at work and at the cafeteria. When work was finished for the day, young and old alike would dash to the time-clock like a flock of sheep.

In the evenings there was always something going on at our place. Time enough for sleep when you're old, was our motto. We played and sang quite a lot and our buddies and gals came around. Our landlady turned out the ones who were too young. Parents used to come to pick up their daughters. Sometimes elder sisters fetched their younger sisters. They wanted some fun, whether they were seventeen or only fourteen years old.

The Hawk was the dance palace where all the young people of Västerås hung out during the winter – that is, ordinary folks Though even some classy chicks would come along now and again and get into the swing. There was action there – the empty bottles would roll in the corners.

One Saturday evening when I came home to Smedjegatan

an undressed broad was lying beside my brother in bed. He was snoring away and hadn't had the energy to touch her in his drunken state. I tried to entice her over to my bunk, but she wouldn't come. So then I got up and carried her across the floor. She was pretty hefty and my backbones creaked so I felt it for several weeks afterwards. I laid her there in the bed, and a moment after I'd finished she suggested that we go up to a room upstairs and have another go at it.

The reason why we went around carousing and raising hell all the time was that we didn't have any foothold in life. I hadn't the slightest notion how to make my life meaningful. It just staggered along without any kind of direction.

The metal industries' strike in 1945 made a break in the daily routine. I was happy not to have to go to work in the morning. I had to manage without any strike pay since I didn't belong to the union. I was lucky enough to get an evening job setting pins at the bowling alley in the Sports Hall. There I earned twice as much an hour as at Asea.

One evening a bowling ball hit me and broke the ring finger of my right hand. My first thought was that I would get eight kronor a day from the sickness benefit fund. Some idiot of a doctor sewed up my finger so that it still looks like a lump of meat. The nail is always split and catches in everything.

The only result of the strike was that the older ones on the team where I worked had to give up a certain percentage on piece-work to us younger ones so that we got an extra ten kronor a week. The team as a whole got the same prices as before. The redistribution made the old guys hopping mad; they kicked up a big fuss and the following week things were back the way they were before. The result of several months' striking was just about nil, and that experience didn't make me more interested in labour unions.

All I did was assembly-line production work, the same every blessed day. In the end I went around in a kind of agony. I asked myself if it was going to continue like that for the rest of my life. It was so aimless I felt like I might just as well be dead.

One evening I rode my bike out to an old man in Lundby. He lived in a place out towards Tortuna together with another old guy who did the housekeeping. It was nice and cosy in the cottage.

We sat in the parlour while he read my hand. He was known to be reliable. You were supposed to wish for two things, but not say anything aloud. The first thing I thought of to myself, was that I wanted to get into a motor vehicle unit when I did my military service, since you could get a free driving licence that way. He turned up a card and said that that wish wasn't worth having.

After that he picked up a black card and I saw that he reacted. Perhaps it was the accident I had in the military that he saw – who knows? My second wish was for a good job, and he said, 'That'll work out, that'll work out.'

Of course fortune-telling is just a hoax, but it can be fun to try. Now and again things do come true, all right.

Half a year before I went in to do my military service I met Britt. It happened one evening when I was sober and had been to the Good Templar meeting hall to a dance. She was almost sixteen and lived in Lekandria, across from Asea's main gate.

Britt and I started going steady right away. It's the best thing that's ever happened to me. My life began to have meaning. Gradually I lost interest in other girls. We were both fond of dancing and I managed to stay fairly sober when we went out together, which we did more and more.

When I was about to go in for my military training in 1946 I asked to take off the week before – that was the custom. But the boss said no. So then I said that if that was the case, I'd give notice to quit and he could write out my reference. And I thought: Asea – never again. My years there are a time I'd rather forget.

At camp I was very nearly killed by a lever which sprang

back when we were re-positioning a cannon to wheel it away. It was in the Second Anti-aircraft Regiment in Linköping and I lay unconscious for several days. Afterwards I was on the sick list for ten weeks.

I did military service for eleven months. Conditioning exercises were fun, especially the obstacle course. It was real sport. The city was terrible, crawling with soldiers. And I was as poor as a church mouse. The state only paid us one krona a day, so we couldn't exactly live it up. It was a sober life we led.

As luck would have it, we got reduced rates on railway fares and I went to see Britt as often as possible. Between times, we wrote letters to each other practically every day. The boys in the barracks thought I was crazy writing that much.

For our mustering-out party my buddies at home sent down some bottles of *akvavit*. I was absolutely stone-broke and didn't even own a pair of civvy socks. And then, the day before I handed in my uniform, a letter came from Ma with five kronor inside – I've never been so glad to see five kronor before.

After military service I moved home to Britt and her Ma. Along with the courting I was a bit of a free-loader too. Her Ma was good at cooking. Good food. She used to take on the cooking for weddings and fiftieth anniversaries.

I'd never thought much about grub before. I was used to eating whatever crap came my way. The most difficult thing was going out to do shopping for her – nothing was ever right. When she went herself, she gave the shopkeepers grey hair!

I got a job as winder at the Aros Industrial Company. The salary was awful, but better that, I thought, than return to Sotebo. (For several years I used to have nightmares where I was running as hard as I could to punch in at the time-clock in time.)

Aros had its factory in the pawnbroker's old premises at Stora gatan 49. The firm had started in a barn in Dingtuna, where all sorts of things were manufactured. On the ground floor at Stora gatan four old women still sat making 'weather cottages', the sort that have an old man with rainboots on for bad weather and an old woman for nice weather.

Even in the barn they had employed a workman who knew about motors and through him the firm began to take on repair jobs – electric motors, transformers, and the like. He wasn't so skilled, but he caught on fast and could fix things, and since Aros had no competitors, it was successful. The Industrial Company soon moved to Västerås and eventually became the Aros Electrical Company.

I started off at 1·50 kronor an hour, only half of what I'd got at Asea, but after a couple of weeks they saw what I could do and raised me to 3 kronor. That was a high hourly wage in those days.

The premises were filthy dirty and without modern conveniences. The heating system was an old producer-gas unit in the cellar in which we burned garbage. That's how primitive a plant could be as little as twenty years ago.

But I was happy there. I worked independently and could see results from what I did. I remember the first motor I wound and tested. It worked the way it was supposed to and when it began whirring around I was happy as a child.

Soon I graduated to repairs. Then I travelled from one place to another where something had broken down. You can imagine the shocks you got sometimes before you'd learned to be careful. No other skilled workmen were in for the digs and gibes aimed at electricians. Folks don't understand how complicated electrical things are, they seem to imagine you can find the trouble immediately. The worst thing is when they've had a look themselves and connected the wires all wrong. Then it can take hours to fix.

Back in the shop I took an interest in the whole business, not just in what I did myself. I started taking telephone orders and checking out machines that had been repaired. The second year I was there, Svensson, who owns Aros, left me in charge of everything when he went on vacation for two weeks.

He gave me a cashbox to look after containing a couple of hundred kronor for freight costs and so on. I felt proud of myself and worked away like a beaver. Several of the others were envious and mad at me.

There was a door leading onto the street with a hoist in it so we could haul up heavy motors and other stuff into the workshop on the floor above. Once I was standing bent over the safety-rail in the door opening and was about to throw down a delivery note to the driver below when the bar, that was loose in its hook, gave way. I had to jump – five metres. I landed on my heels, all my muscles contracted and I lay there unable to move; it hurt like hell.

The ambulance came. The doctor at the hospital said it was only a sprain. They X-rayed me, put me in a cast and sent me home. I had to go for a check-up after ten days. Then they X-rayed me again. The senior physician examined the X-rays and then asked the other doctor sternly in my presence why he hadn't shown him the plates. I was admitted into the hospital immediately and operated on.

So Zachrisson had to lie a month on his back with his legs up and a weight hanging from the operated heel. Let me tell you, it was no picnic, and I must say that I admired the hospital staff for their patience and good humour. I don't know how they stand it – with all the difficult customers there are among the patients!

I was in the same ward as a sword-swallower. He called himself Abdu Rama and he'd cut himself in the throat when he was showing some of his tricks in a bar. He was a funny character who lived a bit of a wild life and had kids all over the countryside. I kept him in cigarettes a whole week. His pals smuggled in wine and *akvavit* to him.

After my stay in the hospital I had to go to Norrbacka Institute for tests and the result was ten per cent in disability compensation. That's the equivalent of 480 kronor a year by today's standard.

I feel the effects of my injury every day. I limp a bit and get a dull pain after the day's work. If I sit watching a full-length feature film on T.V. I have to get up and hop around sometimes when my heel starts acting up. In the evenings it takes a while before I can get to sleep.

One winter I made up my mind to start studying. I had gotten some sense at last. I took a technical course at night school. I didn't get very much out of it, since my knowledge of theoretical things was pretty weak. I only had six years at grade school to go on.

Then I began studying on my own. I bought technical books and worked my way through them a bit at a time. My practical experience was a big help when it came to ploughing my way through the theoretical explanations.

Now I'm an overseer at work but I don't have the credentials for it. I'm self-taught, you might say. A lot of folks are. Of course, schools are a good thing, but the man who has only theoretical knowledge is often handicapped when it comes to solving the problems that come up all the time in a service workshop.

The years go by quickly when you're happy. Britt and I were married on the eighth of October (the name-day dedicated to 'Nils') 1949. Raoul was born in February 1950. I was present at the birth. It was exciting. The midwife wasn't very pleased to have me there. Britt had the baby at home. At that time we were still living at my mother-in-law's. The foetus was in the wrong position. He was all blue in the face when he came out, but that got better after a few days. My mother-in-law ran around in a flap saying he would be a problem child. Now he's already bigger than me and has taken his driving test.

We spent our vacations tenting at home in Kärrbo. After we had Raoul we spent a vacation at my sister Inga's in Lindö. In 1953 I rented a piece of land in Kärrbo for thirty years. It's a good 1,200 square metres and lies on the hill next door to where Sis lives.

In order to have a place to live, I bought a woodshed from Fred Sohlman. It was down along the harbour in Västerås and he used it to store stuff for his boat. I gave him a hundred kronor for it, sawed it in two down the middle, and a neighbour who had a car with a trailer attached helped me transport it half at a time out to Kärrbo.

Pa helped me nail the hut together and then I tarred the roof to make it weatherproof. It certainly wasn't a beautiful place but it was all right for us as a summer cottage. I also began planting a few things there among the stones, a patch of potatoes and a little one of strawberries – things I'd had at home, so it was nice to have the same ourselves.

In the spring we would sit and look through flower catalogues and order seed and bulbs. But it's a lot of work watering and getting the damned things to grow. One year we had decided to have two long rows of tall flowers – I forget now what they're called. Not more than two mangy little plants survived – there was a difference between reality on a bare hillside in Kärrbo and the coloured pictures in the catalogue. Nowadays I'm none too keen on digging and planting all the time.

To start with we didn't stay out there more than on an occasional Saturday or Sunday and on vacation. We took the bus and trudged along with food and the baby in his baby-carriage. That was before everyone had cars.

One year we decided to build a veranda and I got hold of the wood and nails cheaply through connections in the building trade in town. You get to be friends with foremen and other folks, when you're out doing repair jobs. I did them a favour in return, such as mending their irons or vacuum cleaners. When the veranda was finished, we would sit out on it and eat and polish off half a bottle of *akvavit* sometimes on a Saturday night, in the company of the gnats.

Raoul had turned eight and was in his second year at elementary school when Britt-Mari was born. We had moved from my mother-in-law's place to a one-room apartment on Karlfeldtsgatan some years earlier. Later on we managed to swap it for a two-room apartment on the same floor.

Britt had an office job at a real-estate agency and she's still with them. Myself, I travelled around repairing electric motors for travelling cranes and lathes and various other machines, printing presses at the printing works, generators for electric welding sets and all kinds of things.

The ships down in the harbour were worst. The engine-rooms are small and damned awkward to work in when you're doing repairs. Sometimes it was one hell of a circus, especially when everyone on board was drunk, which was often the case. Nowadays there seems to be a stricter control of drunkenness at sea.

By and by I got more and more to do back in the shop, working as foreman and dealing out jobs and supervising them, writing out work-cards, taking orders for repairs – and sometimes also complaints from dissatisfied customers. I became a supervisor by stages, first I was a foreman. When we moved into the newly-built workshop in 1964 I became a full-time shop supervisor.

Here in Västerås the city's management and planning machinery has grown faster than the city itself. It's crawling with new officials down there in that hideous new showcase of theirs (the new city hall). Look at the social services. In a lot of cases they've gone too far with social benefits. A bunch of drunks are living in apartments the city pays rent on and some of them ride taxis instead of the bus when they've got their weekly dole. Meanwhile many people who really need help don't get it because they're too proud and can't bring themselves to ask for money.

People are always talking about alcoholism being an illness, but nothing is done to cure the drunks. We pay taxes until we're blue in the face and they get money from social services so they can go on drinking. You might just as well set out a tub of *akvavit* and let them drink themselves to death in one go, it would be cheaper that way.

Of course the social workers have got their own views on the subject and defend their actions. After all, they've got their jobs to worry about and they sit around their offices acting important. I think the only way to cure drunks is to let them get deprived and suffer a little. Then they'd have to get hold of themselves and change their ways. That's the opinion of most workers.

Our economy has to go to the dogs sooner or later, when so much money is being thrown around left and right. The state doesn't have any Sala silver mines to dip into any more. Everything's getting too expensive in Sweden.

The job situation is tough. Last winter not a day went by at the shop that somebody didn't knock at the door and ask for work – anything at all. At the same time many companies took a chance and 'released' people they wanted to get rid of, mostly older workers. It really is terrible that such things are allowed to happen.

It looks like there are bad times ahead. You're lucky to have a permanent job. 'Course, it would be pretty nice to win a little wad on the soccer pools so you'd have something to put away.

At work we play whist in the lunch break and the two who get the lowest score have to pay the week's soccer pools. We use an eight-row system. Myself, I do a twenty-seven row system with a 'key' of five certainties. It costs 10·80 kronor. I've done this all my life, through the years, mainly for the excitement. Once I had eleven correct and thought I'd gotten rich, but the hell I had. All I got was 600 kronor.

My brother was with a whole gang some years ago and one week they got twelve correct with a lot of draws. They figured they'd win a good deal of money on it and bragged about it and went and celebrated the event at the bar. They thought they had won about 10,000 kronor each, but lots of people had twelve correct that week so they only got about a couple of hundred. They got very fed-up over that.

After all, our most lasting pleasure is the cottage in Kärrbo. When we had been out there for several years my young brother, Åke, rented a piece of land on a nearby slope and put together a fine little summer cottage. So then Britt and I sat in our old hut philosophizing and came to the conclusion we should get hold of a decent cottage instead. We were inspired by Åke and his building.

The following year we set to work. I bought the materials from a Västeråser who was going to renovate his old cottage at Tidö-Lindö, but was countermanded by his wife, who didn't like it at all out there on the island. He'd collected together a whole lot of planks and boards and new shingles, and sold the whole pile to me for 500 kronor, a real giveaway price. I borrowed the firm's truck and drove everything out to Kärrbo.

Pa helped me build. The first thing we did was dynamite a huge rock on the site. I've regretted this, it would have been nice to keep it. We cast plinths, set up a framework of planks, and nailed shingles outside with cardboard between and wallboard on the inside.

We worked every single Saturday and Sunday the summers of both 1959 and 1960. There was enough wood left over to make a playhouse for the kids. The kitchen was the most difficult part, with all the cupboards and the oven – at a first try it jutted too far out on the floor. Then we had a hell of a job puttying and painting to get things nice and smooth and even.

The year after that Pa got himself a plot of land beside Åke and built a cottage too. First he nagged me to build it for him: 'You're *young*.' Then Åke and I had to talk him into it – since he thought he was too old. They had a little money saved up, Ma and Pa. When their cottage was finished they lived out there the whole summer and only travelled in occasionally to the apartment in the city. But now he's alone. Ma died in 1968. Britt and I have worked on our cottage for nine summers now. It never gets finished. Each year we get new ideas for it. We have a room and a kitchen, a sleeping alcove and an enclosed porch. The floor area is almost forty square metres altogether. We've talked about buying the land, but then the next step would probably be to drill a well. We've had electricity installed, so we can watch T.V. in the evenings. We've also thought about renting another lot next door and building a guest cottage where Raoul can live when he gets married and has a family.

Once you've started building a house there's really no end to it. But we're happy there and will most likely move out for good, Britt and I, when we get old. I was born in Kärrbo, and it may be I'll die there too.

Hunting on a Bay

Lars-Erik Andersson

People nearly always called my father Nyby-Kalle. When I grew up I was called Lasse in Nyby, but in the past years it's become Nyby-Lasse. It's handed down from one generation to the next. My boy Hans is sure to be called Nyby-Hasse sooner or later, if he stays on here in Nyby.

When I was a kid, families were generally much larger than they are now. I was the next youngest out of seven children and was born in 1929. We lived pretty comfortably, at least we had enough food and clothing.

Everyone at home had to help as best they could. That's how it always is on a farm. My first regular job was to bring in the wood. The house was big and there were many mouths to feed, so we used a lot of firewood. We always had hired help who ate with us.

Another of my jobs was to clean out the chicken house. My reward was usually some cookies and a slice of sponge cake. Ordinarily all we had with our coffee was slices of plain white bread.

At Midsummer the grass on all the slopes and in all the ditches was cut clear down to the lake. We kids had to help rake up the grass. It looked so nice and neat everywhere, it was a joy to see.

Ma and Pa went to town on Saturdays and they always brought home a bag of candy for us to share. It was divided up in fair portions. Hilma, our mother, was strict about everyone getting treated equally. We didn't have any pocket-money, but people often came around visiting and then we'd get a coin or two sometimes from some relative or good friend of the family.

We were expected to greet people properly and bow when visitors came. We didn't call grown-ups by their first names.

I've never used 'du', the familiar form of address, even to my father. To this day I still have a hard time saying 'du' to older people. I prefer using their name instead when speaking to them.

At elementary school Miss Kant treated us to cookies and Lucia buns on Lucia Day, the thirteenth of December. Before Christmas vacation we practised singing Christmas carols and playing our parts for a Christmas play which we gave at the Christmas Tree party in Lindö or Frösåker. Between thirty and forty well-dressed kids came from all parts of the parish to take part in the festivities and dance around the Christmas tree and get packs of goodies from the brownie who came at Christmas-time.

At home great quantities of food were prepared for Christmas, and on Christmas morning everyone rode by sleigh to the early morning Christmas church service – except the one who had to stay home to milk the cows. When we came back from church we ate Christmas breakfast.

At school I managed to keep up fairly well. I picked things up pretty easily, I suppose, but I didn't really put my heart into it. I didn't do my homework the way I should have.

What you remember most from schooldays are your pals. In secondary school Håkan Bager was one of my best friends. We used to swap sandwiches during our lunchbreak. Mine were made out of home-made bread, which he liked. He took along store-bought bread and something good like sausage or smoked herring or liver pâté, things we never had at home, except on a few rare occasions.

His Pa had some big job at Asea in Västerås and earned good money. They lived in Kärrbo for some years, in the building on the right down by Frösåker. Bager often had foreign guests at his house and sometimes they used to bring Håkan and his brothers lovely playthings.

Here in Nyby two or three schoolchildren from Aggarö boarded with the old-age pensioners in the white house, which the parish rented. Four of us from our family were going to school at the same time. Down by Frösåker there lived even more kids and we often ran down there to play in the afternoon. In the winter, out on the ice in the bay, we played bandy, a popular game similar to hockey.

One day Åke and Boskas and I were going to race each other on our bikes from school down to the store in Valla, where we picked up the mail. At the bend outside the church I crashed my bike and hit my skull on a rock and lost consciousness. They took me home on Birger Andersson's cycle-cart which we used to haul wood in to school. So I stayed home in bed a while. I guess I had a concussion. It cost money to go to a doctor.

As you grew older you had to help with the work. Even when I was in school I drove the milk in the mornings and picked up the cans in the afternoon from the milk-stand up by the road. My Pa was one of the first people in Kärrbo to buy a wagon with rubber tyres and it was nice and quiet when you drove it, compared with the iron-wheeled wagons. It was a big step forward.

In the fall we spent weeks on the threshing, first at home and then in Grindbo and Vallatorp and the parsonage – sometimes as far away as Skämsta and Skysta. The farmer at Valla was a funny old fellow. He used to have the stump of a cigar stuck in his mouth when he drove to the city and it would still be there when he came home again. Folks said that he used the cigar butt several years running and never lit it.

What I hated most was winnowing grain in late fall. Nothing is more monotonous than standing there at a winnowing machine – it was awful.

Pa caught all the fish we needed at home, and from the time I was a small kid I used to go with him out on the lake. I got the fever. I've kept on fishing more or less my whole life.

When I was eight years old we got a new tractor, a green Oliver 18/28 with red iron wheels. It arrived on a Sunday and caused a big stir. We talked about it at school for ages afterwards. We'd had an old Fordson before. During the war the Oliver ran better on producer gas than any other make. I did a bit of harrowing with the tractor in the spring, but mostly it was my Pa or my older brothers who drove it.

Serious work started when I finished school and became a dairy hand at home. I was thirteen years old and big for my age. We had eighteen dairy cows and some young heifers and pigs. You had to get up before five in the morning.

If you'd been out on a binge the night before it could be mighty hard to get out of bed early in the morning. Of course it *was* nice to have animals. Nowadays there's not a single dairy cow in all of Kärrbo. It's become dreary and deserted. The nearest place you can buy milk is the market over in Irsta.

In the past many people worked and made their living on a farm like Nyby. Now my brother, Bengt-Olov, looks after the farm by himself, and the money he makes goes to pay interest on loans and mortgages for all the equipment he had to have in order to manage the work alone. It sort of cancels out, the way it did before.

After the war, people moved one by one to Västerås, not just young people but whole families sometimes. Industry and the building trade were crying out for people. The wages were higher there and the city was growing fast. Farm-work was being rationalized at the same time, and many folks were forced to move to the city because of a lack of jobs around home.

There was a lot of talk about the way folks were moving away from the countryside at that time. Around Nyby here you didn't notice the change so much as in other places because of the summer guests down on the point.

From the start there were two old farm-houses on Nyby Point which Pa rented to summer guests. Towards the end of the thirties Landgren, the bicycle dealer, Wijgård, the photographer, Hedlund, and several others rented plots on a forty-nine-year lease and built summer cottages. During the war that sort of building wasn't allowed, but soon afterwards new cottages began to spring up.

Pa never advertised the plots. It just happened that people who built had friends who also wanted to rent a piece of land, and that's the way it went along. In the beginning the plots were not staked out by the surveyor. The person who wanted a plot would explain, I want this slope, from here to here. Then all they had to do was mark off the piece with a bit of cane in each corner.

The first plots were rented out for between forty fifty kronor a year. Later the prices rose, little by little. I went down and got a few extra jobs from folks who wanted help building a little house or a pier. Other people wanted a load of soil or manure to fertilize their flower beds and garden plots. That way I made a little money for Pa and myself.

Nowadays summer cottage areas have grown up here and there around Kärrbo; at Lybeck, Mårtenshamn, Fröholmen and Lindö works. And there isn't a single farm-house that isn't lived in. Many people from Kärrbo, who live in the city, have got themselves cottages out here and come out over Saturday and Sunday and for their vacations. More and more people make their cottages winterproof and drive out for the weekend the whole year round.

When I'd turned sixteen I got a new bike. Before I'd only had hand-me-downs from my older brothers. At Midsummer five of us boys from Kärrbo decided to ride our bikes to Furuvik. It was more than 200 kilometres and hardly any of us had ever been that far away before, but we'd had a lot of training. It was nothing to bicycle between eighty and a hundred kilometres on a normal Saturday. First in to the city perhaps in the afternoon to have a hair-cut, or to buy a new shirt or a tie, and then home for supper, and so off again somewhere a long way away to a dance.

The day before Midsummer we worked as usual. Around

seven in the evening we loaded our bicycles with sleeping bags, tents, spirit-stoves, lunch-boxes and *akvavit* which we'd gotten hold of, and pedalled all the way out to Gysinge. There we put up our tents on a little point of land in the Dala River, but there were so damned many mosquitoes there you couldn't sleep. We left the place in the middle of the night and pedalled in a long line, taking turns in the lead. In the morning we bought potatoes and cucumbers in the market-place at Gävle.

In Furuvik there were lots and lots of tents and bike riders, many from Stockholm. We danced and had fun on Midsummer Eve and Midsummer Day and drank up all the *akvavit*. I swam in salt water for the first time in my life, and that was quite an experience – of course it was darned cold so early in the summer.

We made our way home by way of Uppsala, and halfway through the woods we met some girls. One of them was sitting on a rock playing an accordion. It was almost midnight but perfectly light; we walked them home on a forest path, and they invited us to coffee.

We didn't get much sleep that night. In the morning we pedalled the long stretch in to Uppsala without a stop. You could see the cathedral tower from several kilometres off. None of us had any money left. We rode the remaining eighty kilometres home on empty stomachs. The following day we had to get back to work again.

My brother, Karl-Axel, started in at the fire department in Västerås when he came home from doing his military service. My sisters were also away working, so when it was time for my next oldest brother, Bengt-Olov, to do his military service, there was only me and Pa left to manage the farm. We couldn't do it, so that's why he rented out the farm on a five-year lease to a man named Nordström.

Then I became something of a freelancer. I was eighteen that year and got work with Hagelin, a bricklayer. My first job was to build a new barn and a garage for housing farm machinery, at Hanved above Orresta. Through the week, three or four of us lived in an empty farm-worker's place. On Sunday Ma fixed grub for me for the coming week. In the mornings we made porridge and coffee on the wood fire where we lived.

I built the brick walls of the garage without having had any apprentice training. A job like that isn't so terribly difficult to do if you've got a little sense about how it's done. It's important to keep the pattern of the bricks neat, so it will look nice, but things like that get to be routine. Bricklaying is fun, a pleasant job.

Then I went with Hagelin to renovate the interior of Bred Church. There was scaffolding all over the place inside. The roof had to be cleaned with wire brushes, and all the cracks had to be dug out, then filled in. This sort of thing takes time. We whitewashed the whole ceiling on the same Saturday as my grandfather had his eightieth birthday.

The last thing we did in the church was to write our names for fun on the steeple. I was earning pretty good money and had bought a lightweight motorcycle, a Husqvarna 120 c.c., to ride to work on. It cost 1,054 kronor, and I bought it with my first cheque and part cash.

Later on I helped with the restoration of Tillinge Church and various other buildings and repair work. In wintertime I stayed home and chopped wood in the forest for Pa and also started to do a little fishing on the lake here in Nyby.

One winter when I had finished cutting timber I was allowed to take the tops and branches for firewood. I chopped everything up – there were more than fifty cubic metres. There was a shortage of wood at that time and I managed to sell it to the fire department in Västerås for a good 800 kronor, if I remember rightly.

Of course a lot of times you were out in the evening raising hell – sometimes on Wednesdays as well as Saturdays and

Sundays. I liked dancing a lot. My sisters had taught me when I was young and we used to practise at home sometimes on the kitchen floor.

On Saturday evenings we'd often down a bottle of booze. Almost all the fellows drank. It was all part of things and that's the way it had to be. But God damn, *akvavit* tasted flat without anything to go with it! Your stomach protested, but you were a man, so you tossed it off.

What a long way we would bike sometimes if there was a good band playing. Almost everyone where the parties were held knew everyone else. We said hello to people and talked, laughed, danced, and had fun. On several Midsummers we had a dance at home in the barn at Nyby. A lot of people also came there.

I changed from job to job. I have driven a tractor both at Springsta and Frösåker. Ral at Frösåker was the first in the district to put lights on his tractor, which made it possible to drive in shifts during the fall ploughing. Another big change was rubber tyres, which meant that the tractors could be used for hauling.

One winter I was on Aggarö – Aggar Island – hauling oak timber: great big logs, some of them more than a metre across. We needed the help of several men to handle these. It's beautiful there on the island, but isolated. There were no spare womenfolks out there, either. We fellows used to go down to Juthällen in the evenings and watch the boats sail by in the narrow channel to and from Västerås. In the spring we rowed through the little islands casting for pike. I went on working out there until it was time for the haying.

Up until military service life is mostly a game. Then you come to an age when life goes on in a different way. You get more mature.

I was in the First Armoured Regiment in Enköping, nice and near. Actually I was supposed to have done my service in Strängnäs, but communications are so bad between here and there that I asked for a transfer. I began service in the spring of 1949.

For me there was intensive motor-cycle drill. I wasn't attached to a motor-cycle unit, but was assigned as platoon orderly. My sergeant – the one I was orderly for – spent a lot of time on a motor-cycle and sometimes travelled abroad for races. He was a good guy who knew his way around – though he could also be very demanding. You sure had to be able to cover fields and forests – all kinds of country.

Now military service involves a certain amount of discipline which I don't think hurts anybody. It's a necessary evil. You'd rather live in peace and quiet, but it's clear: the country has to be able to defend itself if it's attacked.

Looking back this way, of course it's the good times you remember best. Our captain was nice and we were allowed lots of free nights. On weekday evenings we mainly used to sit talking and playing cards. We drank very little *akvavit*; we had no money.

I'd already started going steady with Karin before military service. I used to call on her when I was on leave. She comes from Ängsö. My brother Bengt-Olov also used to pay calls at the farm, as he was courting her sister Greta.

The summer after I was released from military service I worked for Nordström, who was the tenant farmer at Nyby at that time. I also did a little fishing in my spare time. When winter came I went and chopped wood in the forest, and now and again I hauled timber and pulp-wood.

Fishing interested me more than anything else, and I started to wonder if I couldn't exist solely on this. I bought an old car and drove to Västerås and Enköping to sell my fish.

A car was not so common in those days. Mine was a D.K.W. – folks called it a 'chip basket'. I've never owned anything but second-hand cars, ones other people had discarded. It's cheaper that way, at least you don't have to pay for the chromium plate. For a while I had a little Loyd and drove it over the ice in winter. The distances are immense out around Granfjärden.

When I could afford it I bought new nets, but it was impossible to live off fishing alone – the fishing waters belonging to Nyby were not extensive enough. So I continued logging in the forest in winter.

In summertime I worked mostly in the construction business. For several seasons I was with a builder who operated on a small scale, building single-family houses, one at a time.

Karin and I got married in 1954. We didn't make too big an affair of it. Only members of the family were at the wedding, which took place in the minister's home, and afterwards Karin's parents fed us all.

We rented a place in Vedby down by Ängsö Sound, two rooms and a kitchen with central heating, water and drainage. We didn't apply for any state loan for setting up house. We got a little money as wedding presents and we'd saved up some. At low prices I had bought a Victorian sofa, a sideboard, a Pembroke table (with two end-flaps), and some chairs which I'd had renovated before our wedding. It's all good stuff and we still have it around. I like old furniture. Anything else we needed we picked up a little at a time.

We liked it in Vedby and we had nice neighbours, whom we saw often. We had many friends we exchanged visits with. Our way of life didn't change radically when we got married. We had gradually cut down on going to dances and parties when we started keeping steady company.

Our eldest boy Hasse was born in May of 1955. I didn't spend much time tending him; it was his mother's job to look after him, but I did feel a growing responsibility for the family's support. Both Karin and I were set on making a pleasant, comfortable home.

Most of the time I worked for Count Piper in Ängsö, digging wells and laying drains, together with another fellow. Just then there was quite a lot of rebuilding of farm buildings and farm-workers' quarters going on out there.

For a while I was on Måholmen planting trees. All of the arable land had to be planted. It certainly is strange that a farm with eighty-five acres of cultivated ground would just disappear, but then it wasn't in a very convenient location. It's a lot of trouble to freight everything to and from an island.

Besides this the farm-house was beginning to get run down. The Count of Ängsö probably didn't think it worth going to the expense of having it repaired, I don't know. Since then the fields have gone back to forest on other islands such as Lång-holmen, Hallingen, and Fagerön.

There were five or six of us planting trees on Måholmen. The fir-tree plants arrived in large quantities, stacked in boxes, and had to be planted immediately so they wouldn't dry out. The roots are very sensitive to sunlight.

I was only out there helping one season and there was a lot left to be done the following year. We walked around the fields there with the spades we were planting with and talked about how earlier generations had cultivated this earth, wrested it from the forest, how they'd sweated and strained to make it into farming land.

When you walk across overgrown fields and see all the rocks they broke up with primitive tools in days gone by, you feel a deep respect. You wonder how they could have managed. The next generation may have to cultivate the fields again, if industry slows down, with mass unemployment. There's already a shortage of food in the world, and even though we can't foresee the future, we do know that a family can manage to feed themselves, if they work at it, on a few acres of land.

I kept on with my fishing in Nyby during the time we lived in Vedby. It was a good bit more than ten kilometres between the two places, but I combined business with pleasure and paid a visit home when I went to inspect the nets. After a couple of years we moved to Skysta. From there it's only five kilometres to Nyby.

Around the same time I was able to take over the tenancy of the Frösåker waters that border Nyby's. This meant that I now had a large enough territory to be a fisherman full-time, something I had sort of been planning on for many years.

From the very beginning I understood that there was no fortune to be made out of fishing, but as long as I could earn as much money as other categories of workers in the country-side – and in those days you could – then it was advantageous to be a fisherman. It's a free, fine profession, your time is your own and you're independent of any employer.

I needed to buy more equipment so I took out a bank loan of 12,000 kronor to expand my business. Maybe I could have borrowed more, but I had to think about paying the money back, too.

I bought five drag-nets which cost almost 2,000 kronor each and a number of pike-nets. I already had a boat, plus some fish-nets and about a hundred fykes.

By and by I stopped using the fykes. It was bad business hoisting up masses of pike a couple of weeks in the spring during spawning-time and selling them for 1 krona or 1·50 a kilogram, when instead it was possible to catch almost the same amount over a longer period in late winter with fishnets and get very different prices, 3 or 3·50 kronor per kilogram.

The best type of fish here is the pike-perch and I went in mainly for this. You can catch this fish the whole year round and it brought in nice money, since the price was pretty stable at that time.

During the summer months from May to October I fished with the drag-nets. They look like big bow-nets and have an arm of sixty to a hundred metres. The trap itself is about six metres. Since the fish can move freely inside there without getting hurt you don't have to go through and empty them every day.

Fish-nets, on the other hand, aren't so good in summer. There, of course, what happens is that the fish fasten in the mesh, and when the water is warm, they die quickly if they get stuck. Another thing is that fish get lazier after spawning-time in the spring; they move more slowly and so it gets easier to avoid getting caught.

The art is knowing how to place the nets in the right way to catch as many fish as possible. You've got to get to know the fishes' habits. Pike, for example, they come up to the surface in summer and sail with the wind, but when the currents turn colder they go down deeper.

Much of what I know I've learned from other professional fishermen. I often used to ask for advice in the beginning, since I hadn't done any great amount of fishing before.

In the fall when you're out fishing with a net you're very dependent on the winds. When there's a nor'-nor'-westerly wind blowing, then my water, located as it is, gets a good season, because then the pike up here go near land. But if there's an east or south-east wind blowing, the catch is a good deal worse.

The yield in some places is good from year to year, though here too the catch might suddenly decrease. Nothing is absolutely certain, you have to keep experimenting all the time, be alert and stick with it when the fish change their habits.

It seems like fish store up experience in avoiding danger. Long ago, when the first big bow-nets were introduced, for a number of years there were great big catches of pike. Then the volume grew smaller gradually and it got less profitable. They then began manufacturing drag-nets, bigger equipment, which went deeper. And the catches got larger again for some years, only to fall off later. The same procedure was repeated once again. It could hardly have been because the amount of fish declined: what it was is that the fish learned to go down under the arms of the nets.

It's somewhat the same kind of thing with the animals in the forest. I'm also very interested in hunting and have gone hunting since I was a kid. Over the years I've noticed how elk and deer change their course in the forest and fields if they're disturbed or feel threatened.

Actually I don't hunt to *gain* anything, but more as recreation. Sometimes I'll have game within shooting range and I'll let it go. Animals can be so beautiful that you just don't have the heart to shoot them.

Hunting birds is fun because you have to be so quick. But at the same time you have to be careful you're not too quick on the trigger. Good judgement is necessary in all kinds of hunting and you shouldn't shoot until you're absolutely sure of getting your game. I practise shooting a lot, mostly clay pigeons. It helps keep your speed and reflexes in shape and gives you more self-confidence during the actual hunt.

If you're out with a dog hunting hares and it trails a hare to a slope, all you do is stand there and wait. A hare almost never fails to return to the same slope after a couple of hours' absence. Why I don't know. Deer are also quite settled. Elk, on the contrary, move around over wide areas. But they do come back too after long absences.

My fishing went along all right, once I really got going and expanded the business. I covered our interest payments and mortgages and living costs for the family. I was really happy with my life. I've never actually been unhappy – I'm not that kind of a person. But, well, things can be better or worse.

I had much greater freedom than in other kinds of jobs, my time was my own to use as I pleased. By that I don't mean that I had shorter working hours, more likely they were longer, especially in early winter when I worked on my nets weekdays, weekends, and holidays.

Since I was now a full-time fisherman, I joined the Västerås Fishermen's Association which was the fishermen's trade organization. The Association's managing board acts as mediator if problems and conflicts arise between different sides.

The organization was responsible for an extensive programme to stock pike and eels in the waters of Lake Mälar. The fish-spawn comes from various fish hatcheries. Some eel-spawn has been freighted here in tank trucks all the way from Denmark.

In the spring of 1960 my father died. Things were pretty empty after he'd gone. I felt the loss very strongly. He was a man of experience. When there were big decisions to be made I used to ask him for advice. You might almost say that I didn't really stand on my own feet until he was gone.

He also kept me company a lot. In wintertime he helped me with the nets and in summer he came and rowed while I put out the nets and fixed in the poles of the drag-nets. During the latter years he wasn't able to come along as often as before, as he began to feel old age coming on.

When Dad died the main house got too big for Mom to live in alone, so we fixed up the apartment upstairs for her. Earlier my grandfather and grandmother lived there. Bengt-Olov and his family moved in on the ground floor. Before that they lived in the white house which had been workers' quarters.

This meant that that house was empty, so Karin and I and five-year-old Hasse moved home to Nyby. At the same time Per was born, our youngest boy. We had enjoyed those years in Skysta living there on the birch-covered slope, but it was a great advantage for me to come home to Nyby where I was much closer to my fishing.

Summer is the leanest time of year for the professional fisherman here in these parts. In order to make debit balance against credit I helped Bengt-Olov a little on the farm at home here or Torgny at Frösåker, and I also used to take miscellaneous other extra jobs to make a krona or two.

The fall fishing used to be quite rewarding, but in past years the amount of algae and other water plants has increased. The vegetation follows the currents and attaches itself on the nets. It fastens in the mesh so the fish get shy and keep away.

We fishermen call this kind of thing 'greenery'. Usually you'll talk about the water blooming. It always has done this in the fall, but before the greenery used to disappear after a couple of weeks. Now it seldom goes away before the ice has settled and the currents slow. Nowadays the water doesn't start getting clear again before then. I suppose Lake Mälar has been over-fertilized by all the chemicals which are let out through the drains.

In 1961 when the spring fishing was over and the drag-nets had been set out, I started driving excavators for Axel Söderqvist. I carried on with this right up until the ice settled and it was a good combination, since the excavating season came to an end when the ground froze.

The job was quite varied. I went around excavating and levelling all over the Västerås area, Köping, Sala, Skultuna, and Enköping. You got to meet all different kinds of folks. The smallest machine weighed six tons, the medium one nine, and the biggest fourteen tons. It takes quite a lot of know-how to drive machines like those, but after you've been at it a while it gets to be purely routine. To start with, I drove a bulldozer, which is easier than levelling with a steam shovel. If it was crowded on the building sites, you had a guy with you to direct the trucks bringing in their loads, so it all went more smoothly. Sometimes I was out alone digging garages and cellars under houses you couldn't get at with any steam shovel.

My work driving tractors in the summer and fishing in the winter meant I had quite a steady income the whole year round. So Karin and I could build a home of our own, as we'd planned for several years. In 1962 I sent for the surveyor and had the plot staked out here on the hillside.

I really shouldn't have been allowed a permit to build here. All the new residential buildings around here, according to regulations, are supposed to be located in the residential area over in Ullvi. But since I lived by my fishing down here the authorities had to make an exception.

Since then the regulations have been made even more strict. They claim that it's necessary for sanitary reasons, among other things. But God knows! Naturally folks would rather build up around in the hills than out on a field in a rectangular residential area. That is if you had your choice.

A whole lot of applications and other papers had to be written up before the work could begin. I was given a state home construction loan of 27,720 kronor and a mortgage loan of 29,700 kronor. The District Council stood as guarantors for the mortgage loan, as district councils usually do in such cases. The terms are favourable, only 1,000 kronor per year altogether in amortization and a part of the interest costs subsidized by the state.

During our vacation in 1962, I borrowed machines from Söderqvist and dug the foundations and drains and cleared a path down here. The following spring I put in the water and drainage pipes as soon as the frost had left the ground and I laid the foundation, that is the cellar floor.

An architect in Västerås designed the house. Before that the wife and I had studied a bunch of catalogues in order to see which type of house we wanted to have. We decided on a plain, simple house, which works out to be considerably cheaper than one with wings jutting out. Everything costs money and we didn't know how far our money would go.

As soon as the blueprint was ready, I sent a copy of it to Nordenhaag's lumber store in Västerås and got a cost estimate of all the building material needed. Their final bid totalled 22,915 kronor including cost of delivery.

After Whitsun I had a couple of men help lay the bricks for the foundation, and then the basement floor came prefabricated in sections of concrete on a truck with a crane. It took no more than a few hours to put the sections into place.

Then we got down to the carpentry work, first of all the framework of posts, then roof beams and after that rough boards and cardboard, and tar paper on the outside of the walls, and rock wool, cardboard, furring, and sheetrock on the inside. Then there was the roof and the ceiling, partition walls and the floor, windows, and doors. And electricians, plumbers, and painters. Last of all the red bricks of the facade were laid.

There was plenty to do that summer – you couldn't tell Sunday from regular weekdays. At times I was almost sick of it. Some days I just wasn't in a working mood and could hardly get my hands to do anything. But I cheered up when I thought about the house and pitched in again in better spirits.

By Christmas the house was ready and we moved in. Three rooms and a kitchen, hall, and bathroom; eighty-seven square metres altogether. And a whole cellar floor underneath it. When I went in to Nordenhaag's to pay the bill for the building material, they told me I'd been lucky because prices had risen fifteen per cent since they'd given me their bid.

The bills for the plumbing and the electrical installations were also paid and everything seemed more secure, as the money question had worried me quite a lot.

I got the garden into shape in the early summer of 1963. I had done an excavation in Springsta for a granary and was promised the pile of dirt, which was just in the way there. I borrowed a steam shovel from Söderqvist. Bengt-Olov helped me with his tractor and trailer and Torgny Ral helped with two tractors, Olle Åhs with one and Herbert in Skämsta with one.

Each cartload took about seven to eight cubic metres at a time, and we drove like maniacs one Saturday and brought home the entire pile of dirt, about 350 cubic metres. We agreed upon a very reasonable price for everything. It's still the same – you help each other whenever you can, otherwise there'd be a lot of things you could never afford.

I had a good layer of top soil – I could sow grass and plant flowers and bushes here in the garden. The entire building cost about 55,000 kronor; the reason it was so cheap was because I had done most of the work myself.

It certainly is nice to have a modern home. It's also fun to have something of your own to fuss over and keep up. Every spring I get energetic and do a lot of painting and repair work on the house. We'll go on living here even if I have to take a job in the city.

In the evening I usually sit a while in the room downstairs and watch the news on T.V. and the weather report. Doesn't cheer you up. There's war and fighting all over the world. We'll just have to hope that there won't be any more major wars. It's a hell of a world the way it is.

Here at home it's mainly the youngsters making a fuss, kids studying. I think there's something fishy about that somehow. They make demands without having accomplished anything themselves. To a great extent, they're living on scholarships and loans that are interest-free. We working people have to pay for it.

It may not be quite so simple as all that though. I don't know very much about politics, but there certainly are things that deserve protest. And of course the youngsters think it's going to help.

Myself, I'm happiest out on the lake. There's nothing lovelier than setting out over the ice on a winter morning. You go searching for one row of nets after the other, on and on, and you hardly notice the day go by. In other jobs I'm watching the clock, waiting for the lunch break, but out on the lake I completely forget about eating sometimes.

Being a fisherman is no job for anyone who's lazy. Even so you don't get as tired as in other jobs – you don't get tired in the same way. In other jobs you collapse on Friday night and thank your lucky stars that the work week is over. Though before you've had time to turn around it's Sunday evening and then comes that feeling of dread, that early tomorrow morning you're stuck again.

The winter fishing has become a lot easier since I got a snow-scooter. It's cheap to run and it takes just a few minutes to get way out onto the bay. Before I used to use a big sled. It took time and it was tough going when the wind was against you. If there was snow on the ice, you couldn't even use the sled, you had to walk. You can be quite a wreck after trudging ten kilometres through deep snow.

The wind blows pretty strong sometimes, and once when I was out near Skarpan and had stood my sled nearby, it began sliding away without my noticing. When I caught sight of it I started running, but the ice was glassy and the wind got stronger and took hold of the heavy sled with my load of fish. It picked up speed fast.

I ran and ran and several times my finger tips were practically touching the handle. It was annoying – I was panting, putting on bursts of speed, but it didn't help. Then it took off faster and faster and I couldn't even keep up. For a while it looked as if that damned sled was heading straight for Kungsåra Bay. Then I'd have had to walk five kilometres to get it. Luckily it swerved a little to the left and went into the rushes off Lindö and stuck there.

A great many people are interested in fishing and spend all their spare time on the lake. Other people take no interest in it whatsoever. It's the same with hunting and a lot of other things. People are so different. Some are good with their hands, others can't do anything with them; some people are economical, others let money slip through their fingers like water. And so on.

Take both of my boys for example – the elder keeps rabbits and sells rabbit meat to the Italians in Västerås. My nephew Janne is married to an Italian woman and she makes the contacts for him. He keeps track of the money he earns and I'll be damned if sometimes he isn't actually better off than I am. My younger boy, on the other hand, is happy for the present to spend every last öre on ice-cream and candy as soon as he gets any money. They're different.

For me nothing can compare with fishing. What I like best is hunting. I have shot eight elk. Elk hunts are in a class by themselves – they're such big animals.

I've been with a group up in the province of Jämtland for several years, during a few days in the fall hunting elk. There's some real hunting up there. The elk are much shyer up there than they are here, and more difficult to get within shooting range. Down here they're accustomed to the scent of people all over the place and don't shy away from human tracks.

We had hunting grounds on both sides of the Indal River, with long distances to cover. It was strenuous walking over marshy ground, and up steep hills and slopes. The landscape was fantastic, with a view out over undulating forests and mountain peaks far off across to the Norwegian side.

From up high where I stood looking through my field-glasses I caught sight of three elk running across the marsh down below, heading away from me. But damn it! They got the scent of my tracks where I'd just been walking. They veered around and came straight in my direction. I shot a cow. There was also a bull in the trio, but there were mountain-birches and brush in my way so I missed him. Bull elks always walk behind cows and calves.

When you've shot an elk here in Kärrbo you can usually bring back the carcass with a tractor. Up there you had to slaughter it and hang it in a tree overnight, then carry the cut-up meat a long way over terrain that normally you had a tough enough job getting over just by yourself. There were foxes there but they didn't come near the elk carcasses during the night, since the scent of human tracks was still fresh there-abouts.

Hunting is a pleasure. Fishing is work combined with pleasure. That's why I enjoy it so much. But during the past years, winter fishing has been none too good down here in my waters. In the summer I do have other jobs, we wouldn't get by financially otherwise.

The winter of 1967-8 was a complete catastrophe because of the quicksilver controversy. The radio and T.V. were blasting out about the amount of quicksilver in fish and a lot was written about it in the newspapers. Some of the lakes were blacklisted as far as fishing was concerned and it had its repercussions everywhere, even around Lake Mälar here where the fish aren't dangerous to your health. Folks got so scared that they didn't dare eat freshwater fish.

Deliveries almost stopped completely. Sales fell off to a tenth of what they were normally and at the same time prices swooped down to a third of what they had been before. I lost at least 8,000 kronor. Times were hard for all of us professional fishermen. I was lucky enough to get some extra work as carpenter on construction sites, in spite of the fact that unemployment was high.

The fishermen in the lakes that were blacklisted received between 1,000 and 2,000 kronor in emergency relief from the state, and assistance in retraining for another trade. Later they got a sum of money as severance pay. But in these parts no one got an öre, since no restrictions had been set against fishing here.

No doubt you can say that the last fifteen years or so have been good ones for most people in Sweden. But now it looks like we're heading for harder times. Prices have risen faster than wages, and there's a shortage of work. The market is glutted and one factory after another is closing down. For now, you can earn good money while you have a job, but there's no knowing how things will go from here on.

Sometimes I wonder if it wouldn't be just as well to take things a little easier and get by on a little less. The way things are now you're forced to keep slaving away, just to stay alive. Though actually, of course, everybody shares in progress. For example, I don't use a sled any more, I ride a snow-scooter.

Maybe what's most important is to have something to look forward to. A worker can start planning and looking forward to his vacation a long time in advance, for example, and then when it's over he's often glad to pitch into his work again. Or he can look forward to buying a new car or building a summer cottage.

As for me, I'll be satisfied with life if I can stay healthy and live here in Nyby and keep on fishing. The hysteria over quicksilver will probably pass. That's what I'm counting on. So I don't think that I've got any cause for complaint.

Follow the Moonpath

Aina Sjökvist

'If you're quiet, Mama will soon be home with a little Princess for you,' Grandma said to my sister Margit. At that time she was two years old and living with Grandma the days Mom was in the hospital having me. When we came home, Margit said, 'Here comes Mama with the little sessa.' Since then I've always been called Sessan.

Dad was farm-foreman at Frösåker. They called him Foreman-Kalle or just Kalle. We lived in a whitewashed little house by the road near the pier. The apartment had one room and a kitchen.

There were many migrant farmhands on the farm. Pa lived on a farm-worker's allowance too. Wood and seed and milk and lodgings were included in the allowance. In cash he got ninety-six kronor a month.

In the spring he used to stand in the evenings sawing and chopping wood that Margit and I had to stack up. There it stood drying during the summer and in the fall it was our job to carry it into the woodshed. We had a little wheelbarrow which Dad had made and each of us was supposed to haul in five loads a day.

Margit cheated sometimes and didn't take in more than two or three loads. Then we argued and fought and once I knocked her into the stinging nettles by the woodshed. She ran inside crying, of course, and Ma beat me with the broomstick. It hurt me more than the nettles hurt Margit, probably, but I didn't regret what I'd done. After all, she had cheated. Otherwise we got on well for the most part and played together.

I was rather bow-legged when I was little and the grown-ups thought it was rickets. An old woman used to come around to us with a brown salve and rub it all over my body. I don't know if it helped – it was some kind of household remedy. The salve looked like shoe polish, and after it had been rubbed in I was wrapped in a sheet and told to lie absolutely still. It was awfully difficult for me to do this, but the grown-ups said that if I didn't lie still, I would die.

Once someone took a photo of me and Margit at home by the gate. She was standing with her legs perfectly straight. Mine were crooked. I remember I tore off the bottom of the photo so the legs wouldn't show. It was some kind of nutritional deficiency that made me bow-legged, I guess.

There were plenty of kids to play with at Frösåker. We hung out down in the clay pits – where they had taken clay for making bricks before the brickyard was closed down – and in the outbuildings and the barn and all over. Our house wasn't far from the barn and I went there often to play and help clean out after the cows. The cowhands were birds of passage and some of them only stayed a year in the same place. One of them had a big bunch of boys and that may be why I was down in the barn such a lot.

My little sister, Ingrid, is five years younger than me. I was born on New Year's Day in 1929. If I'd been born on New Year's Eve instead, I would have begun and finished school one year earlier and been considered a whole year older.

I went to elementary school in Harkie. It was three kilometres to walk. What I remember most clearly is Grandma calling me to come in for chocolate and a sandwich on my way home in the afternoons.

She and Grandpa lived up in Larsbo. Grandpa had been a forest ranger at Frösåker before he retired. Grandma used to make flat loaves of bread out of sifted rye flour and she cut them vertically into long thin slices. At home we cut the flat loaves into triangles.

Pa kept rabbits. It was my job to give them water and clean out the cages. They had to have juniper branches too, and

Lord, how angry I was every time I had to go and get the juniper. Once I had to ride into the city with a box of slaughtered rabbits. It was during the war when meat was scarce. Ulla Ullberg went with me – we were always together come rain or come shine. She was one year younger than I was but she was bigger and taller.

The box was to be delivered to the Mimer beer café. A whole crowd of old men were sitting there eating pickled herring and drinking lager. We were shy and scared, everything in the city was so strange. It took a long time before we mustered up enough courage to go in with the box, and it was such a relief to be sitting down once more on the bus back to Kärrbo.

I was at secondary school then, in the fourth or fifth grade. The only things I enjoyed there were singing and gym and sketching and handicraft, subjects that hardly counted at all. History was what I hated most, just learning about a lot of dry dates and old geezers. It was mostly about wars and kings, about Karl XII who fell at Fredrikshald in 1732 – or was it 1632? No, of course, that was Gustav II Adolf at Lützen. Anyway, they weren't killed at home.

Geography was a bit better, but that wasn't up to much either. You learned a few rivers in the various provinces: Saga River, Svartån, Kolbäcksån, Hedströmmen, and Arboga River. As well as Lagan, Nissan, Ätran and Viskan. What use is that to anyone? Needlework was more fun. I've still got towels I sewed in handicraft lessons at school.

One girl was near-sighted and wore spectacles and everyone was always picking on her. Kids are cruel. She never did any harm to anyone and sometimes I was kind to her. It was really too bad about her.

At home I was always getting beaten. A kid like me could hardly wait to get into mischief, naturally, and as soon as you did anything they lammed into you. There was never any question of parents trying to talk to their kids and make them see reason. A spanking was in order.

At the start of the war we got a radio, the make was a Radiola. We weren't allowed to touch it – not for anything. Pa always turned it on and off himself in the beginning.

We did have the local newspaper, of course, but we kids seldom looked at it. It was the grown-ups who read the newspaper.

It came with the mail truck. Ma took care of the mail at Frösåker – it was a kind of extra postal-station besides the regular one which the storekeeper in Valla ran. The only things I can remember reading were a few books I borrowed from the library up at the secondary school.

We had a pig at home which got dysentery, and Pa sent me off to Springsta to borrow a hypodermic syringe. I must have been about twelve years old then, but was still so shy that I hardly dared go in and ask for the syringe. It was five kilometres away and I pedalled for dear life so the poor creature wouldn't die before I got back again. When I got home I had to hold the pig, which scared me just as much as when I had to go in and ask for the syringe.

I wasn't allowed to swim down by the pier before the workers' kids from Västerås came out to Snäppan – the children's colony at Frösåker – at the beginning of June, the day after exams. Though Ulla and I went to the clay pits and swam long before that. There were deep pools there with clear water. But of course it got very muddy when we had walked around in the ooze a while.

One summer we had a goose we christened Kalle, and he followed me wherever I went. He liked going down to the pier with Ulla and me and splashing about and swimming out with us. Kalle was so good that he came ashore as soon as you called him. On the way home he used to get tired and lie down, so we had to struggle along carrying him. There were tears shed and teeth gnashed when Dad slaughtered Kalle for St Martin's Day in November and sold him to Mrs Ral.

I had my first job when I was thirteen years old and had

finished school. I became chambermaid for a family in Västerås who had a summer residence in Kärrbo. My duties there were cleaning and cooking. There wasn't much I could do really.

They had a son about twenty-five years old who was crazy. In the beginning I was afraid of him. Every morning when I came he would stand and put his arms around me. He could hardly speak, only a few words. But he could count. I had to play cards with him and if I counted wrong, he got furious. The family had a hired nurse to look after him and to help with the housekeeping.

My wages were forty kronor a month and I considered myself almost rich. I saved and had money left over each pay-day. The summer after this I got a job planting trees on Aggarö together with Ulla. There we each earned eight kronor per day. Later we went and rooted up thistles in the fields out there. That was before the time of weed-killer sprays. The fields seemed unending. It was burning hot and we turned brown as Negroes.

It was a four-kilometre bike ride down to Vretbo, where they picked us up by rowboat – the work began at seven a.m. You had to get up out of bed in time in the morning. Besides Ulla and me there were several others who worked on Aggarö, both men and women.

What I earned I had to hand over at home. I was allowed to keep only a few kronor for myself – I was so mad I could have burst. Still, they let me keep my last wages from Aggarö all to myself, and I bought a new pair of slacks with the money.

That summer Ulla and I and a girl who worked at the colony all went to the amusement park in Västerås to dance. We would ride our bikes any distance in those days. Some Saturday and Sunday evenings we went to Klinta or Östanbro to a dance.

For the most part we three girls used to ride home together too. I pitied boys who decided to go home with us. They nearly pedalled themselves to death. The first boy I went steady with for a while lived at home in Frösåker. His pa was cowman.

The only entertainment we had in Kärrbo was the prayer meetings. Of course, there was a dance at Hagbo now and again on a Saturday night. But on weekday evenings there was nothing else for the kids to do except go to a prayer meeting one evening a week. You went there to meet your pals and because it was free. The audience consisted mostly of us kids, who weren't the least bit religious.

The folks from the Pentecostal church arranged the meetings. The chapel was in Karelen. Now someone has turned the place into a summer cottage. Sometimes one of the Pentecostal people would get up and testify for the Lord and talk about their sins. We thought it was hypocrisy – they considered themselves to be some kind of superior beings.

They had preachers too who delivered their sermons so you could all but smell the brimstone. We didn't take it seriously, to us it was all a big joke. But I thought they sang nicely. The fodderer at Kusta – who was called 'The Potato' – had the job of doorman and of keeping us in order. We knocked around and giggled. That must have been a thankless task for him, hallelujah!

Afterwards we used to swipe apples at Ral's in the garden at Frösåker if it was the right season. Sometimes he was outside sneaking around waiting to catch us. So we'd lie as flat as we could on the ground by the pond. He never caught any of us – we were better at running than he was. Most of us had apples at home. It was for the sport of it that we snitched the apples.

In the fall, the same year I worked on Aggarö, I started in a cafeteria in Västerås as errand-girl. I took around food on a delivery bike to the folks who worked at the bank offices. First I made a trip with the food and put it in the warming ovens and set the table. Then I made another trip after lunch to pick up the dirty dishes.

The employees at the County Savings Bank, the Commercial Bank, the Farmers' Bank, and the Bank of Göteborg had lunch tickets. The first day I picked up the dirty dishes from the County Savings Bank some small change was lying in a pile on the table. I thought someone had forgotten the money so I left it there. The next day they asked me why I hadn't taken the coins. It was a tip. After that I got a tip practically every single day.

I went around making deliveries on the bike for half a year. It was fun. Well, of course I also had to help in the kitchen – delivering food didn't take all day. Once I dropped a dish of hash on Stora gatan, but I was too embarrassed to stop and pick it up. I rode back to the cafeteria instead and said that there was a dish missing.

My wages were ninety kronor a month and I got a free uniform and my food. I was fourteen years old and lived on Åsögatan with Astrid and Martin Ullberg, Ulla's Mom and Dad. They had moved to the city and Martin worked at Asea.

The following year my parents also moved to the city. I think Dad had a falling-out with Mr Ral or else it was just that he was tired of farm-work after twenty-six or twenty-seven years at Frösåker. Mama would probably have liked to move back there again. She was born there, after all. She didn't like the city. But Dad did.

First of all he got a job in a cement foundry – that was in 1944. His next job was to guard the railway's coal piles at night. Not all locomotives were electric then. I guess he and the other watchmen sat and played cards a lot at night between rounds. Later on Ma began working as well. She had shift-work washing the dishes at Sjöhagen – Lake Meadow Restaurant.

We lived in a two-room apartment in Stensborg by the deep-water harbour. We got our water from a tap out in the yard. At work I had advanced to counter assistant by that time. I stayed four years at the Dairy Bar and became one of its veterans. There were girls who stayed only two or three days and then you never saw them again.

One day you'd work in the morning from five forty-five a.m. to one thirty p.m. and from one thirty p.m. to ten thirty p.m. the next day. There were about ten of us on each shift. The last half hour after closing-time in the evening was spent cleaning up. Several old guys used to remain sitting, not wanting to get up and go home, and some probably didn't have any place to go.

In the mornings the tables had to be wiped off before we opened at six a.m. and then the breakfast rush was on. Most of the men who ate there worked at Asea and wanted their porridge and their coffee and an egg. After them came the boys who were studying at the Technical College. The job was quite fun and I had good fellow workers.

All types of people ate at the Dairy Bar and we got our share of drunks. Once a drunkard gave me five kronor for cleaning up after him when he had vomited in the bathroom. He had drunk up a bottle of 'Keratin' hair lotion, and apparently wasn't used to it. That's why he'd thrown up. The old soaks who drank wood-alcohol could take anything.

Busloads of American airmen used to come and eat at the restaurant, flyers who had made emergency landings in Sweden in big military planes that were called 'flying fortresses'. The Yanks had a lot of money to get around on and many Västerås girls went wild over them. When the war was over they went back to the U.S.A. Some of the girls went with them. One went over of her own accord to see her Yankee, but when she got there it turned out that he was married and had two kids. She was out of luck.

At the restaurant one of the girls I worked with was called 'The Horse'. She had *akvavit* in a vinegar bottle with her one Saturday. It was the first time I had tasted liquor. We dipped ginger snaps into the *akvavit* and then we went dancing at The Hawk. The next day the other girls at the restaurant said we'd been drunk. I didn't remember a thing. I was sixteen years old at the time, I think.

It wasn't so appetizing at the old Hawk with the stench of pee and vomit in the ladies' room. But gee, what fun we had! There was always a line outside The Hawk on Saturday evenings. You had to be there in time in order to get in before it was full. There was a line just like it outside The Shack on Sunday evenings – that is, the old community centre.

The Hawk's still there and I believe Ekman's still play, the same orchestra as when I used to go there. Many of the folks who danced there twenty to twenty-five years ago still go there now, some of them with their children. It's almost impossible to get tickets, people say. You have to phone to Sundkvist beforehand to get them.

Lasse and I met at The Shack. I hadn't intended to go there that evening, but the other girls nagged me until I agreed to go along. He came over and asked me for a dance. I'd never seen him before. We danced. He was eighteen and exactly two years older than I was, since he was born on New Year's Day too.

Afterwards he walked me home. His buddies teased him: 'You gonna walk all the way to Stensborg tonight?' They must have recognized me, I guess. It was in December – wintry and snowy. Well, that's the way it went.

We often went out dancing and had only occasional fights, which is the way things should be. In the summer we went to People's Park on Saturday evenings like everybody else. Though mostly we were out on the lake. He had an open canoe, a Canadian one. We used to go out alone to some little island. That was during the early summer of 1946.

On our vacation we paddled to Frösåker first and camped. We cooked food over a spirit-stove. We walked to Valla to do our shopping. One evening when the moon was shining and the lake lay clear as a mirror, we started out towards Strängnäs. Everything was fantastically beautiful.

Lasse wasn't really sure of his directions out on Gran Bay. Then a big steamboat came along in the channel with people standing on the bridge, and Lasse called out and asked them.

Before they had time to look at the marine chart the boat had
steamed along a good ways. They took the megaphone and
shouted, 'Follow the moonpath – and good luck!' We did, and
came directly to Strängnäs Sound. The canoe glided like a
piece of down over the water, we paddled at full speed. After
five hours or thereabouts we arrived and put up our tent in a
glade by Perch Mountain – Abborrberget.

In Strängnäs Lasse had an aunt who invited us to eat with
her. We had to go to her house every single day to eat. She sort
of felt responsible for us eating properly during our vacation.

The thing with relatives is that you can visit them at any
time, without any fuss. Though my family didn't socialize
much with each other. I had never seen my grandfather (on
Pa's side) before Sis and I got the idea of renting a tandem
bike and pedalling away to Hallstahammar to pay him a call.
He lived at the old folks' home. My goodness, how pleased the
old fellow was when we came and told him who we were. He
took us with him to visit an aunt and uncle who lived in
Hallsta.

Pa also used to go and visit him sometimes, but it was a long
way to bike from Frösåker, some forty kilometres. Pa had a lot
of relatives. Ma had only one brother. He lived at home with
Grandpa and Grandma in the summer so we did get to meet
him.

If it had been fine weather when we paddled to Strängnäs,
it was certainly anything but that on the way home again. The
waters of the lake were rough. We had to go ashore on Fagerön
and empty the canoe – we were sitting in water nearly up to
the rail.

The trip home took over twelve hours, and when we finally
arrived at the canoe house in Västerås we were so exhausted
after all our paddling against the wind that we just collapsed on
the pier and slept. We slept several hours before we woke up,
so cold our teeth were chattering. All our things in the canoe
were soaked.

There was no baby from that vacation, but later on in the winter it happened. I was still working at the Dairy Bar. Lasse had a job at the Metalworks laboratory. He was actually going to be a chemist, but it meant too much studying and he didn't care for that too much. So he started at the Acetylene Gas Works instead.

Then, when I was expecting a baby, I moved to his parents' home on Pilgatan. We lived there several months until Ann-Britt was born, 22 September 1947, the same week Lasse went into the military. The kid was born on Monday morning, so he had time to see her before he reported in on that Wednesday.

He couldn't get a pass for Saturday. They hadn't even been given their uniforms. He was stationed with the First Air Force Division, on Hässlö, just outside the city. In order to come and see me he had to crawl out through a hole he found in the wire fence by Hälla. When he walked into the maternity ward he had his khakis on.

We got married on 18 October. I was eighteen and he was twenty. Lasse's Mom and Pop and brother and sister-in-law came to the wedding. My Ma and Pa weren't there. They were a little put out, as they thought I'd made a mess of things. But it blew over.

The day after the wedding we moved out to Gäddeholm, where we had got hold of an apartment through answering an ad. in the newspaper. Lasse was allowed an overnight pass after we were married and was able to come home in the evenings. He had an old lightweight motor-cycle that he rode.

The entrance to the Air Force Station is on the Västerås side, and it was a long way to ride all around. If he cut a hole in the fence he only had to drive straight across the airfield home to Gäddeholm.

So that's what he did, but an older sentry, a former pilot, who had been kicked out for drinking too much, mended the wire fence each time Lasse cut a hole. One day Lasse told him how things stood. After this he was able to keep his hole.

If it had been discovered both of them would probably have been locked up.

We didn't have much saved up when we married – we'd been taken rather by surprise. But we had enough anyway for furniture for one room: dining table, chairs, linen cupboard, and sideboard. We bought the furniture for 350 kronor at an auction. We got some second-hand furniture from Lasse's parents. I'd sewn clothes for Ann-Britt before she was born. Grandma helped me.

Rent and money for fuel we got from the military, plus a few kronor a day in family and child allowances. It was enough to live on, but it was skimpy, all right. Lasse had given me a two-kronor silver piece which I wore on a velvet ribbon around my neck as a necklace, it was the fashion just then. On it were engraved the letters L.E.S. (Lars Egon Sjökvist). One day I had to take the two-kronor piece and go buy baby-cereal, that's how poor I was.

We liked it very much in Gäddeholm. The apartment had one room and a kitchen, running water, and a wood-stove. The neighbours were nice; there were three families, including us, living in the building. Outside I had a little vegetable plot with cucumbers and other vegetables in the summer. Lasse and I borrowed a rowboat from the gardener and rowed over the Sound to Björnö and went swimming.

I had learned to play poker out there the year before. It was one Sunday in summer and we were sitting under a birch tree, Lasse and I and Grandpa and Grandma – that's what I called my parents-in-law even then, after all the baby was already on the way. We played for small stakes, either one or two öre pieces. Since then I've played a lot of poker.

Usually no one bets more than five kronor when we play, but once on a New Year's Eve I was there when they played 'sky's the limit' and then the pots went up to sixty to eighty kronor. We continued playing until seven in the morning and I won 120 kronor. Lasse also won a little. My Pa was there too and he lost, and the family whose place we were at lost too. Lasse's Pa was also with us, but he was O.K., he almost never loses.

Lasse was discharged in September 1948, and then he worked a year at the co-op slaughter-house in the city. He commuted on his lightweight motor-cycle. It was a chilly pastime in winter, but luckily he managed to get hold of a big coverall with a sheepskin lining.

The following fall we moved to Berga in Skultuna. Lasse took a job there as cowman, and stank of cow manure from a long way off. The apartment was beautiful and of course I was happy about that. Until I discovered it was crawling with bed-bugs. So the fumigation people came and sprayed in every last nook and cranny, and they also looked up the family who had lived there previously and fumigated them too. I went on seeing bed-bugs long afterwards, even though they had all disappeared.

While we lived there I got to vote for the first time. It was in a local election. Both Lasse and I voted, but otherwise we didn't take part in politics. We never have.

At Berga Lasse was third cowman, and he didn't stay there more than a year. Then we moved to Vallbylund in Rytterne. There were fewer animals there, and he tended the barn by himself. He preferred that. But the house was worse, with only a hand pump in the kitchen and poor heating.

I stayed at home. We had gotten some chickens and a pig. In the spring of 1951 Kerstin was born. Then I had my hands full looking after the two babies. Ann-Britt was in her fourth year.

We took a trip to Furuvik one Sunday to look at the animals. Lasse had bought a motorbike. My sister Ingrid looked after the kids. It was my first time in a zoo and we wandered around for hours looking at the bears and reindeer, goats, ponies, monkeys, penguins, and lots of birds. We should have been home before evening, but the motor-cycle gave us trouble.

Outside Östanbro I had to push it to get it started, but I didn't have time to hop on myself and Lasse didn't dare stop. There was something wrong with both the kickstarter and the clutch. So there I was walking alone through the dark and almost in tears. Finally a man in a car stopped by Gottsta hills and gave me a lift. He was a minister. I caught sight of Lasse again on Pilgatan in Västerås by the railway crossing.

After a year at Vallbylund Lasse got tired of being a cowman, and we moved to Lindö, back in old Kärrbo. There he took to chopping wood in the forest. We lived in a little red cottage with one room and a kitchen opposite the greenhouses. It was so cold that you had to have the heat on full blast the whole time in the winter.

A neighbour's daughter looked after the kids when I went to Valla to do my shopping. She had changed Kerstin one day and when I came home the pants lay frozen to the floor behind the bench. The workers' quarters in Kråkslottet – Crowcastle – up on the hill were warmer. They had been repaired and modernized.

There were quite a lot of folks working at Lindö. We were good friends with a family called Nehrén and used to spend practically every evening with them, and on Sundays Lasse and Holger Nehrén used to go out onto the lake and bob for fish.

You earned good money in the forest. We were never without money and could even save a bit. Lasse belonged to the farm-workers' labour union. He had always been a union man ever since he began working.

Some time in the spring Mr and Mrs Ral from Frösåker came and asked us if we would like to move to Frösåker. They had already spoken about the matter with Sture Ral at Lindö. We would get to live in the cottage at Larsbo – ten minutes' walking distance from Skyttebo, where Grandpa lived. He had been alone since Grandma died in 1939. Fru Ral used to keep an eye on him and occasionally pop in to see if he needed anything.

We had a week to think it over. We accepted and moved in. Lasse was, I think, also promised a bit more money, as a sweetener.

Of course Grandpa was pleased that we had come to live so close to him. He had helped my uncle build the shack in Skyttebo when I was at school. He had been promised that he could live there the rest of his life. Uncle used to be there in the summers. Grandpa died in August 1954, when he was eighty years old.

Larsbo, where we lived, was set off a little apart, on its own. It was lovely there – not modernized, but lovely anyhow. I fetched water from a pump outside and there weren't any drains so I had to use a slop-bucket.

Lasse earned good money in the forest, and I contributed a bit too with my rose-hip picking towards the fall. There were lots and lots of rose-hip bushes among the ruins from Gammelgården in the direction of Hammarbo. I took one kid on the front and one on the back of my bike, and rode out there in the morning to pick a bag of rose-hips every day. If you kept up a good pace you could earn 3·50 kronor an hour, and that was a good hourly wage in 1952.

My big girl Ann-Britt, who was five years old, had to look after her little sister Kerstin, who was just over a year old, but I kept an eye on them both, of course, as I was picking. We took sandwiches with us, and we'd get no farther than Gammelgården when they'd declare that they were hungry, even though they'd just eaten.

On Sundays Lasse helped with the picking. Once a week he rode into the garden market at Västerås with the bags of rose-hips. At that time, we bought a used car, a '32 Chevy we named 'Hulda'.

Now and then I used to help Lasse in the forest. Sometimes he put in some work on Sundays too, and one Sunday when my young sister Ingrid had biked out from town with a boy friend to look after the kids, I peeled the bark off thirty cuts of pit props. I got blisters on my hands into the bargain. I've also helped fell timber with a two-man crosscut saw, though that really was tough work for a small person like me. Of course, Lasse isn't so big either, but he's hardy.

One time Ral got it into his head that Lasse was earning too much money, so he gave him some poorer forest. It wasn't so surprising that he earned more than the other lumber-jacks. They weren't from these parts, and they were bachelors who drank and took time off quite a lot. Later Ral bought a power saw which Lasse used and it was much faster than a handsaw.

Once in the spring of 1953 a gang of painters came and sprayed all the houses and outbuildings in Frösåker Swedish red, and then Lasse was invited to paint all the loft-rafters, and the corner-rafters and around the window frames on the houses. This took him several months. It was supposed to be piece-work, but no price was settled upon, so when it was time for payment he quarrelled with Ral and quit. But he got his money.

He then became a travelling fishmonger. So he traded in his car for a small delivery truck which he got from a guy who had been selling fish around Västerås. At first he bought his stock from a fish market, but soon enough he began ordering his fish directly from Göteborg and other fishing ports.

We stayed on at Larsbo. After a couple of months we were given notice to leave. We didn't have anywhere to go. A Finnish family in Vedby at Ängsö Sound helped us. We knew them from when we lived at Berga in Skultuna.

Lasse had just traded the little delivery truck for a bigger one, and in it we hauled our things to Vedby and filled the whole cellar. What we didn't have room for in the cellar, we put in the Finns' apartment, and we lived there for a couple of weeks until we got this shack here.

We've lived here at Lövsta in Dingtuna for over fifteen years. A family called Broman, old acquaintances of Lasse's parents, lent us 4,500 kronor so we could buy the house. The whole property cost 7,000 kronor. It was dirt cheap. Why, it's only about ten kilometres from the city.

The grounds then took in 1,276 square metres, now they are 2,273 square metres. We bought 997 square metres of extra ground in 1964 for seventy-five öre per metre. It's meant a lot for our budget that we've been able to live so cheaply, compared with what an apartment in Västerås would cost. Neither Lasse nor I could imagine living in the city. We're happiest in the country.

When we came here there were only two rooms and a kitchen downstairs. Outside, the southern wall was completely covered with woodbine. It had grown across the windows and in under the tiles on the roof. We tore it down so we could make repairs and paint the house copper-red. It was stupid of us, but we dug up the roots too. It would have been nice to have had the vine left and to have trained it.

Inside the house was in bad shape, draughty and with cracks between the walls and ceilings everywhere. The wood-stove in the kitchen kept the heat in, but the glazed-tile stove in the big room didn't warm up no matter how many times you stoked it. The little room didn't have any hearth at all. We had to use kerosene stoves, and they kept the place somewhat warm as long as the kitchen stove was burning. When it went out at night the house got ice-cold. It was miserable and the kids were still small, only two and six years old.

Lasse kept on driving his fish-truck day in and day out. He also had vegetables and canned goods and cucumber pickles which I put up in considerable quantities. At Christmas-time I made 'lutfisk', soaking stockfish in lye in big wooden tubs.

In spring 1954 we started to fix up the shack. We pulled down all the old wallpaper and covered the walls and ceilings with sheets of insulation. On the floor we laid heavy masonite and then we put on wallpaper and painted. We did everything ourselves in the evenings and on Sundays. We used all our spare time on it.

We didn't change the windows until later when we had more time and money. You have to do one thing at a time. Eventually we had a bathroom, central heating, an upstairs bedroom, and a deep well. The water is good, though it does contain a lot of lime and use up a good deal of soap. But it doesn't taste bad at all.

In the garden we have planted flowers and fruit trees – pears, plums, amarelles, raspberries, and currant bushes. The chestnut tree growing outside here was planted by the son of the people who lived here before us. He buried two chestnuts in the ground forty-five years ago and one came up. Now it's covered with blossoms in springtime. It's older than I am and will go on growing long after I've passed away.

That's the way it goes. We'll fade away just the way Mama did. She died on 1 November 1954, and was buried out in Hovdestalund. Before she died, she was partly lame in one arm after a brain haemorrhage seven years earlier.

It's strange when you really start to think about dying. Of course that's how it has to be, you just have to go along with it.

I think about death quite often. For a while I used to think about it in the evenings. I lay there wondering what it must be like when you're going to die, for that matter, whether you're dead when they put you away in a coffin. Sometimes I imagine that I'll be around even afterwards. But I guess that's just wishful thinking.

Anyway, I *do* believe that there's a God, because when you think about all the animals and flowers and trees and people, all of life – it must have come from someplace, why, it couldn't have come out of an empty void. Someone must have made it all some way or another. Though I don't know how.

I go to church sometimes. I admit, it's a good while since I went last. I like sitting there, listening to the minister, it's so peaceful. But Lasse, he never goes to church unless he's forced to, to confirmations, weddings and funerals, and a baptism once in a while.

Even when I was young I sometimes tended to be a little churchy. Deep down I'm really a decent person, in between times at least. Though sometimes it goes to the other extreme too. It all depends how things go. But in any case I'm not religious. Well, that doesn't stop you from believing in different things. You have to believe in something, don't you? But you don't have to go around sounding off like religious folks do.

The fish sales were going very well until deep-frozen fish came in. Then it didn't hold any longer. Lasse had to take a job at Asea. He was there for about a year and liked it pretty well. Ann-Britt had started school in Miss Berg's class by then. She was very kind to the children.

When Lasse finished the factory job, he started hauling lumber at Nordenhaag's. He kept that up for a couple of years. He liked to drive a truck, and when they cut back their trucks he got a job with a trucker. The owner was a widow and when he had been driving for her a while he bought the trucking business from her. He had to pay over 20,000 kronor for the truck and the licence. The truck was old.

He hauled every conceivable thing: gravel, asphalt, dirt, garbage, and so on. There was plenty of hauling to be done then at the end of the fifties, and he earned considerably more on his own than he'd made working for somebody else. It made a big difference, and we could afford to buy a number of things we couldn't afford before.

I was also a driver, though only part-time. I drove kids to school. The younger ones had to go to Dingtuna and the two last grades, seventh and eighth, to Jakobsberg's school in the city.

I drove for Andersson across the road here – he owned the Volkswagen bus. Then I got a commercial driver's licence and I started driving taxis for him as well. I made my debut on Midsummer Eve in 1956. I picked up passengers all through the night until four in the morning. I was only a substitute taxi driver for Andersson when he was away. I kept on driving for two to three years.

Naturally during the Midsummer holiday you'd rather be off-duty, no matter what job you have. There are three families, including us, who always celebrate Midsummer together. We've done this ever since the kids were small. The other two families live in Stockholm. We met them through the sister-in-law of one of the wives we met at Frösåker.

First of all we gather here at our house on Midsummer Eve and then we take the boat and chug away to an island out here in Blacken. The island is called Gräggen but we've renamed it Groggen. We stay there with dogs and kids and tents until the evening of Midsummer Day, regardless of the weather. It seldom rains out there.

Generally we begin by cleaning up to make it look nice and neat. If folks would just quit breaking empty bottles and slinging cans with sharp edges all over the place. Ourselves, we set a good example when it comes to keeping things clean.

We take a whole lot of food along for the Midsummer celebrations. And of course *akvavit*. We grill sausages and chops and eat 'Janson's Temptation', herring in fried potatoes, and baked Baltic herring, and all kinds of things we wives have agreed upon beforehand.

We use one of the pine trees on the hilltop instead of a Midsummer maypole and we deck it with flowers, which we stick into the cracks on the bark. We dance in a ring around the pine tree and sing. It's so lovely out there and we have fun together – eating, drinking, being happy. We also dance in couples to music from the radio.

The night is quite bright, and nobody wants to sleep. The sun rises at half past two, but the dawn has begun long before this. As Evert Taube, our national troubadour, sings, 'The tips of the pines are a-flame.' Just then it's really wonderful to be alive.

Sometimes all the celebrating can be almost too much of a

good thing, even though you can stand more when you're out in the open air dancing and moving around. We usually swim too, when it's warm on Midsummer Day. But it sure isn't at all warm in the water.

We also get together at other times during the year. Sometimes in the fall we go to one of the families who live in Tyresö and have 'sour-herring parties'. I love fermented Baltic herring. In the berry and mushroom seasons they usually come to visit us. We never play cards together. Instead we listen to the radio and dance. They usually come during the New Year's vacation, since both Lasse and I have our birthdays on New Year's Day.

After my extra job as taxi driver I was a housewife for a while. Kerstin had started school by then. She went to Näsby for the first two grades, and then the school was closed down and she had to travel to Dingtuna.

My next job was at the Mälar Restaurant in the community centre. I needed to earn some money, and they wanted extra help washing the pots and pans while their regular was away on vacation. After this I was to have a better job. But the woman who usually washed the pots and pans never came back after her vacation.

It took several months before I got away from those pots and pans. It was a tough job. And unrewarding. As soon as you washed a pot they came to fetch it for the kitchen, where it was immediately used again. It was sickening too, the smell of food almost made you nauseous at times. Some of the pots were so big you nearly disappeared inside them.

The job was in shifts. The afternoon shift finished at ten at night. I would fix food in advance at home, so Lasse only had to warm it up at night. The kids had to look after themselves when they came home from school.

Three evenings a week I worked as an extra in the community centre's A-hall, where there was dancing. The Mälar Restaurant did the catering in the A-hall, and I washed coffee cups and beer mugs. First there was my regular dishwashing job in the morning or afternoon, then the extra dishwashing until one a.m. on Saturday nights and until midnight on Sundays and Wednesdays. I earned pretty good money.

At home there was also a lot to be done, cleaning, washing, ironing, and work in the garden. There was never a dull moment. Lasse was also working full speed at his trucking business, and sometimes drove evenings and on Sundays as well. When I got out of washing the pots and started washing dishes and working in the restaurant kitchen, things got a little easier. After about a year I quit and became a housewife again.

Then I relaxed a bit. On Saturday evenings Lasse and I used to sit on the sofa and have a drink. Now that we have Saturdays off we sit drinking on Friday evenings instead, having a good time, watching T.V.

For a while we drank wine that the Italians in Västerås fermented. That was when Lasse was working with his fish-truck. He gave them boxes of small fish and they gave us bottles of wine in return. We started drinking wine at every meal. After a while we had to stop so it didn't become a habit.

We Swedes certainly are well-off – all we have are little worries. Out there in the world there's war going on and people are being killed outright. What the poor people have built up is being bombed to the ground, so they get even poorer. The rich want more land than they've already got, I guess. They want to rule over others. Relief funds and assistance aren't enough when so much is being destroyed all the time.

I puttered around at home for a whole year after the restaurant job. Then I started at Tempo department store, where I worked half days for four and a half years.

By 1963 Ann-Britt had gotten so big that she began working too. First she spent a year studying business at the Technical School, and after that she was hired at the Central Shoe Store.

On Sundays and vacations we went out on the lake in the

boat. We've had a boat for many years. The first one, an open rowboat with outboard motor, we bought way back before Kerstin started school. Then we've gone on trading gradually to bigger boats. Our pier is down by Tidö, about three kilometres from here. We put it up ourselves. We pay seventy-five kronor a year in rent for the boat place.

Lasse does most of the steering. I usually lie on deck sunbathing. Once when I was navigating I ran the boat aground outside Fuller Island pier. There is only one underwater reef there and of course I had to head right into it. No mortal sin could be worse.

Sometimes at vacation time we take off for the Strängnäs area with the boat and stay a week. It's so beautiful out there. We usually anchor by Kolsundet on Selaö.

Both Lasse and I like fishing. On summer Sundays we often pull our dinner directly up out of the lake. It's the same in the winter. Now and then Lasse doesn't have any driving during the week so he sits out on the ice bobbing instead. Sometimes he comes home with twenty kilograms of perch which I clean and fillet.

I go bobbing for fish too, but I haven't gotten so crazy about it as Lasse has. We're members of the Aros Anglers' Club and usually take part in the club championships. The bob-competition lasts four hours and is divided up into men's, ladies', pensioners', and juniors' contests.

In 1962 at the district championship I was chosen to take part in the Swedish Championship, which was held that particular year in Hede in the province of Härjedalen. When the pistol fired, we gals hurtled off like a herd of reindeer across the ice. There were sixty centimetres of snow on top, and I was completely exhausted by the time I'd shovelled my way down and drilled a hole through the metre-thick ice.

And then it was cold sitting still there. Only my head showed above the mound of snow. Towards midday the sun shone and then it was better. I came in fifth in the contest and

was given a little copper pitcher as a prize with the inscription:
'Prize donated by the post-office girls in Hede – Ingrid,
Gunnel, and Bojan.'

To begin with, my job at Tempo consisted of unpacking and
marking prices, down in the supply room. Eventually I wound
up in the store as a salesgirl. More time went by and I was
moved down to the supply room again where I supervised the
supply of goods to five departments, gloves, mittens, and
stockings; lingerie; toys; handbags; and shoes. I got a certain
commission on everything sold, which gave me about a
hundred kronor a month extra.

For a time I worked in the employees' cafeteria, and then at
the grill in the public restaurant. I also sat in the staff-purchase
department a while, and after that I became assistant cashier in
the food supermarket. Hell, I was everywhere. But my co-
workers were awfully nice, and for the most part we all got on
just fine together. It was fun working at Tempo.

One day Ann-Britt came and said she was expecting a baby.
I didn't say anything. What was I to say? After all, I was only
eighteen when I had *her*. Now it was her turn.

She had been going steady with Tommy for quite a while
then. He is a paint-sprayer. Naturally they went to the Housing
Bureau and there they advised them to get a doctor's certificate
saying she was pregnant, which would help them get an
apartment faster. But it didn't help. The Bureau couldn't find
anything for them.

They lived with us for a while and then with Tommy's sister
for a bit. He's one year older than Ann-Britt. Joakim was
born on 6 May 1966. Soon after I managed to get an apartment for them quite by accident. An acquaintance of mine was
moving to an apartment that came with his job as ambulance-
driver, and Ann-Britt got to take over his old one. What
luck!

Lasse and I paid her deposit, which was 4,600 kronor, and
bought some furniture for them for a little over a thousand

kronor. We also had to act as guarantors for the apartment lease, since neither of them was of age. The rent was 240 kronor a month.

Now they live out in the new area at Bjurhovda. Here's how it came about: Ann-Britt was working in a store and a neighbour lady was looking after Joakim in the daytime. And so this 'day-Mama' was going to move to Bjurhovda. Ann-Britt and Tommy said they wouldn't have any other day-Mama but her, and she wouldn't have any child but Joakim to look after. But it was too far to commute morning and night, and they didn't want Joakim to be away the whole week and just see him at the weekend. So Ann-Britt telephoned the Västerås building agency and was lucky enough to get hold of a three-room apartment out in Bjurhovda where the day-Mama was going to move. She and Tommy moved there at Easter in 1968. Of course the rent was much more expensive, 528 kronor a month, but the apartment is spacious, eighty-seven square metres, and really nice. I don't know whether they'll get married, they haven't said anything about it.

Now only Kerstin is left. Though she's already been running around with a lot of fellows. It's her turn for that now – youth has to have its fling. Sooner or later she'll be tied down too. But for the present it seems she loves Putte most of all – the dog, that is. She calls him Panther.

When I worked in Tempo's supermarket I applied for a week's subsidized winter vacation, which the chain store arranged at the mountain hotels way up north in Storlien for their staff throughout Sweden. I didn't figure I'd be picked, but I was, together with two others from Tempo in Västerås.

We only had to pay 158 kronor for the trip and full board at the hotel. The other two-thirds of the price was paid by Tempo In addition you got to borrow skis and ski clothes free of charge.

I think it was the loveliest week in my whole life. The entire hotel was crawling with Tempo employees, mostly women.

But there were other guests there, of course. We came after Easter.

The food was fantastic and you got to eat as much as you wanted. I put on two kilos. We skied every day, both in the morning and afternoon. One day a gang of us went up to Bånggården on our own instead of taking the ski-lift. But Lord, you got sweaty.

I hesitated before going downhill again. And then a little fellow of about five or six came skiing down a much steeper slope, and I thought to myself, if that little rascal can make it, then so can I. Though I hadn't ski'd for many years.

There was a dance three evenings a week, and we danced to a southern-European orchestra. They played beautifully and my, how we danced and drank wine! A fat Norwegian executive was being very generous and treated me to a hamburger and a drink. Well, if that pleased him, who was I to refuse, I thought. When I came home I was so sunburned that my neighbour said I looked like a mulatto in the face.

Since the summer of 1966 I've been a housewife. I sew quite a bit too. I used to sew everything myself, even coats and costumes, but now I buy quite a few clothes ready-made. The last few years I've begun to make lace, which is interesting and good for your nerves. A neighbour lady and I have been making Easter witches out of pipe cleaners – we dress them with scarves on their heads, shawls over their shoulders, skirts, and brooms to ride on. We make a couple of hundred every year and sell them for two kronor each to friends and acquaintances.

On Easter Eve the kids in the neighbourhood dress up in old long skirts and paint their faces with soot and rouge. Ann-Britt and Kerstin did exactly the same when they were little. They have brooms and coffee-pots and little Easter cards that they sketch and colour themselves and they go around tossing them in to folks in their houses. Then they stand and wait for the people to come out and give them cookies and good things to eat.

Sometimes I drive for the automotive vehicle corps, which is a voluntary association connected with defence. I became a member of the Västerås women's motor corps because I think it's fun to drive a car.

First of all I took a thirty-hour driving course here in Västerås and in the First Armoured Division in Enköping. We listened to lectures about how military organization works, and read about sections and regulations, but most of the time went on learning about motors and driving trucks and jeeps and drilling in auto-manoeuvres.

We went to Enköping one night a week and there we changed tyres on the big trucks. The tyres were so heavy that you could hardly budge them. But it was fun. There were eighteen or twenty of us women and a captain who was supposed to keep us in order. He was swell. Sometimes he hollered and screamed but we didn't take it too seriously.

We kept it up in the midst of winter, in the snow out among logs and rocks in the forest. The captain drove one of the jeeps down into the snow so we would get training in hoisting it up with the winch. It worked fine. We were given big sheepskin coats and uniforms and caps. The ski boots were our own.

To wind it all up we drove to Veckholm one Saturday and hid the cars under the trees and put up two large military tents to sleep in, with a big stove in the middle. At night we roasted sausages and sang and it was a lot of fun. We slept in sleeping-bags and each one took a half-hour turn watching the fire. Since then I've taken another driving course which lasted fifty hours.

I've driven dogs and their trainers when the Dog Owners' Club had their cross-country races, and I drove the figure skaters between the Stadshotel and Rocklunda when the European Championships were held in Västerås. I've chauffeured officers on military manoeuvres several times. It's all voluntary work and I'm in it because it makes for a little change in the daily routine.

But if there's war it wouldn't be voluntary any longer. Then I would drive a truck, probably regular truckloads of supplies to stores and so on. But I don't think there will be a big war. I don't think anyone will dare to start, now that they've got atomic weapons.

It's hard to know how things will be in the future. We can only hope that the economic situation will stay the way it is. They're laying off folks in many places and closing down industries. Jobs are getting more scarce. Things aren't humming along the way they used to. Lasse has had exceptionally little driving to do the past winters. Things are at a standstill.

Last winter there were several people who were forced to sell their trucks. They couldn't make the payments. When Lasse bought his new truck it cost 120,000 kronor – that's a lot of money and now they're probably even more expensive. There are only a few thousand kronor left to pay off on the truck now, so we're managing quite well and don't need to count every krona any more.

When it comes to money, I'm not worried about the future. I can always take a job again if necessary. If there *are* any jobs, that is. It's worst for the youngsters, who have a hard time getting jobs. Kerstin has been out of work since she was laid off from the beauty parlour in Hökåsen where she went as a trainee for fifty kronor a week. I drove her there in the mornings and picked her up in the evenings, for there are no buses there any longer. It was a hundred kilometres' driving a day, round trip, and she hardly earned more than I spent on gasoline. When I was her age you could get a job anywhere.

The best thing around here is the lake. Neither Lasse nor I would dream of living without it. We've traded in our boat for a converted lifeboat which is ten metres long by three metres wide. It has a four-cylinder Albin engine which runs on kerosene and is cheap to operate. It can do ten knots. It has a cabin both fore and aft and a lounge in the middle, and closets, cupboards, pantry and larder in the keelson. The only thing missing is a refrigerator.

We put up 15,000 kronor cash when we swapped our old boat, which we got 5,000 kronor for. We have bunks on board for eight people, but if we double up a bit we can make room for ten or twelve. And we have a lot of friends who want to get away from the mosquitoes on land. It's a boat that will last us all our lives, and it's the last boat we'll ever buy.

Dust Right in Your Mouth

Herman Andersson

I've forgotten most things about my childhood. But one thing I do remember quite clearly was when I was six years old. Ramström's boy was seven years old.

His Ma lived alone with three little kids in the forest by Gäddeholm Road in a shack called Eriksberg. Ramström himself was away with the emergency relief crew, building a road at Svanå. It was in 1933 during the time of unemployment. The family got food tickets from the community to buy food with.

Ramström's kid and I went along to Valla to shop, and down at the very bottom of the ticket his Ma had written one hecto coffee. The old biddy in the store started whining: 'You can't have that, I can't give you coffee – that's a luxury.'

The boy had to go home without any coffee. That's something I'll never forget.

At home the cottage was full of kids. Pa rented Fallet, 22 acres, from the Count of Gäddeholm. That's where I was born. Pa was born at the other side of Kärrbo parish, in Skämsta.

I had to watch the cows and drive the horse and harrow the fields before I started school. The thing I hated most was walking to Valla on fall evenings to get the local newspaper. I was as scared as hell of the dark forest. We shared the newspaper with the family in Persbo. It was about three kilometres to Valla.

We kids said evening prayers. Pa didn't believe in God nor in the devil. When we were alone we said a different version, which went like this:

God, who loves us children dear
Keep me safely in thy care
In bed wherever I might be
A big bug darkly leers at me.

On birthdays we sometimes got soft drinks and cookies. When we had our party to 'strip the Christmas tree', kids from the other shacks and cottages would come along. We danced around the Christmas tree and played circle games. The little bags of goodies were the most important things to us – with apples, crackers, ginger-snaps and so-called Christmas tree candies, which had icing sugar and bookmarks stuck onto them.

At elementary school the minister's boy, Dag Tiberg, happened to rip my shirt one day when we were playing. Mrs Tiberg bought me a new one. It was the first ready-made piece of clothing I'd owned and I felt very proud. Otherwise Ma made all our clothes.

The way Ma had to work was inhuman really. Sometimes she sat up until past midnight, and then she had to be up again around five a.m. to start work in the barn. It was considered embarrassing for a guy to do the milking.

The tenant farmers' and farm-workers' wives were the community's Negroes. They were worn out by the time they were forty or forty-five years old. Pa didn't have anything to do with the milking until Ma got sick, and then he had to. Afterwards he went on doing it.

He worked like an animal too. In wintertime he hauled timber in Gäddeholm's forests, using horses. He left home before it was light in the mornings and wasn't back until it was dark outside. In the kitchen in the evening, he mended shafts or anything else that was broken.

I still have a scar under my chin from one time when I was leaning over the back of a chair watching him while he was riveting something – the chair tipped over and I fell down onto the anvil which he had brought in and stood on the kitchen floor.

We had a kerosene lamp hanging over the kitchen table. Pa sat there reading the newspaper in the evening and we kids had our homework to do and Ma needed light to see at the stove. When I was in third grade, Gunvor was in the fifth, Ellen in second, and Eva in first grade. Our other brothers and sisters hadn't started school yet.

Ma churned butter which we kids had to take to Gäddeholm on a Friday evening to sell to Axelsson who had the delivery truck, and then buy margarine and other things for the money we got. It was six kilometres there and back and we had a lot of stuff to drag along, and earlier in the day we'd already walked the same distance in the opposite direction to and from school.

In 1937 Pa took over the lease on Rosendal and we moved from Fallet. The places are situated alongside each other, so we kept Fallet too. Small farms were combined and run jointly even in those days. Besides these he rented land in Tellbo, Hagen and Persbo. Including these small plots in the forest there, we had a total of fifty-four acres of tilled land.

The land was owned by Gäddeholm and Pa paid the rent by hauling timber in the forest and doing day work at the sawmill in Gäddeholm. But damn it, you can't tell me that he and other tenants didn't do a lot of day work for nothing and didn't have to work much harder than the rent was worth. Beyond that, he wanted to earn some ready money.

The bigwigs have always been good at lining their own pockets. Surely the estate owners have stolen lots of earth and forest from the poor farmers through the ages. Why, counts and barons were in command of soldiers in war, and in peacetime they certainly must have had forces stationed on the estates sometimes. There's no doubt about it: it would have been really strange if they hadn't taken advantage of their superior position to help themselves to other people's property.

They say that the forest at Limsta once belonged to the Olsta farmers, but that the Count of Gäddeholm used his soldiers to confiscate it.

The farmers were often no better themselves. When a farmer made a servant-girl pregnant, it was a common thing for him to get one of the farmhands to marry her, and in exchange, the farmer would give them a patch of ground which they could clear and cultivate. Then after they had sweated and strained year in and year out till the ground was cultivated, it happened that the pig of a farmer would come and take everything away from them.

Some gentlemen have preserved the old mentality to this day. Hamilton of Hedensberg, for example, had a feud with the minister there because he wanted his own pew in church. Nobody else would be allowed to sit in the pew, not even when none of the Count's family was there. This happened as recently as in the fifties. I seem to remember that he lost the fight; I read about it in the newspaper.

You really start to wonder what makes that sort of person tick. They seem to think that they can still do just what they like – and in church, of all places, where, if any place, all people are supposed to be equal.

Sure, it's the big shots in the community who make the decisions now too, but at least ordinary mortals have a little more value than they did in the thirties and before. These days you just can't bully people around any old way. In Kärrbo, for example, it was the estate owners and the minister and some of the bigger farmers who made the decisions.

In secondary school my first teacher was old man Nyström. Sometimes, as we came along the dirt road from Täby to school, other kids would be standing by the milk-stand outside the church, and they'd shout out, 'The old man's got so drunk he's sick again, so we get to go home.' That made us happy.

When we were very busy with the farming, I could ask to be absent a few days now and then to help with the work at home.

Our first and main concern was survival. Going to school was of lesser importance. So we didn't get to learn very much.

Börje Thunell sat at the desk in front of me at school, and once when he was trying to catch a rat by the stove, Nyström got so angry at him for not sitting still that he threw his bunch of keys at Börje. It hit the wall beside him and made a hole in the plaster. 'Better luck next time,' was the old man's comment.

'What's the motto on a one-krona coin?' he asked me one day. I didn't know that, I'd hardly ever seen one. Vera Mälberg knew the answer, of course – 'With the people for the fatherland.'

Once we had a substitute teacher from the city – he was between sixty and sixty-five with a pudgy face. He went around feeling up the girls in school, that old lecher.

Then we got a new teacher named Håkansson. He tried to get me to sing. I refused. It wasn't regarded as manly to sing. In reality, I was too embarrassed. We weren't as fearless as the kids are today.

Another one of Håkansson's ideas was to get us to borrow books and then report on them. I got out of it two Fridays running, but then on the third Friday it was my turn. I couldn't think of anything worse than having to stand up all alone by the teacher's desk and give a talk. So on the way to school, up by Gryta, I threw myself off my bicycle and cut my knee and my trousers. Then I limped and whimpered and put on so when I got to school that I was allowed to go home.

Four weeks later it was my turn again to give a report, but then I said that it was such a long time since I'd read the book that I'd forgotten what it was about, so I got out of it.

I did borrow books to read all the same; among others, two by Karl Gunnarsson called *A Farmhand Among Swedish Farmers* and *Immigrant in Canada*. I was really too young to borrow such books, but I said they were for Pa, so they let me have them. Of course they were relatively innocent, though perhaps a bit naughty for those days.

I read several other books too, but I don't remember what they were called nor who wrote them. Pa, he read too, sometimes in the evening by the dim light of the lamp, or on Sundays. Electricity wasn't installed in Rosendal until 1948. When he retired, he read so much that he got fed up with it for a while.

When the war broke out we didn't have any radio at home, but in 1940 Pa got hold of an old one with a separate loudspeaker. It ran on one acid battery and one dry one which now and then we had to take in on the bike to Fryxell in Irsta and leave it to be recharged. He loaned out batteries that we could use in the meantime.

Håkansson, the teacher, had an automobile, which was uncommon. During the war when we had producer gas we school kids used to have to push the car to make it go. He changed his name later to Hernmar. For a while it was very popular to change your name. Axel in Täby changed his too, to Hedermo. His name used to be Pettersson.

I finished school in June 1940, and in July I was thirteen years old. Then I had to work on the farm from seven in the morning till seven at night. I was grown-up now and didn't have to ask permission to go out in the evenings any more.

In the fall I met the minister one night outside Valla. When folks talked about him they referred to him as 'paperlips'. 'You will be coming on Friday to confirmation classes, won't you, Herman?' he said to me. 'I've no time for such nonsense,' I answered.

If I hadn't given the mare a lash with the whip and ridden away quickly, he might have hit me on the head with his cane.

'A person can never be too busy to become a true Christian,' he said just as I rode away.

Actually Pastor Tiberg was a decent fellow, all right. Come to think of it, he baptized both of my oldest kids. We had the ceremony at home in Rosendal.

The reason I didn't go to confirmation classes was because the other kids were always razzing me about one of the girls who was fat. We were the same age, and since I was a little on the heavy side too, they always used to say we'd make a lovely couple. So I couldn't bring myself to go read for the preacher the same time as she went. That's why I wasn't confirmed.

Of course, my decision also meant that I didn't get a new suit for confirmation. But I earned the money for one myself instead by collecting scrap-iron and selling it to the junk-dealer on Malmabergsgatan in Västerås.

When I had finished the six weeks of continuation school – that is, classes which the school teacher ran during secondary school's Christmas vacation, three weeks before and three weeks after Christmas, for two years in a row after you'd finished going to school – I began logging in Gäddeholm Forest. It was heavy work for a fourteen-year-old, and it didn't get any easier when I started at the brickyard in the spring.

The meaning of life was in working, we knew of nothing else. Our fun had to wait until the evening. My sisters sometimes had girl friends who came to visit and then I'd try to grab hold of their breasts, of course, or touch them on the cunt if we could. It was really just a game – why, we were only young boys.

I never learned to dance, but I went to a lot of parties, of course. Once in the winter Pa took me and my bike to Kärrbo church by sled. The road through the forest was never snow-ploughed. A gang of us were going to ride our bikes to a dance in Östanbro. 'You can find your own way home,' my Pa said.

Low-cut shoes were a must, even if your feet nearly froze off, especially on the way home. The only way to get blood circulating was to run alongside the bike for a kilometre or so. On the way there we generally had some *akvavit* along to warm ourselves up with.

I got six or seven kronor too little on my first pay-day at

Gäddeholm's brickyard. My fellow workers started talking about it right away and threatened to stop work if I didn't get what I had coming to me. Workers stuck together much better in those days than they do now.

In July when I had two weeks' vacation from the brickyard I worked at home helping Pa. We were out stacking hay to dry one day and I asked him if I could borrow his permit-book in order to buy a half-litre bottle. Bengt-Olle and I had planned to buy *akvavit* and I was thinking so hard about how I could get hold of a permit-book that the question just slipped out.

My Pa looked at me. I wasn't more than fifteen years old, and I thought to myself, I'll regret this. But he just said, 'Since you ask, I see you've started drinking, and you'll be better off borrowing my book than running around worrying other folks for theirs.'

Later on, when I was sixteen or seventeen, Pa would offer me a drink at home sometimes.

I wouldn't let my own boy have *akvavit* just like that, if he asked me. We don't have permit-books any more, but he can't buy liquor himself at the state liquor store, since he isn't old enough. He is seventeen. He's never out chasing around. Instead his girl friend comes here to see him in the evenings. They may drink a little when they're alone together on Saturdays, though I doubt it. He's been going steady with the same gal for a year now. Kids are so faithful these days.

At the brickyard I only worked the rest of the summer. Then I had different jobs in Kärrbo, Irsta, and the city. One winter I was employed with a drayman. The horse I drove had his stable in Romfartuna and it was almost thirty kilometres for me to ride my bike there in the mornings. It didn't work out in the long run. I went on doing that for just a short time, then the horse was moved to Skiljebo. There it was much closer for me – seventeen or eighteen kilometres.

You had to jump out of bed damned early in the morning in order to have the horse groomed and be on Vitmåragatan at the freight-yard by six forty-five a.m. at the latest. Sometimes when we unloaded used brick the boss had bought out of railway cars we had to carry on working until eight thirty in the evening; he couldn't afford to pay night rent on the wagons.

After two months with the drayman I got a job at the Old Brewery. I was delivering oakwood there one day when Omstedt, the brewery foreman, came along and suggested that I work for him. He didn't think that the sweat and grind of delivery work was anything for a young fellow.

Omstedt was a good guy and he saw to it that since I was the youngest there, I got lighter jobs to do than the others, who were older and bigger. I was given all sorts of jobs, and sometimes I rode along with a drayman in the city as errand-boy.

The gals at the brewery drank gallons of beer and the fellows went around pinching and squeezing them. As a matter of fact, the women were just as horny as the men. And yours truly had quite a lively imagination too. One of the guys was especially fresh, but one day the women got together and ganged up on him and took all his clothes off. From then on, he toned down some.

I biked the eighteen kilometres to my job in the city every morning in the cold and I was obliged to carry my bike the first three kilometres from Rosendal to Gäddeholm if it had snowed hard during the night. Towards spring I got run down. I was coughing all the time and lost almost ten kilograms from all that bicycle riding.

One summer I worked as blacksmith's helper in Irsta. It was quite an easy job compared with the brickyard or logging in the forest. Ernst, the smith, was quite nice. The trouble with him was that he stuck his nose into other people's business. He tried to get me to stop smoking and God knows what else. I could hardly afford to smoke anyway with the pay I got: fifteen kronor a week.

I had lots of fun those years. We used to ride our bikes in a gang to various dance places round about. In Tillinge dances were held in a meadow, the same as in Badelunda. We also used to ride to Frögärde, beside the shooting range in Björksta.

Sometimes we rode by boat with the Nyby boys to Hässel-byholm in the province of Sörmland on Saturday evenings. It took half an hour or three quarters over the lake. I fell overboard once when I was stepping ashore – the planks on the dock were loose and I was drunk.

Another time some kid fell in. I was going to look after the motor while he undressed and wrung out his clothes. He was drunk, too. Suddenly there I was sitting with the tiller in my fist. The pin was just lying loose in the outboard motor. The God-damned boat went around and around so it nearly turned over.

The last day of April one year there was a dance in a school down by Ängsö. There were three of us standing outside in the garden polishing off a half-litre. Bengt had just taken a swig when I saw the minister coming. I grabbed the bottle away from Bengt and shoved a soda-pop into his hand. The minister asked us if we were standing around consuming intoxicating beverages. But of course we weren't. Bengt showed him the bottle of soda-pop and asked if he'd like a taste, but he said no. 'I believe you,' he said, and went on his way.

Boozing in public places is disorderly conduct, according to the law. If it weren't, things would really be a mess. Here in Västerås the cops jailed thirty people for drunkenness only last Friday night.

Once a whole gang of us was standing down by Kärrbo Church, on the way home from some dance or other. A kid we didn't know had followed along with one of the girls all that way. We thought we'd have a bit of fun with him, so one of the Kärrbo boys went up to him and asked him how come he dared to ride down this way all by himself. He got so scared he didn't say a word, but figured he'd be on the safe side of things, and beat it.

In 1947 in the spring I met Disa. Earlier I had never gone

steady with anyone, but just gone home with some gal now and then to get fucked. But with Disa I was serious right from the start. I was running after her all the time. I sometimes pedalled to town four evenings a week to see her, and sometimes she came to see me in Rosendal.

She lived near Arosvallen with her stepfather, who was a soldier in the Salvation Army. She was too, until she met me. Nowadays she's not so obsessed by it, though she can't imagine that there isn't a life after death. The hell there is, I tell her; but actually we never talk about religion and that sort of thing any more.

That summer I was working as a tractor driver at Frösåker, and in the fall I moved to the city. I was twenty years old then and fully developed. Disa was nineteen when I met her. We got engaged in October.

I lived in a room in Haga. The landlady was religious, but she was nice. When I rented the room she said that I couldn't have girls there after ten at night. 'I happen to be engaged,' I said, 'so it'll probably be a bit later than that sometimes.' Then she said, well, if I was engaged, it was a different matter. What she meant was that she didn't want a whole lot of comings and goings and running around in the house at night.

My first job in the city was at the Metal Works. I stayed there one day and fifteen minutes. I started on a Friday. I was put into the wire-drawing plant and the words of welcome I got from several Norrlanders who worked there were: 'Now this new bastard'll come along and bring down the rates!' I was so angry I went to the foreman and asked him to give me another job.

No, there weren't any other jobs, just stay in the wire shop, it'll be all right, he told me. On Saturday morning I told him, 'Give me a leave permit and you won't have to see my face any more.' You had to have a paper in order to get out of there.

'That was a short guest appearance,' said the guard, when I went on my way at quarter past seven on Saturday morning. On

Monday I got a job at Sotebo (Asea). It took until the following week before I got paid there and the sixteen kronor I'd earned at the Metal Works didn't come until three weeks later. I sat in my room and ate bread and margarine in the evenings sometimes instead of a cooked meal. You were poor as a church mouse.

At Sotebo I worked in the foundry. I removed the cores from castings with a pneumatic crowbar. The cores were made out of sand, horse manure, a little clay, sawdust and oil, and some other things. It was hot, the mixture was smouldering and you breathed in the blue smoke from it. You were black as a chimney sweep all the time and it didn't do your lungs much good either. Later when I was put on another job grinding away rough edges and flaws on metal the dust went right into my mouth. That wasn't any better than the smoke. But the pay was comparatively good in the foundry.

Disa and I got married in February 1948. We lived with her father on Vasagatan, in a separate room. In March I went in to do my military service. When we reported in I picked the coastal artillery because I thought that then I would be stationed somewhere on the mainland. But the hell I was – I got sent to Fårösund, way out in the Baltic.

There was hardly a civilian to be seen out there, just sheep and juniper bushes mainly. We had a pass once a month. When I went home in October by boat for Pa's fiftieth birthday there was a gale blowing twenty-eight metres per second. It doesn't really matter where you're stationed, since wherever you are people regard a serviceman as some weird kind of creature.

We rowed and went in the water there, but I never learned to swim. Everyone was like one big family and on familiar terms with all the non-commissioned officers. If they could help a guy with something they did: they weren't stupid and malicious and there never was any trouble. Sometimes the sergeants came around to see us on Saturday evenings to play cards and do a little boozing.

But my God, how dull and boring it was. I just gave up thinking, because if you didn't it was unbearable – the whole system *means* that other people do your thinking for you.

At Christmas we were discharged. Everybody had a package sent from home for the mustering-out party. Disa sent a litre of *akvavit* in a shoebox and wrote on the wrapping paper that the box contained a bottle of juice. They all grinned. From the total weight of all the packages, the post office figured that there were at least 115 litres of *akvavit* among us in the company.

When I got home we had got a two-room apartment through Asea. Disa also worked at Asea, as a secretary – she still does. That day was the happiest, proudest in my life, all right. For the first time we were entirely independent.

The apartment was brand-new. The only furniture we had was a sofa-bed in the big room. Disa had bought it for 325 kronor – she had a sense of what was most important. Then we went out to shop, with the 1,500 kronor we got from the government to set up housekeeping. It was enough for two armchairs, a coffee table, a floor lamp, kitchen table and four kitchen chairs, a linen cupboard, a double iron bedstead, and a table to stand flowers on. We had a sewing machine too, which Disa had inherited from her Ma. The make was a Solidar, inlaid with mother-of-pearl and with an ell-measure on the wood part in front.

There were only three Swedish families in our part of the building; the rest were southern Europeans. We lived in Hammarby, right in the middle of the area where all the foreigners lived. They didn't bother me at all. Disa complained that their womenfolk tried to get out of their turn at cleaning the staircase.

They may have been a little bit noisy, especially the Italians, but on the other hand, I never met a drunk Italian or one who scrounged cigarettes and money when you were on your way home from a late shift or who started threatening you if you refused. The ones I've met who were begging like that have nearly always been Swedes and in a few cases a Finn.

I've worked together with many foreigners and nearly all of them have been good at their jobs and decent guys who've worked every day. But of course, some of the dregs have come here too – the ones who never do a good day's work, but run around wasting their time and then apply for sick benefits and stay away from work. People like that take advantage of every benefit they can find and have no conscience whatsoever about becoming a burden to the rest of society. A lot of them sit around at the Dairy Bar at Tempo all day long instead of working. It's not race hatred on my part, but the simple fact is that some of these foreigners are so sharp that Swedes can't keep up with them. When it comes to Finns, I've met a few who've been all too eager to jump, when management and the higher-ups tell them to.

When I came home from military service I went on working in the foundry at Sotebo. After a while they discovered a new way of forcing the cores out of the castings. Instead of a crowbar, a kind of pistol was used which blew water and sand out in a powerful jet. Axel Ullberg, who also comes from Kärrbo, and I were given this job. In the beginning a whole lot of technicians and engineers and other jerks came around looking at the new method.

It was a wet, dirty job. We wore rubber clothes and a hooded cloak that went all the way down to the waist with a glass window to see through – this was rinsed clean with water every five seconds and air blew inside the helmet so you wouldn't suffocate. It was a clumsy outfit and you needed another guy to help you get it on and off. But it meant fifty öre an hour more.

24 February 1950 Maggan (Margareta) was born. Disa quit her job before she was born and became a housewife. If she had stayed at work she could have had a part of her salary for three months in maternity benefits, but we didn't think of that.

Almost exactly a year later, 1 March 1951, Gunnar was born. When he was six months old Disa began working as a secretary again.

We spent our vacations at home in Rosendal and then there was usually the haying to be done during the two weeks of the vacation. I didn't have my first real vacation until Pa gave up farming towards the end of the fifties. By then we had another son, Janne. He was born 23 March 1956.

When I started work at Asea I became a member of the Swedish Foundry-workers' Union. But I never went to any union meetings. There were just a few guys who used to go to meetings. The foundry-workers were fairly united and backed each other up in the shops. Later on when automobiles and all those things started coming in, their solidarity wasn't what it used to be. A lot of them started getting careful about what they did and said because they were scared that they wouldn't be able to make their payments if there was any trouble at work.

As a union member you were affiliated to the Social Democratic Party, and one year a number of us signed a petition that said we didn't want to contribute to the Social Dems' party funds any longer. There was one hell of an uproar. The Social Democrats in the labour union attacked us and claimed we were Communists. So then a lot of them struck their names off the petition, because they were cowards. In the end there were only a few of us who stood for what we'd said.

When I come to think of it, I've often been called 'Red' just because I've said what I thought and then stuck up for it. But I've never been a member of any party. I steer clear of party politics. Of course, it's better to have a Social Democratic government than a Liberal or Centrist or Conservative one, but maybe there isn't all that much difference between them.

If Social Democracy had continued the way it was meant to from the start then we'd have had a dictatorship here. It can never be a good thing for just a small clique to be able to do and say just what they like, while the rest of the population have to keep quiet and do as they're told.

In the Soviet Union there is a ruling clique whose members make the decisions. Though you find it here too, of course, at least to a certain extent. That's how it is everywhere and no doubt it will go on being the same for as long as mankind endures. Though it may not be around that much longer. Both the U.S.A. and the Soviet Union have weapons enough to wipe us all out.

In the spring of 1954 after the storm-broken trees had been cut, I took an extra job at Gäddeholm Forest. I had my regular shift work at Asea, from five a.m. to two p.m. one week and from two p.m. to eleven p.m. every other. When I was on the afternoon shift, I rode my bike from home early in the morning and worked six hours in the forest before it was time to ride to the foundry. When I was on the morning shift I rode directly out to the forest in the afternoons. It was fifteen kilometres to pedal. I earned thirty to thirty-five kronor extra per day, but it was exhausting and I didn't get much time for sleep.

The first day after my vacation that year I gave notice at Sotebo. The engineer said, 'In a week's time you'll be standing in the doorway begging to be taken on again, but if you'd asked me instead of giving notice to quit, I would have been able to arrange a job for you in another department.' I told him that I wasn't planning to beg him *or* Asea for anything.

What I had in mind was to become a construction worker. Even before the vacation I had made inquiries at the building companies, and had been promised a job at three places. But before I could begin I had to have a card stamped by the public employment office.

The official at the employment office refused to stamp my card. I told him that I'd worked at Asea because that was the only way to get a place to live. I thought I had a right to change trades if I wanted to and asked him who he thought he was –

some kind of dictator over workers. He got furious and shouted at me – he said I was an industrial worker and had to work in industry.

So I couldn't get a building job. According to what I was told, the construction companies had agreed not to take people from Asea and the other industries, where there was a labour shortage. I suppose the union leaders were probably in on the deal.

Several days after I'd given notice to quit, a note came from Asea saying we had to move. The apartment was in a company building. Disa went to her boss and asked if we couldn't stay there since she'd worked at Asea for almost ten years. He told her that as long as she was married and the apartment was in her husband's name, there was nothing they could do about it. However, if she were *divorced* she could take over the lease and remain there. She told them that if it meant having to get divorced, they might as well forget the whole thing.

I was a member of the Tenants' Association and they helped me take the matter to the Rent Board. The Rent Board's decision was that we'd be allowed to stay in the apartment eight more months.

There I was – without a job and soon without an apartment too. Anyway I'd made up my mind never to work at Asea again. Instead I took a job at Limsta, which is a part of Gäddeholm, and worked there a couple of months on the farm.

Then I borrowed the horse from Pa and hauled timber in the forest several weeks, and after that I got a job in the city at Myggbo Sawmill.

The pay there was lousy, but after a couple of months I had an offer to cut woods which Myggbo had bought as standing timber at Lilla Promenaden north of Billsta. It was a good job, I cut timber and pulpwood and earned good money, quite a lot.

To begin with I used a kerosene-powered saw which Myggbo lent free of charge. You had to warm it with a blow-torch in order to get it started. It was damned heavy and one day I stumbled and nearly cut off my nose, but I managed to stop the blade in time, luckily.

The power saw was extremely dangerous so I went back to sawing by hand again. After three weeks a guy from Myggbo came along and wanted to work with me, so we bought a two-man crosscut saw. It was too long, so we broke off a tooth, took the saw along to the hardware store and said that there was a flaw in the manufacturing – they gave us a new one instead, this time a shorter one.

After Myggbo I worked in a cement plant. It was hard work – I drove 140 cement blocks at a time on a two-wheeled car and got so black and blue I could hardly get out of bed in the mornings.

Right across the street from the cement works they were putting up a building. Gunnar Gustavsson from Gäddeholm worked there, and he came over one day and passed the word to me that they needed more people. I had talked to him before and he'd had a word with the overseer about my wanting to start in the trade.

The overseer was a decent guy who knew the lay of the land. He advised me not to say a word, either to the public employment office or to the construction trade union, until I had been working a little while as a builder. So when a couple of months had passed I went down to the construction union and asked them to transfer my union card. The man in the office just said that since I already had a job, he couldn't stop me. So eventually I was able to become a builder, but I had to go a long way round.

Just before we were going to be thrown out of the Asea apartment, we got hold of a new one through the housing authority. It was on the eighth floor of a high-rise building. Since the kids were small, we swapped it for a different apartment on Karlfeldtsgatan. It had two rooms and a kitchen, and we lived there for eight years before we traded it for this three-room apartment on Pettersbergsgatan.

Now I've been working as a builder since 1955, with different companies (it works out that way). The biggest company in Västerås is Paul's building firm (Bygg-Paul). The Trade Unions' Building Production is not far behind, they're the leading residential builders. I've worked for both big and small firms, and it really doesn't matter where you are, it's about the same all over.

The most crucial factor in determining whether you like a place or not is how well or how badly you get along with the others, fellow workers, foremen, overseers, and engineers. And of course it all depends on how well the work is organized. In some places the work is in such a mess that you just wouldn't believe it.

The jobs must be organized so that they flow without interruption. Otherwise you won't earn a prayer. If you're going to get by and earn enough to live on, everything has to mesh perfectly all the time. You have to work so hard at piece-work rates, that you just don't have time to stand around waiting.

When I started in the construction trade, I got about eight kronor an hour. Now average wages have risen to around thirteen kronor. But in actual fact you were better off then than now, since everything has got so damned expensive during the years in between. For example, I believe the cutback of working hours has brought about decreased wages. It's been said that shorter working hours have been offset by percentage wage-raises but this has been swallowed up by rising prices.

Construction work has some variety to it and pays somewhat better than factory work, but you have to work like hell for your money. I've done cement casting and finishing, plastering, excavating, I've stripped lumber, put up partition walls, and a bit of everything.

I've worked mostly building apartments and houses. The city's growing. I've been in on the work in East Malmaberg, Viksäng, Hammarby, Råby, Pettersberg and on Bangatan. At present I'm out at Bjurhovda and work will last there for a good while, we hope. During the last fifteen years Västerås has grown from 65,000 to 110,000 inhabitants. Though some of the growth is due to the fact that the city has been incorporating neighbouring parishes. Kärrbo has been a part of Västerås for several years now, too.

On weekdays you work on a construction site to earn money and on Saturdays and Sundays you spend it all on your own construction work.

It began almost ten years ago when a buddy asked if I wanted to rent a little summer cottage which he had rented. He didn't need it any more since he was building his own. Both Disa and I thought that the shack was situated wrong. We used to drive out to Kärrbo and this shack was located in the opposite direction, in Sevalla. But anyhow we did rent it for fifteen kronor a month.

We had a lot of fun there and partied on Saturday nights now and then. A family we were friendly with used to come and stay with us. We rented the shack for five summers.

There was no well there, so we had to fetch water from a neighbour. He was a bachelor and had a little farm. His house was in bad condition and needed repairing. We agreed that I would help him repair it, and I managed to get hold of some cheap lumber when they tore down the barracks in Sjöhagen where the Italians had been living.

When I brought the wood to him, he said that I was welcome to his other shack there. I thought he was joking. Three weeks later I asked him if he was serious, and he said, hell, yes, he'd been serious.

We started talking price. The cottage was originally a spare building that his grandmother and later his father had lived in. I asked him how much he wanted for the shack, and he asked me how much I was prepared to give. How should I know that, I said, you'll have to name your price and then I'll dicker afterwards.

So then he said 'You can give me a thousand kronor for the shack and the ground it stands on.' I took it, of course. Then he said, 'You can take the triangular patch behind too.' I told him that I couldn't accept that for the same price, so we agreed on a thousand kronor for the shack plus its ground, and five hundred kronor for the three-cornered patch.

The surveyor who staked out the plot thought that the cottage wasn't worth more than a couple hundred kronor in the ramshackle state it was in, but that the ground was worth the money. That was in 1963.

The rain leaked into the room through a hole in the roof. It was draughty and uncomfortable. The wallpaper was nailed directly on to the log walls. Under one of the kitchen windows the logs had rotted. In the main room I had to lift up the outer wall with jacks and put down a new foundation.

Sometimes I worked night and day. I spent all my free time out there. The cottage is called Gustavsberg and is located twenty-five kilometres from town. The first summer I used to go out there nearly every evening right after work and keep at it till midnight. Weekends too. I was never tired then, but now I begin to feel it sometimes.

I have built on to the room so that it's almost twice as big, and I've cemented the floor and fixed the outside walls to make them a little bit straighter and I've nailed up new boards outside and insulated with rockwool and put fibre-board on all the walls inside. I've relaid the outer roof and repaired the chimney and built an open hearth in the room. The entrance hall I've rebuilt, and I'm going to make a lavatory there later with an electric toilet. Up in the attic I've built three bedrooms and a staircase leading up, and I've laid new steps outside and set tiles in the kitchen cupboards and closets. I made the kitchen cupboards myself out of scraps of chipboards, I couldn't afford to buy finished cupboards. Then I've glazed and puttied and painted and wallpapered everywhere, and I've dug a well and laid the pipes for a kitchen sink. I'm thinking of putting in hydrants so we can have running water, and I'll make a bathroom and a sauna bath in an outbuilding I have in the garden. I also built that myself. And then I'm going to plant berry bushes and fix the road and put in a potato patch. Everything takes time, but maybe when we're old we can live there permanently. There's electric heating all through the place.

I would have finished all the repairs by now if I hadn't helped everybody else with their building. It's hard to refuse folks who can't help themselves.

I have no idea how much money I've spent on material, I don't save the bills. A large part of it I've got cheap. I may have spent about 10,000 kronor, and then there were all the hours of work. But it's also been fun doing it.

You need a place of your own where you can be yourself, where you can get away from the crowds and the bustle of the city, where you can be in peace. In the city you can't wear what clothes you like, either. I've never really felt at home in the city.

Actually, I'm sure I'm at least as much a farmer as I am a city-dweller. Most of all I'd like to live the free life, hunting and fishing. Before I started work on the cottage, I used to go fishing every Sunday and also sometimes in the middle of the week. I still hunt a little too, but not for the meat. My brother and his brother-in-law and I rented hunting grounds in Möklinta and I also hunt in Sevalla sometimes on my neighbour's land – he's a farmer.

Nowadays work in the construction trade is a good deal easier than it was before. Everything is done by crane now. Constructing factory buildings and that type of thing is always much tougher than building apartments. In shops the ceilings are always much higher and the prefabricated construction parts are bigger and the area you have to run back and forth over is much larger.

When we constructed Asea's new shops on Finnslätten we had to work in shifts and haul in wheelbarrows all the concrete for a floor that was about 700 square metres and had to be laid in one piece. It was no good having any seams since heavy machines were going to stand on the floor. Christ, how we worked!

For a while I stood passing up bricks to the bricklayers. We figured out that you walked about thirty kilometres a day with the mortar and the bricks.

There are many different sorts of folks in the construction business. During one lunch-break, we were sitting talking about death and one guy said that he couldn't bring himself to kill a rat, since it could be his uncle – he believed in reincarnation. There were more people than I could have imagined who had thoughts in that direction.

I've never met anyone in the construction trade who has read the Bible. I meant to read it myself some time but I never got around to it. The oldest scriptures ought to be the most accurate, to my knowledge; they've written and rewritten the New Testament to suit their own needs.

A young man who works in construction today and wants to be sure his future is safe ought to try to get a job in the union. There they sit safe in the saddle until pension time. Nobody's income rises as steadily as a union official's. And they're the ones who make the decisions. The members are too dense. We don't give a damn about going to meetings. Nobody speaks out, so it's the officials who run the show.

I went to the union meetings sometimes in the fifties, but then I stopped going. Mostly because I thought there was too much party politics mixed up with union policies, at least in the construction trade. Here in the city Social Democrats and Communists are about equally strong in our union and all they do is try to outvote each other at the meetings instead of getting together on important issues.

Unionism has gotten to be like an industry too, prices and everything are all worked out ahead of time, they have fixed guidelines to stick to and the construction bosses never give away an öre spontaneously. In the fifties, when there was full employment and a labour shortage, the union management said that if we were modest in our demands, we would get preference later from the employers when times were bad. Which was an exceptionally stupid claim, since naturally all employers are always out to rake in as much profits as they can for themselves.

A lot of union work could surely be handled in a much simpler way. Now it's nothing but red tape, like everything else here in Sweden. You used to pay your dues to a guy at work who collected it. Nowadays you have to go to the post office and pay it. I think it's done by computers, like so many other things. I'm convinced that only half the population will be able to get work in the future, and the rest will have to live on welfare without a chance for a real job. Even now it's hard for someone to get work if he isn't completely healthy or is over fifty years old.

Anyone who doesn't have a profession will be redundant. I've told Gunnar, my eldest boy, that he ought to think about that and learn a trade. He could be an electrician, for example, but in that case he'd have to be an apprentice with low wages for several years and since he's already used to earning money, he doesn't pay any attention to my warnings.

Maggan studied at the Fryxell School. But she's not too sure what she wants to be. She's talked about seeing a bit of the world, of travelling to England and learning the language well. But I guess she'll start working instead. She'll probably wind up in some office, and be badly paid – that's the way it goes. Now she's gone and got engaged, too.

I just might like to go abroad too, for a vacation. But there's a lot I haven't seen in this country. Gunnar and I went up to Norrland one summer, otherwise I've been at home mostly. There's always a lot to be done during vacation month. It's true it might be fun to travel outside your own country, but I guess I never will.

A Foundation to Stand On

Eva Sjöqvist

My grandfather fished and farmed on Aggarö in Kärrbo. Dad stayed at home helping until he got married. Mom was the daughter of the machinist at the sawmill in Gäddeholm, but she lived with her grandmother in the neighbourhood of Mullsjö down in the province of Västergötland her whole childhood and through her teens. When she was twenty-one her mother died and then she had to go back to Gäddeholm to look after the house. She was the eldest of seven children.

Mom and Dad met on one of the regular passenger boats that ran on Lake Mälar in those days. At first, I believe, Grandfather was against Dad courting his daughter, but later on they became good friends. After they were married, Mom and Dad settled in Kolbäck, where I was born in 1924.

About a year later Grandfather became a widower. So then my parents moved back to Aggarö Haven, as the farm was called, and took over the lease on the land and on the fishing waters. They also rented Juthällen, next door.

My eldest brother, Ingvar, was born in 1926 and then came a long line of brothers: Sigvard in 1927, Hugo in 1929, and David in 1932. I got quite fed up with brothers, since I was eldest and had to help look after them.

When I was four years old or so Dad bought Vretbo on the mainland in Kärrbo right opposite Aggarö. We lived there about three years. At the same time he rented Harkie for a few years, but then he sold Vretbo and we moved back to Aggarö Haven just before I was due to start school.

Our house there consisted of two rooms and a kitchen downstairs and two rooms upstairs. We had glazed-tile stoves in the rooms, and some of my earliest memories are of fetching wood and lighting fires.

In summertime it was just like paradise out on Aggarö, and there were lots of summer visitors, and I used to go and sell fish to them. We often had guests at home too. Relatives and their friends would call on us, and I remember them sleeping in the hayloft sometimes on Saturdays and Sundays.

Mom and Dad were always together when they were away from home – they still are. On Saturdays they would go to town to sell fish in the market place. Not just fish, but flowers, blue wood-anemones, primroses, and lilies-of-the-valley in springtime, and meadow flowers in the early summer. There was a lot of trading going on at the fishmarket.

We kids were allowed to keep the money for the flowers we picked. I remember once buying shoes with the money I earned, and being allowed to pick them out myself. Most of our clothes had been made over and the boys had their hand-me-downs.

We also used to pick wild strawberries and raspberries. There were plenty of raspberries on Aggarö but neither blueberries nor lingonberries. Dad paid us five to ten öre per litre for the raspberries we picked, as an incentive. It wasn't such fun to have to pick loads of raspberries.

One of us kids was allowed to go along with our parents to town on Saturdays. We were particular about taking turns and got jealous if somebody got to go more often than the rest. The ones who were left at home would go and sit on the rock late on Saturday afternoon and keep a lookout for Dad's boat in the direction of Västerås. It was very beautiful there and we used to watch the big ships come and go in the channel.

We could recognize the sound of Dad's boat from a long way off, it went chug-chug-chug. It had an inboard motor with an ignition that had to be warmed with a blow-torch before starting.

Dad was very kind. We weren't in awe of him like many other kids were of their fathers. He never hit us. Mom didn't either, but she did tell us to clear out sometimes when we were making too much noise.

Winters, on the other hand, weren't much fun – everything was so quiet and dead out there on the island.

I started elementary school in Harkie in 1931. Dad had to take me over in the boat every morning and pick me up in the bay at Harkie in the afternoon. When the lake was in the process of freezing over, I had to live with the schoolmarm for a week. It was fun living away from home.

Later when the ice was thick enough to hold you, I would walk to the channel through the ice where Dad picked me up. The channel was made for the sake of the boats and there was always a lot of confusion when the schoolkids were being dropped off and picked up.

When my brothers and I were older and started in secondary school up by Kärrbo Church, we lived away from home the whole week, except for Saturdays and Sundays. We didn't go to school on Saturday. You often got homesick, of course, and Mom and Dad were very happy to have us back again on weekends. The smaller children may not have been quite as glad.

During the week we boarded at Aunt Andersson's, a widow who lived in the white cottage at Nyby. The cost of our lodgings was paid partly by the rural district and partly by Dad. Naturally we played and had a whole lot of fun with the other kids at Nyby; altogether there were about ten of us.

Aunt Andersson told me a lot about her childhood and how her married life had been. We got on well together. All the while she talked she knitted stockings for her grandchildren. I also read a lot of books, which I borrowed from the school library or from the public library.

Dad had two hired hands to help him with the fishing when

we were little and Mom had a girl named Karin to help her. She came to work with us when she was fourteen and liked it so much that she stayed until she was twenty-one.

The men wanted herring and potatoes and porridge for their breakfast, so every evening I went down to the beach to clean herring and put it to soak. I remember, on summer mornings, how the fellow named Knut would stand turning the cream-separator and sing: 'I fell in lo-ve wi-ith you be-neath the oo-old oo-oak tree-ee . . .'

Though it wasn't me he fell in love with – I was too little then.

Both Mom and Dad were Nonconformists and members of the Pentecostal Church. Grandmother was a Baptist, and Grandfather became one in later years. Earlier generations of our family have also been nonconformist.

We weren't able to go to the meetings very often from Aggarö, but Dad used to have family services at home on Sundays. On the second day of Christmas we went to the Sunday-school party in Västerås, the whole bunch of us. We rode with Mr Hålldin, and it was the only day during the entire year that we took a taxi. Mom usually had a lot of trouble getting all the boys neatly dressed.

Somebody read a passage from the Bible, then people sang and acted out little plays, and there were games and packages of goodies. About three hundred kids from the Pentecostal Sunday schools in the neighbourhood of Västerås took part. Sunday school didn't start in Kärrbo until I was a bit older, so I never went to one.

I can't remember us kids ever being razzed during our school years because we were religious. Everyone knew us for what we were. We didn't make a big thing out of it either – we were really no different from anybody else.

The Evangelists used to like to visit us and we would hold meetings sometimes in the kitchen. Folks from Aggarö and even from Harkie came to these meetings. In winter we occasionally rode over the ice by sled to Ridö and went to the meetings at Hugo Andersson's house. He was the man who regained his sight after an operation in 1968, after having been almost blind for thirty-six years.

Most often the Kärrbo group's prayer meetings were held in Karelen. I think the cottage there was owned by the Workers' Community in Irsta, and they would rent it each time. The congregation in Västerås employed two Evangelists who lived in the Elim Chapel in Kungsåra, and who were sent around to help the local members with their meetings. The local members would speak up or sing, according to their ability. Once a month members came out from Västerås to 'the outposts', and there was usually singing and music. Between times, assembly days were held for the members in the neighbourhood.

My little sister, Ingegerd, was born in January 1935. I remember distinctly when Dad went for the midwife. It was cold and there was a full moon, and we were sledding down the slopes at home. Mom was walking around upstairs, big and stiff with pain. The same night Ingegerd was born – we call her Inga.

My brothers and sister weren't confirmed. We went to the Pentecostal Church but were not members; you're counted as a member from the time of baptism, which doesn't take place at any special time, but only when you yourself decide. Some children were baptized when they were eight or nine years old. I was baptized in 1938, when I was fourteen.

I had made up my own mind then. Faith probably comes through preaching, actually, and I had heard a lot of sermons. Naturally your environment plays a role too. Mom and Dad wanted us children to follow in their footsteps. Most of the young people we went around with were believers too. I still belong to the congregation. You feel secure having a foundation to stand on.

At baptisms several people are usually baptized at the same time. First of all you have to make a confession in front of the congregation at a meeting; you tell how you were saved and when you really began being a believer.

Some were a little shy but generally believers are less shy than other people, since they want to do something to spread the faith, or at least try. It makes it easier too that there's a sympathetic atmosphere when the youngsters make their confession.

I was baptized along with three or four others. We wore white baptismal robes which reached down to our feet and white stockings, but no shoes. The robe had weights on the hem to prevent it from floating up during the ceremony.

We stood together in order of height, and then the minister who was to perform the baptism read from the Bible about baptism and its significance. One at a time we stepped down into the baptismal pool.

The congregation sings one verse of a song after which the act of baptism takes place, when the minister says the name of the person to be baptized and reads the baptism ritual. Then the one being baptized is immersed under the water and at that point the old person is buried. At the same time the congregation sings verse two of the hymn.

Afterwards we went out through a side door and got dressed again, and then the members of the congregation welcomed us and talked to us, saying how joyful they were that we'd been baptized. I had promised to live a Christian life and to me it was a great day. I received my membership card some time later.

About five a.m. one winter's morning Mom looked out of the window and saw a guy walking in the yard. It was Joel Greis, one of the Estonian-Swedes who came to Sweden before the war. He didn't want to disturb us so early in the morning so he thought he'd wait until we woke up by ourselves.

He was a believer and a good speaker who often testified at the meetings. Dad contacted him through an ad., and he worked for us quite some time. When we moved from Aggarö he took over the fishing from Dad.

Joel couldn't ride a bicycle when he came to us, but since everybody else had a bike he went to town one Saturday by bus, bought a two-wheeler and rode it home, in spite of the fact that he had never ridden one before. He must have gone into the ditch many times, though he didn't like to talk about it. It's a story that's given Dad a good laugh many a time.

Actually Dad went over to Estonia by boat once before the war. In those days boats from Sweden went there regularly.

From Aggarö Haven we moved to Ekensberg by Frösåker. Dad rented Horneby and Grissle and a little place farther into the forest called Lunsängen, where we just had hay. Altogether the ground was about sixty acres, but the fishing was the most important thing. Dad's always really been more of a fisherman than a farmer.

We rented the house in Ekensberg. There wasn't enough room for us, either in Horneby or in Grissle – both cottages were too small for a household for ten people. We had eight or ten milk cows, as well as heifers and calves. The barn was in Horneby, more than one kilometre away from the house.

We had a man who helped us, whose name was Fredén. He was a widower and had come with us from Aggarö; he used to bring us coffee in bed at five in the morning. He would sleep an hour in the middle of the day to make up for it. Evert Holm also worked for us at that time.

Those cold winters during the war I helped fish on the lake. We had lots of nets and I used to stand and chop holes through the ice. It was deadly dull work, and I froze doing it, but you had to keep at it if you wanted to stay alive. Fish prices were good and everyone bought like crazy, especially in the city, since meat was rationed.

One fall, Dad fell down from the tall pear tree and Sigvard came running home screaming, 'Dad's dead, Dad's dead!' Mom rang for an ambulance, and then we all rushed down to

Horneby. He was lying in the grass beneath the tree. The ambulance came, and Mom went with it. We hardly dared believe that he would live.

He had cracked several vertebrae, and had to have a cast around his whole body and be in the hospital for a long time. There were some folks in Kärrbo who went around saying that he was dead. But in spite of everything he got well. He had fallen more than ten metres.

There was so much I wanted when I was young and yet at the same time I didn't have any idea of what it was I did want. I used to ride in on the bus to Västerås on Saturday evenings to meet pals my age; I'd stay until Sunday and sometimes even until Monday. Dad muttered a bit about my using so much money on bus tickets. I rode my bike in summer.

We used to go to prayer meetings on Saturday evenings. Sometimes we had crayfish suppers and parties or else we'd go to some *konditori*. Once when I came back on a Monday morning Mom scolded me, and as a punishment I had to stand the whole day washing clothes in the wash-house.

In order to get away from home for a while, I went down to Mullsjö and visited Mom's relatives a couple of summers. Most of the farmers there in the parish were related. One of Mom's cousins had a boarding-house in the main building of his farm which would accommodate thirty guests.

The Pentecostal folks had their annual conferences in Mullsjö and in the neighbouring community of Nyhem, just like they do now. About ten thousand people used to gather there. The place was full of life and activity and many young people took part. I used to see to it that I arrived the same week the conference was in progress.

I was very nearly married off to a farmer's son down there. My parents were all for it. I myself was a bit doubtful about the prospect of becoming a farmer's wife. It fizzled out. We wrote letters to each other, but you can't go on keeping company with someone you never see – it's bound to fade and die.

One summer I fell desperately in love with a boy from Stockholm. He lived with a family who had a summer cottage by Frösåker. When I milked cows he would sit on the stool with his back to mine. He was my devoted companion the whole summer. In the fall when he returned to the city we wrote letters. But it wasn't as everlasting as we had imagined.

I was supposed to take a cookery course at Margareta Housekeeping school in Jönköping, forty kilometres from Mullsjö, but I had so many friends of my own age who lived around home, that I decided to learn how to sew properly instead, and became an unpaid trainee at a dressmaker's studio in Västerås.

The proprietress tended to be a bit peculiar. She was from Stockholm and didn't address anyone by their first name but said 'Miss' this and that, and everyone was expected to call her 'Miss' too. I wasn't used to that kind of complication. The seamstresses who worked there were frightened and submissive. She was expensive too – her clientele was composed of the city's gentry, the ones with the money.

I stayed the three and a half months of the trainee period, then I moved home to Kärrbo. During the time I was at the dressmaker's studio I had been living with an aunt in the city.

Actually I wanted to get away from home, but I didn't manage to. I wasn't enterprising enough, I suppose, to find myself a job. My parents wondered why I wanted to work away from home when there was so much to be done at home. Mom needed help. She worked from morning to night. She never stopped making food, three meals a day for nine to ten people.

I didn't know what to do. My relationship with my parents was good, so good that I didn't want to break with them and go against their wishes.

What I had in mind was marriage. Mom and Dad had the same idea, so they did a bit of investigating on my account. I didn't know whom I would marry, none of my acquaintances were in the picture.

In late winter of 1945 Dad bought Harkie from Ivar Törngren. We drove the load of belongings over the iced lake by horse. The house there was much roomier and better than the one at Ekensberg. There was a boiler in the kitchen and central heating, instead of glazed-tile stoves. In summer Dad rented out the top floor to summer visitors, and then we had to crowd up a bit for a while.

At Ekensberg we had also rented out the second floor in the summer. Captain Jahn from Västerås rented it, and I often used to go up to them and help out. In their city house sometimes when they had parties, I also helped them. They would have food and drink on long tables, and dancing to four or five in the morning. I waited table and thought it fun to be among so many happy people.

In the fall of the same year that we moved to Harkie, I became engaged to Ingvar. I knew him before he started courting me, though there wasn't anything special between us then. We had just met on the bus, for example, and talked a bit, the way people do.

Suddenly he was in love with me and I wasn't altogether unmoved. He wasn't at all shy, he came to Harkie and sat and drank coffee and talked, and after two weeks he wanted us to get engaged. He was as forward as anything.

I hesitated and wanted to wait a year, but after three or four months we exchanged rings. That was in September. I still felt uncertain and we didn't put the engagement notice in the newspaper until October.

Even before we were engaged he introduced me to several of his relations, and we used to meet some of them at Tage's *konditori* in Västerås, which was where folks from the countryside met on Saturdays.

One evening Ingvar introduced me to his grandmother, a farm woman of the good old stock, determined and with a feeling for tradition. She lived in Olsta. I was to her liking, so she showed me her cupboards containing linen and household articles and offered us Madeira wine in glasses off a silver tray. She was a sort of tribal mother to Ingvar's family.

My Mom and Dad were also favourably disposed and when it was getting on towards spring in 1946 Mom set to and got ready for the wedding. We were married one cold grey Sunday in April in Kärrbo Church by Pastor Tiberg.

It was a solemn and sort of scary feeling to walk down the aisle right up to the altar, with everyone's attention centred on me. You felt like the most important figure.

Afterwards we had the wedding dinner at home in Harkie for fifty people. What a job it had been beforehand making the food and getting everything ready. Dad gave a speech where he said: 'Well do I remember the day Eva was born, that was the time I was so sick . . .' The accent was on him being sick and everyone burst out laughing.

Ingvar also made a speech and 'thanked for the bride' as it's called, and for the presents we'd been given. Several of the wedding guests stood up and congratulated us. Ingvar's father was there, too, and his mother with her new husband.

Our first home was Mullbacken in Irsta, a farm which Ingvar's grandfather had got for Ingvar when he was doing his military service. We were given a few things from both our family homes to start with. Dad gave us an old harvester. Most of what we needed we bought at auctions. We bought new furniture for the house and got bedroom furniture from my mother.

The farm consisted of forty-eight acres and we had cows, horses and young stock, and a lot of hay in the summer. There was plenty to do all the time. You can never relax and enjoy life when you're a farmer's wife; there's no time to see and appreciate the beauties around you. When I think back on farm-work and farms, I could almost puke.

I was too young for it, in the beginning, and didn't look upon it as my own possession. We managed quite well for money. We didn't have any real debts, though what we earned, of course, all got spent. Actually I don't think you should be so well off when you're first married, because that way you have too many expectations. It's better if your income increases slowly bit by bit.

Ingvar bought a small truck second-hand in the winter, and we used to travel in it a lot home to Harkie, to prayer meetings, and to the city. He was a member of the Elim congregation, maybe mainly for my sake. It was very cold in the cab of the truck and the windshield got covered with ice. We had to scrape away peepholes in order to see the road.

On 14 March 1947 we took over the lease on Måholmen outside Ängsö. As I had grown up on an island it didn't bother me. Ingvar, on the other hand, had lived in Irsta all his life. But what he had in mind was to get more land; we both agreed that Mullbacken was too small.

Most of our machines and tools we took over there in our truck during the winter when the ice held all the way out to the island. That old truck got good use. When we had arrived on Måholmen and got settled there, I said that I never wanted to move again. At the same time I thought it was fun to come to a new place.

In those days there were a lot of people on Ängsö. The Count had sixty tenant farmers. Nowadays it's as dead there as it is in Kärrbo. There aren't even a hundred permanent residents on Ängsö.

In the house on Måholmen there was a huge kitchen and two rooms downstairs and one room upstairs. There wasn't any water or drainage, so it was hard work running the place. But we did have electricity and a telephone (though it was out of order pretty often).

We lived out there just under one and a half years and during all that time we never got up later than four-thirty a.m. – otherwise we wouldn't have been in time to catch the milk truck on the mainland at six-thirty a.m.

Those were beautiful mornings in the summer of 1947,

going out early to fetch the cows from meadows far away. After that we'd spend the whole day working in the fields. The farm included over eighty-four acres of land. Sometimes the tractor broke down and made things rough on us.

I was never through with the work before nine-thirty in the evening. Then I'd put out the thermos bottles with coffee on the table to get ready for the next morning. It was no use thinking of recreation since it took too much time to go out. If we drove to Harkie in the evening, we didn't get home until the middle of the night.

You never had enough time to sleep properly, and went around continually tired. We managed it all only because we were young and strong.

I was expecting a baby too. When we were haying at the hottest time of the year, I had a miscarriage. It was worse than being in labour. I was sweating all over and had a terrible pain in the small of my back. The following morning I rang my mother, and she told me to lie still and not to get up until she came. Actually it felt strange to lie in bed in the morning.

When Mom came we rode in to the hospital in Västerås where I lay half a week, and after that I was in Harkie a couple of days before Ingvar fetched me. He was a bit touchy and anxious that I wouldn't be able to have any more children. A cousin of mine came to look after the household while I was away and stayed to help me for a while when I returned. I didn't get so very much rest anyhow because there was such a lot of work to be done.

Elis Vidlund on Långholmen was our nearest neighbour, a tough, wiry, man who had been a sailor. When he settled on Långholmen he became a boat-builder and fisherman. He helped us on the farm in the summer without any definitely settled wages. His wife often came to see us from over the sound, we were good friends and our two families were often together. They figured they ought to have a cow, so in the fall they took over one of ours as part payment to Elis for his work. They had that cow a good many years.

In late fall when the lake was freezing over and in the spring when the ice was neither solid nor thawed, I had to take care of the milk at home, so I churned butter. We had about twenty cows. Meat was still rationed and you weren't allowed to sell calves and pigs freely. Sometimes an assigned controller came to inspect. There was one of these in every parish who counted the animals and was known as the 'calf-spy'. But on the side the farmers still sold to butchers in the city anyway.

In wintertime the island was quiet and lifeless. The house was badly insulated and only the kitchen and the room beyond where we slept could be kept heated. I didn't bother to light the fire in the main room, or the parlour, as it was called in the country.

We moved from Måholmen in the summer of 1948. Three Finns took over the lease from us and paid 35,000 kronor for the animals and equipment. Ingvar's father handled the transaction. He had started a real-estate agency. The Count of Ängsö also had to give his approval.

In November we bought Östergården just behind Irsta Church. Ingvar, Elis, and a carpenter fixed up the cottage there. It was unmodern and was pretty run-down. During the time it was being repaired, we lived down by Harkie in what used to be the schoolhouse. There I was able to get some peace and quiet for a while, big and swollen as I was.

Bertil was born on 10 November. It was snowing when Mom and I went into the maternity wing of the hospital. It certainly is an experience having a child; it's a great moment when you get to see your own baby. Though the first time you think mostly about the pain. I was twenty-four years old.

The house at Östergården was quite nice, with a new wood-stove, a sink, and a hand-pump in the kitchen. The john was outside. We moved there in the spring and agreed not to have so many cows to bother with all the time.

The farm consisted of about sixty acres of cultivated ground and 120 acres of fine forest. It was the forest we were interested in, because prices for wood were high just then. The fields weren't worth very much since the soil was poor and full of rocks. We hired men with stone-pulleys and gadgets to remove the rocks from the fallow fields; my job was to keep them supplied with coffee and food.

In the summer I was always out helping drive the tractor and bring in the hay and the grain. I've always liked doing that – I've never been one of your sewing-bee ladies, content to sit with their sewing and embroidering.

Birgitta was born on Ascension Day in 1950. A little girl was more than I'd dare hope for. In my parents' home it was practically all brothers and in my daily life I talked and worked with men all the time. So there was something a bit special about having a little girl. She was exceptionally pretty too, with long black eyelashes and fine features. Even folk I didn't know would suddenly exclaim: 'My, what a pretty baby!'

One summer we spent a vacation driving around Southern Sweden for almost three weeks. Ingvar's mother and her husband Harald drove their automobile and we drove ours. Relations looked after the kids for us while we were away. We drove down the east coast and over to Öland, and then continued farther south where we put up tents and swam. From there we took a trip over to Copenhagen and also looked around the Danish countryside a bit before driving home.

Actually we did take a vacation every summer, even if it wasn't for very many days. We travelled as far as Lapland once and I really appreciated its barren loneliness one morning when I was driving between Lycksele and Vilhelmina. Ingvar was lying asleep on the back seat. There wasn't a single building there, nor an animal, and we didn't even meet another automobile. All I saw was unending rows of marsh-pines for a hundred kilometres. But it was beautiful in the north with all those big winding rivers and huge forests.

At home in Irsta we associated quite a lot with other farm families in the neighbourhood and had small parties and gatherings. Sometimes there was a lot of liquor and then it wasn't so pleasant. Ingvar and several others drank more than was good for them and I never did like that. But there are a lot of things you have to get used to in this life.

On 15 April 1952, I had Göran, the third child in three and a half years. Well, then I thought to myself, this is enough, so I went to the doctor to get a pessary.

It got a little tiring with one on the breast, one wanting to hang around my neck all the time, and one who went around pulling everything down all over the house. I could never have things looking nice and neat but had to hide away every single thing. They had children's ailments one after the other.

When I was outside working I took all three kids with me. One day in the fall I just happened to be helping Ingvar fix two tractor wagons when I got caught between them. It would have cost me my life if I hadn't managed to scream in time. Ingvar jerked the front wagon away with the tractor. I was unconscious and collapsed on the ground.

Before the ambulance arrived I came to again. All my ribs down one side were crushed, one was sticking into my lung, and one of my collar bones had broken off. I lay on my back for three weeks in the hospital, then I had to start practising to sit up. I felt the effects of the accident for several years afterwards.

In 1955 we built a new house to live in at Östergården, with five rooms and a kitchen, bathroom, toilet and hot water. Living was much easier when we had moved in there. You didn't have to heat up the dishwater any more, and it was easy to keep clean. Before we always washed ourselves in a basin in the kitchen.

Two years later we moved from there to Olsta. Ingvar's mother had got divorced and Ingvar didn't want the home farm to go out of the family. We gained better land in the deal but worse living quarters – the farm-house at Olsta is big as a barn and quite cold.

It wasn't so that Ingvar made all the decisions while I had no say in matters, and just went along with him. We discussed everything together and weighed all the pros and cons before we made up our minds on different things.

I didn't mind trying something new. Naturally the thought of having one's own place had had something to do with it; to trade a smaller farm for a bigger one means a kind of advancement. Farmers have always thought in terms of acres.

Out in the countryside people have been hungry for land all the time because of all the new machinery. Large machines take large land areas, otherwise farming doesn't pay. Olsta was combined with Mullbacken and Grimsta when we took over the farm. The total acreage was about 120 acres.

The first four years we farmed without animals and grew grain only. There was a grain drier, and this I looked after in the fall. The drier had a wood-boiler which used up a lot of fuel. It was before the days of oil heating. You had to keep firing in it all day, and on up to midnight.

By this time the kids were so big that they were going to school. None of them was crazy about farm-work. Gittan (Birgitta), though, liked animals, and we kept three cats. One was run over on the road outside and she was almost inconsolable.

I often drove the tractor all day long and later, when we got some cows, I had them to look after too. It was terribly tiring to have cooking and washing and other housework to do and be outside working at the same time. But since it was the outside work which brought in the money, that had to come first.

We managed quite well. I felt respected and could treat myself to a few things, like having a hair-do and buying clothes for myself and the children – there was never any argument about it. The problem was that Ingvar began drinking heavily, which led to discord between us, and finally made us tired of the hard work on the farm.

After seven years at Olsta we sold the farm and moved to town. We bought a nice house to live in and there I was the whole summer of 1964 with nothing to do, except the housework, of course. I swam and sunbathed and really gave myself a break, resting and relaxing.

But I wasn't used to having so little to do, and in the fall I began a course at the hospital to become a nurse's assistant. During the first ten to twelve weeks we just had instruction in theory – anatomy, pathology, therapeutics, civics, organizations and social welfare – and we also learned a whole lot about how medical care functions. The County Council is in charge of all medical care in the county and we pay for it by means of our taxes.

Most of the people in the course were young. I was forty years old. It was interesting and quite fun to sit at a school desk again. We had a lot of homework and sometimes we had to give a report. We went on field trips now and then. There were eighteen of us in the course and it lasted eight months.

I wasn't paid anything during the time it lasted, except my food and a scholarship of a few hundred kronor. After the instruction in theory I did three months' practice at the nursing home. There were mainly old women who lay half-crippled and helpless. It was something entirely new to me, working among sick people. At times I thought it was the worst thing in the world, working at the nursing home.

Then I moved to the gynaecology department, which was more interesting. You had more contact with the patients there. My job didn't have so much to do with actual nursing, but consisted mainly of asking them what kind of sandwiches they wanted for breakfast, whether they would like crisp or soft bread, and so on. The porridge and *filmjölk* (sour whole milk) came from the central kitchen and I made the sandwiches myself.

In the evenings they had to eat whatever food was sent. Nowadays there are electronic ovens to warm up the food, which only take a minute. I worked there part-time, in shifts, mornings and evenings.

I liked the job, and when my student period was over I joined the regular staff. After a little more than a year, they started a rationalization programme in order to cut down costs, and there was no end to the experimentation and trying out this and that. They wanted to find out if it was cheaper to use paper mugs than to wash coffee cups, and all kinds of things like that.

One full-time and one part-time job was going to be cut back. The superintendent of the clinical section had discussions with us and we gave her our opinions; there were also information meetings where the management presented their point of view, and we had labour union meetings and so on.

Of course a lively debate went on among the staff about the new methods and working hours. Sometimes you got angry with all the newfangled ideas, and many experiments had to be rejected because of resistance from the employees. At the same time we were aware that the realities of the situation were what it was all about – each patient costs the County Council 200 kronor a day.

There aren't really very many class distinctions any longer in the medical care profession. Everyone is on 'first name' basis with everyone else, at least in some of the departments. You get a feeling that you're working together and sharing responsibility. There are, of course, a few exceptions; people who don't care too much about the crowd at work.

In March 1966 Ingvar moved to Enköping. *By then we had decided definitely not to continue our marriage. We'd sold the house, but the children and I stayed there over the summer. The new owner was to move in on the first of September. I was lucky enough to get hold of this apartment which we live in now, but I had to go through a big fuss beforehand.

* Ingvar Sjöqvist died in May 1968.

The lease didn't get finished by the time we had to move, so we were forced to lug all our furniture and clutter into one of the hospital's apartments on the third floor and store it all there a week before we were able to move here.

Our whole existence was turned upside down. At the same time I went to Örebro to help Birgitta move in. She was starting a two-year course there that fall to become a pharmaceutical technician. First she had heard from Stockholm that she had been accepted in a similar course there, so we put in an ad. and found her a room which we went to look at. Then came the answer from Örebro, and we decided that was better, since the city isn't so big and is closer to Västerås. It was a hectic time.

Oh, the kids knew that they had to learn a trade. There was no trouble from their side, we all stuck together. Bertil went to the Zimmerman Institute and graduated in 1967. Now he's an engineer at the public works office here in the city. The youngest boy, Göran, goes to a vocational school and is going to be a plumber.

To go with all the other troubles, in the fall of 1966 I was rationalized out of my job as well. But it didn't really matter too much since I wouldn't have been able to go on doing only part-time work anyway. The money wasn't enough, so I had to take a full-time job instead at the hospital. Then after that life seemed to be working out all right.

My new job was in an experimental unit. Lots of things had to be tried out before moving over to the new hospital complex that was being built. I worked odd hours to begin with, and then we had to test consecutive working hours and a new meal schedule. This meant that the patients began the day with coffee and sandwiches instead of porridge and *filmjölk*.

Lunch was earlier and the food came already stacked on trays. All the dishwashing on the ward was done away with – everything was returned to the central kitchen instead. In May 1967 we were given a new work schedule with concentrated working hours that we all liked much better.

We also got out of doing any cleaning, which had been a large part of our work before. This was taken over by special cleaning people. The rest of us got more time to give to the patients.

The experimentation went on, of course. The nursing assistants, to give an example, took charge of all the bandaging for a while, then suddenly it became the student nurses' job. However, the business about being able to concentrate more on the patients didn't mean that you had much time to talk to them individually. But it was better than it had been before.

I was going to spend a vacation on Gotland in August, but right before that I was out driving one evening with somebody I knew, and as we turned around on a road another car ran into us. Both automobiles were smashed up. Nobody was seriously hurt but I landed at the hospital in Fagersta for a week.

My vacation was postponed until October. Then my sister and I and two acquaintances from Stockholm were going to take a trip to the Canary Islands. We were going to fly from Arlanda airport on a Sunday morning, and on that Saturday afternoon I started to pack my bags for the train trip to Stockholm.

Suddenly I discovered that my passport was missing. It was locked in a bank safe-deposit box, and the bank was closed. I telephoned them in Stockholm to tell them I couldn't come, but they began calling the bank officers in Västerås and then there was phoning back and forth all evening.

The president didn't have a key to the bank vault, but there was a spare key in another bank, and an officer there very kindly got hold of it for us. The cashier also had to be present, as well as the president, according to the regulations. They also got hold of a policeman to turn off the burglar alarm. Everyone was kind and helpful and looked upon it almost as a game, to solve the problem.

Nine people finally congregated there on Saturday evening when we filed in to get my passport. Then it turned out that more keys were needed for another door in the vault. The whole expedition was in vain.

The others called from Arlanda on Sunday morning and told me not to give up, but to try to come on a later plane. I phoned the travel agency on Monday but didn't get any answers. So on Tuesday, thinking I'd rather be safe than sorry, I travelled to Stockholm to straighten things out.

The people at the travel agency were nice and generously offered me a completely new trip for that Friday. It was several hundred kronor more expensive, but I got it for the same price in spite of the fact that I would be staying at a fancier hotel, with a double room and bathroom and wall-to-wall carpeting. The trick now was to get time off from work. I went back to Västerås and talked to the supervisor at the hospital – the outcome was that I was given an extra week off work.

It sure did feel good when I finally got going. My sister and the two from Stockholm stood waiting to welcome me at the airport in Las Palmas, with flowers in their hands, and we all laughed and joked.

The weather was wonderful, and we swam and basked in the sun, enjoying ourselves all the time. We bought chicken and wine and took it back to eat in our hotel rooms, and in the evenings we went by taxi to restaurants up in the mountains.

One day we flew to the Province of Spanish Sahara. It was unbelievably hot when we got there. Six taxis stood waiting at the airport, and we drove right out over the sand to an oasis – an old man living there invited us to tea. He had several wives but we didn't get to see them. Some camels also came around, as if to order, and were given water.

From there we drove to a Bedouin camp with tents and crowds of kids. We sat down on soft mats in a circle in one of the tents. It was scorching hot and full of flies. The kids died like flies too, I guess. Then they showed us some dances done to a little jingly music, and the old man who ran the show invited the tourists to dance with him. There were camel rides too,

you could ride on a camel a hundred metres or so if you wanted
to, but I didn't.

After this we rode to a garrison town and ate camel meat
with chicken and rice and grilled meat and other dibs and dabs
on a skewer. It wasn't particularly good to taste, though of
course we ate it. You wouldn't believe how hot the sauce was.

The town was called Al Aiun. It was small and had buildings
with white domes. We went around the bazaars shopping and I
bought a silver bracelet. The heat was terrible. Everything was
so poor there; it was hard to imagine how they could survive.
One short day was enough for me – I couldn't have stood it
there for a week, although it was certainly interesting to see
how they lived.

On the way home I sat looking down at that glittering, end-
less surface of water – the Atlantic. It's lovely to fly. I'm
overjoyed every time I get up in the air. I'm not afraid to fly.
I'm actually more afraid to get in an automobile. The shock
from the collision in 1967 is still with me.

When I came back to work, the move to the new hospital was
being planned in the most minute detail. We took part in a
whole lot of information meetings and read through piles of
typed bulletins. Once at a meeting they yelled out through the
loudspeaker that the staff from unit nine had to go back to
work. That was where I worked.

The new hospital is twelve stories tall, with a unit on each
floor. All the units are exactly alike, and everything is in the
same place; the general wards are identical and the lounges are
replicas of one another. The idea is that the staff will be able to
find their way around everywhere, no matter which unit
they're on.

When we moved, nothing was taken with us from the old
hospital. Everything was new – linen, furniture, everything. It
must have cost huge amounts of money. A new hospital bed
costs a thousand kronor, to start with.

There are intercom phones everywhere and letter chutes and

a corps of messenger girls, who weren't there before. An extensive orderly service has been introduced too. When a patient has to go for an examination you ring for an orderly. That's so that those of us who work on a unit won't have to leave any more often than necessary.

Of course, it's nicer to work in new surroundings. I like it very much, even if they do keep you busy all the time. On the top floor are beautiful staff lounges and a small kitchen where we can warm up our food. And on the roof there's a sun terrace.

The only disadvantage really is that sometimes it gets very hot around the glass walls in the summer. There's no cooling system, but then, there aren't very many days of the year when it's hot in this country.

I'm happy to be through with farm life, and I don't want to go back to the country. It's better in the city, and there's more equality. Maybe it's just that the differences don't show up so much.

Here I live my own life, and I like that. I still have the children with me, and that's fun for as long as it lasts. If I had time I'd socialize with people more often, but time doesn't allow. I have kept up with the Pentecostal Church over all the years, and it's given me strength and companionship. Without the Church and God, I certainly would have felt alone and abandoned many times, but in the Church I have my spiritual home.

We ought to be happy as long as times are as good as they are. But they won't last. It's going to get worse. You can read in the Bible about what's going to happen, and whatever's written in the Bible will come to pass.

It would be best if nations and groups would forego any great changes, because once the avalanche is set in motion there'll be no stopping it – not now when they have such great resources, with atomic weapons and other means of destruction.

You have to try to work towards the triumph of good over

evil. It's insane that they keep on fighting wars in so many places. No matter what happens, it's nice to have a faith and conviction that you're in the hands of the good Lord.

I believe that on the whole common folks are the same all over the world – they want to work and live in peace.

If I had more money I would go abroad every winter, south where the warmth makes people more open and life easier. I adore the sun and the warmth. In winter I really get to hating the cold sometimes.

They all worked in the daytime from seven in the morning to seven in the evening and to half past three on Saturday afternoons. Then sometimes they played at dances on Wednesdays, Saturdays, and Sundays in order to earn a few extra kronor.

There was music in the place when the whole band came home to practise. On summer evenings they practised outside on the grass underneath some big oak trees.

Later on Alm got burned. It happened when he was going around with a spray gun on his back, spraying the barberry bushes. He had spilled some of the inflammable fluid on his clothes, and when he lit his pipe, he caught fire and was burned to death.

In 1935, the same year I started school, Ekevi was sold. The land was enough for three private farms. The state bought up land and divided it into small farms in order to create jobs. Westerdahl at Kusta sold several outlying farms at that time during the farm crisis. It was the only way to get hold of ready cash. He didn't make very much on it, but he had no choice.

All private farms were built on the same model with the same houses and outbuildings. Each farm consisted of about thirty-six acres of fields plus forest. The State Rural Resettlement and Home Ownership Board owned the farms and rented them out.

They made three private houses out of Ekevi, and named them Ekevi, Rönnbacken and Borgen. At Rönnbacken the shack stood between two slopes covered with mountain ash trees, which is where the name came from. Borgen got its name from an archaeological relic up here, the foundations of a fort surrounded by the remains of a stone wall 125 metres long. Classes of schoolkids come to look at it sometimes.

Pa rented Borgen beginning 14 March 1936. The farm consisted of thirty-eight acres of arable land and forty-six acres of forest, and we had two horses, eight cows and some calves, pigs, and chickens. He was lucky the first year – the harvest was

Part-time Farmer

Karl-Erik Söderkvist

My Ma turned forty-four the year I was born. I sort of got in at the tail end of things. We lived in a tenant farm-house near here; there were seven of us in a kitchen and one small room. Two of my sisters had already left home when I came into the world in 1928.

The farm was called Buskebo. There were four acres of land, enough to feed two or three cows. When Ma had milked the cows and made breakfast she would stand in a poky little hole inside the kitchen, turning the cream-separator. It would rattle as it turned.

The noise from the separator mingled with the sound of morning calisthenics on the radio, led by Major Uggla: 'Now we're going to open those windows and breathe out that night air,' he began as he breathed the air out of his lungs. It went whew-whew-whew.

My Pa was farm-foreman here at Ekevi, which was then an adjoining farm to Kusta. He used to take me out in the fields with him. When I got tired of walking I slept on his leather vest.

Once I was awakened by a whistling noise and I saw a pilot in a parachute, coming down over the forest. I thought he landed just up the slope, but Pa said he was farther away. The following day he read in the newspaper that the pilot had landed at Limsta and that his biplane had crashed even farther away.

Ma played the guitar and sang sometimes. Pa knew how to play the accordion and harmonica.

My brother Axel played the accordion too. He was conductor in the Italia Chapel where my sister, Thyra, played the banjo – Alm and Södergran played the violin and Fröjdfeldt the drums.

so good that it wouldn't all fit into the barn. Birger Andersson had to come over with the thresher so they could haul the grain in and thresh it at the same time.

I had begun elementary school the year before. Christ, I was scared the first day. I didn't dare go alone, so Ma had to go along with me. There wasn't anything to be scared of, though – Miss Kant was the nicest person you could ever imagine. She gave us milk chocolate.

If you'd done your lesson well and been good there'd sometimes be a piece of candy in your desk. 'The chicken's laid an egg in the book,' Kanty would say when you asked about it, but we *knew* that she was the one who put the goodies there. I used to pick bunches of flowers to give her. After a while you thought it was such fun to go to school that you hardly wanted to go home in the afternoons.

At home there were fun things to do too, like harrowing, for instance. When you drove the horse all alone and jogged along on your short legs in the furrows behind the harrow – then you were a man. You *never* got tired then. Later, when I was older and had to follow the harrow all day long, then I was tired all the time.

In secondary school I had Nyström for teacher in the first year. He was a bit partial and favoured the big shots' kids, the rich kids. On Saturday mornings we liked him, then he was in a good mood. On Mondays and Thursdays he was hungover and mean.

I don't know if I ever did learn anything at school, beyond a little reading and arithmetic. You can't say that we got any insight into the way society and things operated. What little I do know I've learned afterwards.

I remember clearly the outbreak of the Finnish War in 1939. We heard about it on the radio in the morning at home and then we looked at the big map of northern Europe in school. We realized how close it was and felt insecure and a little scared.

Then came posters that said 'Finland's cause is ours,' and

every schoolkid went around selling paper Finnish flags and all kinds of badges to help the refugees. Then kids dashed around like crazy to be first around the cottages. I ran like the wind down to Täby to beat the Rosendal kids. The ones who sold the most badges and flags received some kind of diploma.

When war number two began between Finland and Russia two years later, we had a Finnish guy at school for a while. His name was Yrjö and he had been evacuated from Helsinki with his brothers and sisters. They lived down by Frösåker. There was a big commotion at school when Yrjö came and told us at recess how one Finnish soldier could lick two hundred Russians.

I helped weed fodder-beets at Springsta for several summers as soon as our school summer vacation began. We tied sacks on our knees but bruised them anyway crawling in the beet field. We kids didn't think it was great fun exactly – weeding. Sometimes we amused ourselves by throwing clods of dirt at one another. In the evenings we rode our bikes down to Springsta pier to swim.

When the weeding was done we went and hoed the whole beet field two or three times until the tops had grown so much that they completely hid the ground. The best part of it all was signing for your pay and then pedalling home with money that you'd earned yourself.

On Whit Sunday 1942, I was confirmed, and on the same day I went on the National Road Walk. I rode my bike home from the church at top speed, changed my clothes and then raced back again to be in time. We went up to Väsby Wood and back. The entire parish turned out, young and old.

It was a sort of endurance test between Sweden and Finland. The idea was to get as many of the competitors as possible to walk ten kilometres in a certain amount of time. I don't remember how long you were allowed. The ones who stood the test got the right to buy a blue-and-yellow badge they could parade around with.

We were in good condition, all right. I'd been walking in the fields all day long during the spring farming. We would never think of riding on the harrow. It probably wouldn't have made the slightest difference if we had, weighing as little as we did, but the old man bawled you out if you tried. You were supposed to walk.

I walked so much that I got saddlesore. The skin between my hams got red and burned like fire. If I complained to Pa he just said, 'It'll go away. When you've been walking a few years you'll have an ass like leather.'

That was all the consolation you got. It was the same in the fall when I did the ploughing and could hardly manage to pull back the plough at the corners where you turned. 'Practice'll make you stronger,' he said. It got so you would cry sometimes over that damned plough. But you just had to keep on.

The winter I was fifteen I went to cut wood in Kusta Forest. You got 2.75 kronor a metre. I managed three metres a day – that is, cubic metres. The grown-ups cut more and I tried to keep up. I couldn't, of course.

We had tramped up a narrow path to the forest. The snow was deep that winter. In the mornings I could take the path all right, but on the way home I was so tired that I staggered and veered off the path out into the snowdrifts. I hardly had the energy to eat in the evenings.

The grown-ups managed six to eight metres every single day. 'Course it depended a lot on the way they stacked the wood. You can stack wood in many ways. If you stacked loosely so there was more space in between, you earned more.

Sometimes I had to be at home working, helping the old man haul the manure piles out to the fallow field, for example. The manure had to be out by Christmas – that was tradition. Some years we didn't drive the dung more than 150 metres. If we'd let the manure lie there outside the barn, and then carted it out directly onto the fields in early summer, instead of putting it in a new pile over the winter, we'd have saved ourselves half the work. But nobody thought of that. It was just supposed to be that way.

In summertime I went and played football at the secondary school almost every evening. The new schoolteacher had taken the initiative in making a sports field where before there had been only swamp-land and a whole lot of rocks. Zacke and the Ullberg brothers did the dynamiting there. More than a metre had to be filled in at the end nearest the church. We schoolkids lugged broken rock down there during the recesses and Ma got furious because we tore the front of our clothes.

A kid called Uno and I always played back. We used to brag that nobody could get past us with the ball. One summer when we were playing especially hard we had a number of matches against Irsta and Gäddeholm. Mostly we just had practice games, though.

Later it gradually fell apart. We couldn't get a team together. Some of the guys got tired of playing and many of them moved away from Kärrbo and took jobs in the city. And there was no grown-up to lead at all when the teacher fell sick.

Twice a year we were inspected at home by a director from the Rural Relocation and Home Ownership Board in Stockholm, plus his errand-boys and a consultant from Västerås. The occupants were submissive, afraid of the bigwigs, who were in complete control of their welfare.

The inspectors went all over the farm, and Pa was supposed to go along with them and be at their service. They went into the barn every time, probably to count the animals. There had to be a certain number of animals, so there would be enough manure, among other reasons. They snooped into every nook and cranny of the barn and the outbuildings and even in the house.

Once Ma pointed out to the director that the stairs were too narrow, so that there wasn't room for more than your toes on them. They were like a rickety step-ladder and so steep that you almost grazed your nose on them when you walked up.

But the director didn't consider it anything to belly-ache about. 'Our wives in Stockholm sometimes have to go down three flights of stairs to the cellar to fetch a bottle of juice,' he said.

'Maybe that's the only thing they do all day,' answered Ma, who had a mind of her own. She was so angry she couldn't stand him any longer. Of course no changes were made to the stairs, but from that day forth they were never invited to coffee again in this house.

I wasn't so old then and to me they were just disgusting dictators, overbearing bullies demanding that folks should crawl for them. Nowadays the thing has been reorganized and they're there to help folks, so they say, but it's the same damned thing. They're the same kind of bullies who won't lift a finger to help folks who don't cringe from them.

When I was fourteen years old I began to shoot, and when I was fifteen I bought a Mauser ninety-six. At first I was refused a permit to buy a gun – on two occasions – because I was too young. But Richard Westerdahl helped me write new applications as soon as the refusal came – long applications they were too.

The authorities who issued the licence for a gun wanted to know just about everything about me from the time I was born. I had to have a certificate from the Child Welfare Committee to say that I wasn't a criminal, and from the temperance board to say that I didn't abuse liquor, and from the parish constable and I don't know who all. Last of all the government had to approve the licence because I was underage.

You also had to be a member of a rifle club in order to have a gun, but I already belonged to a rifle club in Kärrbo. Earlier there had been a rifle range at Skämsta. It was the parish meeting place, even for those who didn't do any shooting, especially on Sundays, when a lot of people came.

Shooting is a fair sport. You have to have control over your body and be in trim. You need luck at the beginning of the season, then it's like an injection of self-confidence. Otherwise it can be damn difficult to get into swing later on.

You can't come to a competition with a hangover. You have to keep sober and get some good sleep the evening before. Shooting tends to restrict a person's partying, though some folks have to have a couple of drinks before they can shoot. It's something to do with the nerves.

When I started it was an expensive business, it cost eighteen öre a bullet. Thirty bullets in a contest. At a practice session you could lie there and blow off seventy-five bullets. It took 1,000–1,500 each session.

Then I started earning a bit more and was able to buy a box of 1,000 bullets with two öre discount on each bullet. The box stayed up in the attic so the ammunition wouldn't get damp. As soon as it started to thunder Ma told me to take the box outside. But I left it where it was.

The Kärrbo authorities were stingy with the appropriations. The district was poor. The rifle club was allotted only seventy-five kronor a year. The membership fee was five kronor. The sports club got four times as much from the district – 300 kronor.

Before the war the clubs in Kärrbo, Kungsåra, and Irsta combined as one rifle club. We managed a part of the finances by having parties in Skyttebacken in Irsta. We took in a lot of money this way. I helped with the work, selling entrance tickets, tending the dart booth, the air-gun shooting range and so on. Free coffee and free admission was my reward. There was never a question of anyone getting paid, except the dance-band of course. Luckily we had good weather most of the time.

Some of the members backed out of the work. They didn't have time and made all kinds of excuses. But they were quick enough to come to the dancing – they had time for that, all right. On Sunday afternoon we had entertainment for the family and the prizes were given out.

At the annual meeting the various jobs on the rifle range were divided up and a written schedule made for when you were going to be shooting lead, scorer, and so on. The juniors were sticker-boys who put patches over the bullet holes on the targets. On the Sunday you were shooting leader, you had to be at the range no later than eight a.m. and stay until three or four in the afternoon.

We had many challenge cups to compete for. As a rule they were donated by the proprietors at Kusta, Gäddeholm, Lindö or Frösåker; they were posh-looking cups with the donor's name engraved, worth up to 400 kronor. Ordinary mortals could donate presentation prizes. If these cost more than thirty-five kronor they were allowed to have their names engraved.

Shooting is fun but it takes up a lot of time. I have been doing it for twenty-five years. For a while I almost gave it up, but now I've taken up seriously again. It's fun to tussle with the youngsters, especially your own. They get so big-headed at times and think the old bastard's done in. But there's life in the old boy yet.

We have had many fine marksmen in the club over the years. The members are divided into five classes plus juniors and veterans (that is, those over sixty). This is the only time they go by age, but the veterans can continue to belong to the big fry in class five, for example, if they want to.

When I began there were no women there on the rifle ranges, and that's how it was right up to the beginning of the sixties. Now we have fifteen girls in the club between the ages of fourteen and sixteen, and thirty to forty young fellows. Those who don't have their own rifles can borrow them from the club. The divisions are the same for both boys and girls. The number of adult members is around 150.

There are a lot of Västerås people in the club out here. They say there's a friendlier spirit in a small club. On summer evenings we practise two or three times a week. The hard part about having small clubs is that this means a lot of rifle ranges, which are expensive to keep up. We get a certain amount of state support but not very much.

Västmanland's Rifle Association wants us to combine with Björksta, Ängsö, and Tortuna and use a bigger range. Hardly anyone rides a bike now and folks have cars instead, so it doesn't matter that some people have a bit farther to drive.

Ammunition is free for the young folks nowadays. The costs are financed by bingo games. It's thanks to bingo that we've got the rifle club going like we have, and it's the same in many other kinds of clubs. You have to admit that on the whole, bingo has brought nothing but good with it.

I've been chosen four times to compete in the county championships. One year I came first in class four, and another year I got second place in the same class. Once I completely disgraced myself, shooting wide of all the targets, and I don't remember how I made out the fourth time.

I also joined the Home Guard when I was fifteen, mostly because of my interest in shooting. In Kärrbo, Klas Karlsson – his name is Rognestedt now – had got the Home Guard going at the outbreak of the war. He was a sergeant in Strängnäs but he skied home to Kärrbo over the ice almost every Saturday – it was about twenty-five kilometres. Then he would train the Home Guard on Sundays and ski back in the evening over Lake Mälar to Strängnäs. He kept in shape!

It was a big day for me when I signed for my Home Guard uniform and came home in full dress. We practised sniping with old worn-out rifles. You couldn't use them for a range greater than 300 metres. The barrels were not changed until after the war, when the rifles became usable. This was done after various complaints, and it was about time!

We had defence drills over and over. It was mostly sentry duty at military stores. And mobilization drills. The boss might phone home one evening or on a Sunday morning, and then you had to go like a shot to the gathering place in your mobilization district.

We held field practice against the Home Guard from neighbouring parishes and got an idea of what it was like to defend an area. Setting mines was fun; the land mines exploded like crazy when someone stepped on them. If there was time we would set out trip-wires lengthwise and crosswise between trees and bushes. The wire is so thin you can hardly see it, and is attached to detonators which explode if someone runs into it. Even a hare can cause an explosion, which did happen sometimes.

If we had a long-distance manoeuvre we had to start off on Friday evening and keep at it until Sunday evening. It was O.K. if you were attacked, then you had something to do. Otherwise it could be boring as hell. And cold too. We had no tents, just a shelter, and we weren't allowed to make a fire because that would have given us away.

If we didn't have anything else to do we'd eat sandwiches and see who could eat the most. The women's auxiliary looked after the cooking, and paid for it themselves. Imagine how good it tasted when they came and brought us coffee and sandwiches in the morning after we had been lying out the whole night long. They had mountains of sandwiches with them. Some of the older Home Guard boys always managed to get sick for night manoeuvres. You wouldn't catch them lying out in the forest all night with hardly anything to do.

On one or two occasions we'd have a festival, beginning in church and with a parade of women's auxiliary and Home Guard, their banners flying, and continuing with coffee at the rural community centre and a speech by some visiting big shot, and then they would give out the medals. You get the first medal after being in the Home Guard for ten years, and after that there are medals of increasing value every five years.

Nowadays the Home Guard gets cooked food. On paper plates. The time of the old snuff can is past. The state pays for the food. But up till 1967 the women's auxiliary were responsible for the cost of all the grub themselves.

As you got a little older you became mainly interested in girls, of course. For over a year I went out with a gal who worked at Kusta. She was from Hallstahammar. The idea was that I would move in with her there. Her dad had arranged a job for me at the works – he was one of the ones in charge there. We were the same age, she and I – eighteen.

But that job was a factory job and not my sort of thing. So when the time came I backed out, and neither of the plans came to anything. I decided to stay in Kärrbo. I was born here and it looks like I'll stay until I'm buried in my grave. I can't exactly say that I've travelled widely.

After that love story there were several shorter affairs. And you did some carousing. Drink up and let yourself go. Pa took a swig too sometimes. Ma wasn't so holy either. But she wouldn't abide any remarks slighting religious matters.

No fathers have ever thrown me out of their houses. I've always got on well with both them and the moms. I never got into trouble with the other guys, like when you were with girls down in Gäddeholm, for instance. It was quite common for other kids from up here in Kärrbo and Irsta to find their bikes had been hidden down there when they were about to head home.

I left my bike outside without anything happening. But there were several guys from here who wouldn't dare go down except in groups of three or four. When you are younger, sixteen or seventeen, you seldom stayed overnight. You were too green for that. Though it happened occasionally.

The gals you went out with you almost always met at dances. Where else would you meet them? There were dances at outdoor amusement places and in barns and granaries. You missed out on a lot of gals, a lot of fine opportunities, on account of booze.

There was much more of a difference between guys and gals

at that time. The girls never drank in those days. Now they drink practically as much as the guys do. Actually most of it was really only play-acting when you were drunk, and it's probably the same now. They stagger around shouting their mouths off in order to get some attention.

I met Gun in 1947, at the Anund Race. Everybody from all around flocked there to see the bicycle race. She was with a gang from Kungsåra, and I'd come with Ture Hellström, another guy from Kärrbo. We hung around together a lot.

Well, then things rolled along. Gun and I have been together ever since that Sunday at Anundshög. I walked her home from there and the next Sunday we met again. She was fifteen and I was nearly nineteen.

She worked in Ro then, in the store. I used to sneak my way in there so as not to be seen – she was so young, after all. The storekeeper also used to slink around, spying – there was a sort of mutual stealth.

We went to the pictures a lot in Östanbro on Sunday evenings. Her mom had just died so we didn't go dancing that year. Now the custom of a year of mourning has almost disappeared, which I think is quite sensible, because once you're dead you're dead. It won't change anything if relatives go around in black clothes afterwards.

Her father had died one year before. She used to stay with her aunt and uncle in Sevalla sometimes over the weekend.

When we had been going steady a year, Gun came visiting at home here for the first time. Then she started coming here almost every Saturday and Sunday. It got to be like a second home to her here. I had a room up in the attic but we slept apart, she was downstairs and I was up in the garret. She was probably seventeen years old before decency allowed her to sleep up here with me.

We were split up in the same way when we went to visit her relatives or mine sometimes. Though later on they realized that we were keeping steady company.

We used to go camping in the summer with another guy and gal from Kungsåra. He had his pop's automobile, which we all rode in. Once we drove to Mariefred. It was pouring rain the whole night. Our tent kept the rain out, but theirs leaked so they got soaked.

Then on Sunday the weather was fantastic, so we went to Gripsholm Castle and had a look around. There were some old cannons standing outside which I think were captured in Russia two hundred years ago. I wonder how they managed to freight them home. They're great big hulking things that weigh tons.

Another time we went to Skokloster camping. There are no end of things to see in that castle. I've visited the place several times later when I was driving classes of schoolkids on school outings, and then I've looked through one department thoroughly each time.

There are weapons and armour, furniture, and big Gobelin tapestries, portraits, and silver which has been won in wars, or rather, taken. When you see all the old things you get a kind of connection or link backwards in time. They probably weren't any different then from what we are now.

Ma died on the twenty-third of February 1949. She lies buried in Kärrbo churchyard. She had stomach cancer and weighed next to nothing at the end. She never complained, it was not her way.

In March we auctioned off the animals and all the equipment. Pa gave up the lease and we moved to a house he bought in Badelunda, called Nybo. There I went to work for Torsten Andersson in the gravel pits until it was time to do my military service at the beginning of June.

Gun and I were engaged at Midsummer. She finished working at the store in Ro that year and moved to Västerås, where she found a job in a milk store.

I had it good in the military. I was stationed at the First Armoured Division in Enköping. I drilled for two months, then I never had a field uniform on me again during the remaining seven months.

I was drafted to be staff chauffeur. One of the reasons was that I had a commercial driving licence. I had worked as an extra for my brother Axel, and driven the milk-truck some Sundays and other times. He has a trucking business in Kungsåra.

Being a chauffeur, I got out of doing sentry duty, since I had to be on call to drive whenever I was needed. I was allowed to sign out a swanky new De Soto at the auto firm in Enköping – it was a seven-seater, big and low-slung. I drove the major in it.

I often had to drive him to Stockholm in the evenings. He went visiting women. And oh boy, what women! They were neat-looking broads around twenty or twenty-five years old – I wished I could have got rid of him and stayed myself. The old geezer was over sixty.

I might get an order to come and pick him up in the middle of the night and then I had a long chilly wait. Sometimes he was so drunk that I almost had to carry him, but he was good-humoured then. If he happened to be sober and found me sitting dozing in the automobile, he would bark and roar at me so I had to leap out and open the car door for him.

He was like two different people. In a sober state he played the dignified big shot, but that was hardly ever. In his normal state, when he was a little tipsy, he was well behaved and pleasant. In the beginning it bothered me getting bawled out, but you get used to it. My job was fine, and I was never bored – I was always out driving all over the place.

Right at the start he said that the ordinary, official, coarse homespun uniform wasn't appropriate for a chauffeur, so he wrote out a requisition for a uniform made from thin, fine twill, the kind worn by non-commissioned officers, from sergeants upwards. Plus black gloves – it had to be elegant, you know.

Sometimes he must have had a guilty conscience because of

all those visits to the ladies, and on those occasions he would give me money and order me to buy a cake and take it home to his wife. And I would sit there for a while in their house, drinking coffee with her.

The very best thing was that I got a daily expense allowance of twenty-five kronor each time I was away on duty and unable to eat and sleep in camp. Often I made a clear profit since I ate at the nearest regiment. I had a ticket that entitled me to eat at all military camps. And I slept in the car, at least in the summer.

The year after I was mustered out, I read in the newspaper that the major had got kicked out. He had socked a recruit who wouldn't stand still when he gave the order for attention. The recruit was so cold that he couldn't stand still. The major was reported and dismissed from the army.

After the service I became a truck driver for my brother. There were four of us drivers and two truck driver's helpers working in his trucking firm. I drove milk from Kärrbo in the mornings from quarter to six until about twelve or one p.m. All the small farmers had cows then, except for Eriksson in Täby. He was the first one in Kärrbo to start just farming the land, with no animals.

It must have been all that milk driving that ruined my back. It's a tough job tossing fifty-litre cans up from rickety, low milk platforms onto the back of a truck, yes sir. Sometimes you would drop cans at the road bends and then the farmers would put up a big fuss. It was easy for empty cans to roll off on the way home and you had to hunt around in the ditches to find them. If you happened to drop a can of whole milk, you'd have a word with the weigher-in at the Dairyman's Association and he fixed it so the farmer in question didn't get a deduction for a smaller delivery.

The driver who had the Kärrbo route before me had been too kind. He stood waiting for the farmers to bring their cans. They were spoiled and started coming later and later. I didn't wait. If they didn't have their milk ready, they had to keep it at home. This was the only way to teach them to get up in time in the mornings.

Some had milk platforms that were half rotten too, so you just happened to knock them over with the truck. The farmer got the message and built a good, new platform. Some farms' platforms were too low, so on these you crashed down a can full of skimmed milk so the boards broke off. If they were sturdy boards, the farmer couldn't for the life of him understand how they could break. So then you explained that it was because the platform was too low.

Of course the farmers were furious and bawled us out. But you just turned a deaf ear. If they called Axel, the trucker, and complained, it was water off a duck's back. 'Speak to the boys about it,' he would answer. I had a helper, so there were always two of us.

On Sunday mornings there was a race to get to the Dairyman's Association and unloaded, so you could get home as early as possible.

When you saw the milk truck from Orresta coming along Tortuna Road you stood on the gas pedal across Lundby field. You might even swing in on the wrong side of the safety island on Kopparbergsvägen in order to save a few seconds. All the milk trucks came in so hot on each other's heels that you might have to wait in line up to two hours if you didn't get a move on.

On weekday afternoons when we were through with the milk deliveries, we drove timber and gravel and grain and other stuff. Sometimes we unloaded big rolls of paper from railway cars for Eriksson's wholesale company. Tore Skogman worked at their warehouse; he was a nice guy and a good worker. Even in those days he sang, but that was before he got famous.

We usually weren't through until late in the evening, nine or ten p.m. The company gave us coffee and sweet rolls and pastries or cake. Thore was always the one to look after that detail. The boys often got him to sing a little and then he'd sing a couple of peppy numbers with a kick to them. He was quick with the comebacks.

At that time he was travelling to Stockholm for singing auditions at the phonograph companies. Then he made it big with one platter and he stopped moving paper. Now he earns loads of money, but he hasn't got conceited – he still seems natural. When you see him on T.V. he's exactly the way he used to be.

I watch T.V. when I get time. They show a lot of good programmes, both entertaining and serious ones. You get an inkling of the horrible conditions some people in the world live under, even in many parts of Sweden.

Sometimes you see demonstrations. It's certainly understandable that the young people protest against war and misery, but you can't help getting mad at the way they behave. I could never be a policeman, I'd get so angry that I'd beat up any troublemakers who made fun of me.

Gun and I were married in 1951. We rented a shack from Lundgren in Kungsbyn to live in, two rooms and a kitchen for sixty kronor a month, wood fire, toilet and shower, but no bathroom. We liked it a lot there.

I earned 125 kronor a week as a driver and 50 kronor extra on Sundays. There was no question of a honeymoon or a vacation. Gun continued to work in the city and commuted by bus. We used to borrow my brother's car and go to Östanbro to dance even after we were married. She quit her job just before Kent was born. He came into the world in August 1952. Since then she's been a housewife.

For a time I drove a lot of pulpwood up to Skutskär. I had Kjell, my helper, with me – he was my brother's kid. We loaded in the mornings from six a.m. to about ten. What a strenuous job it was – we loaded by hand, thirty-five cubic metres, twenty-three tons. The heaviest load permitted was thirteen tons, but you always took ten tons overweight, otherwise it wasn't worth driving.

If you were caught by the police you just said that the trucker had given orders for the loading. We didn't take the rap. The trucker paid the fines. Nowadays it's the driver who comes out worse than the owner. If he's carrying overweight or is caught speeding, they mark it on his licence, and after the third mark, they take away your licence. So now the drivers always have one foot in jail, but they still drive with just as much overweight as they did before.

The drive up to Skutskär took between four and five hours. If you were unlucky you might have to stand in line for the same amount of time. So then you lay down and slept in the truck, or sat in the café shooting the bull if there happened to be a trucker you knew from around these parts. Many truckers and truckhands were great at lying and spinning wild tales. That's the way it's always been with men who are on the road.

A lot of them boozed. No one checked that so carefully in those days. Later there seemed to be a definite decrease in drunken driving for a few years, but now it's on the upturn again. Folks can drink themselves to death for all I care, as long as they lay off when they're driving.

Unloading at Skutskär took only ten minutes with overhead travelling cranes and cables. Then you turned around and headed south. If all went well you would be home by nine p.m., but if there was a mix-up it dragged on till past midnight.

Once when we had a flat tyre in pouring rain, we didn't get home until half past three in the morning. Axel drove out looking for us in his own car. We met him outside Uppsala, changed to his car and breezed home and ate supper or whatever you could call it. We grabbed an hour's sleep before the next day began – there was no question of having a day off or even of starting a bit later.

Gun may not have been completely happy about such a life,

but at least she had the boy as company and was certainly used to folks working.

In wintertime there was the snowploughing. It was fun driving if there wasn't too much snow, but when you got snow-drifts and snow that was packed hard then it wasn't too much fun. You drove at a speed of seventy kilometres an hour and had five cubic metres of gravel on the back of the truck to make it hold the road.

Sometimes you might suddenly come to a dead stop so that the cab creaked and you nearly crashed your skull through the windshield. If the snow kept falling you had to keep driving day and night until it let up. In return you earned pretty good money in times like that. I liked my driving job, it had some variety to it.

In March 1954, I became a farmer. It was quite by chance, and not something I'd gone around planning for a long time. We were visiting my sister and brother-in-law down here in Rabo around New Year, and they told us that the man who rented Borgen was on his last legs. After a week or two had passed I went in to see the Agricultural Board in Västerås and asked if it were true that the farm was going to be available, and the answer was yes.

They had already started contacting people who were in line to rent a farm through the Board, and I was put on this list too. Two weeks later I received a piece of paper saying that I had been accepted as a tenant. They took into consideration that Borgen had been my family home, but what carried most weight was perhaps that old Westerdahl at Kusta vouched that he knew me to be honest and trustworthy. I had worked there one summer when his son Thure Westerdahl, the present owner, had been farm manager for the old man.

Well, then it was just a question of getting the wheels turning to borrow money. I needed machinery and tools and animals to get started farming. I myself didn't own more than 2,000 kronor. Pa and my brother Axel stood as guarantors for the lease, which was 1,050 kronor a year. The Agricultural Board stood as guarantor for the 10,000 kronor I was able to borrow from the Rural Credit Society.

The tenant before me had thrown in the towel. I settled his debts with 5,000 kronor and got a Ferguson tractor, a binder, a mower, and a few old tools. It was a good buy.

The first animal I bought was a sow. After that I bought six cows. The price was about 1,200 kronor a head. Then I was broke.

You couldn't get the 10,000 kronor in cash from the Rural Credit Society. When you bought equipment that way, bills were sent to the Credit Society so they could keep a check on how the loan was spent.

Earlier the borrower had been able to get the whole sum in cash, but it turned out that many people had trouble handling the money. They used some of the borrowed amount for useless or not so necessary articles, like automobiles.

I continued to drive trucks for my brother all during the first year that we had the farm. It was mainly my wages we lived on then. Of course the milk we sent to the dairy provided some income, 700 kronor a month maybe. But we also had a lot of expenses, insurance premiums and shares in farming co-operatives which had to be paid. Gun was the one who looked after the barn.

When you are a farmer you buy and sell practically everything through the producers' co-operatives, like the Swedish Milk Producers' Association, the co-op slaughter-house and Arosbygden. It's Arosbygden that buys up and sells the members' grain, and you can buy all kinds of fodder, fertilizers, and machinery there.

You can get seed and fertilizer for the spring sowing on credit from Arosbygden, to be paid on the first of October. At one time there wasn't even any interest on this loan over the summer. Now you pay about one per cent. After the first of October you have to pay full interest on what you owe, and it costs money. Although usually you do pay off the debts before-hand by delivering grain after the harvest.

But there are several members who sell all their harvest, or part of it, to private grain-dealers and keep the money instead of paying off their debts at Arosbygden. You can manipulate the credits from Arosbygden, at least for a time, because the regulations don't say that members must deliver there. How-ever, the private buyers have a limited share of the grain market, less than a third.

When we started, Gun and I often sat in the evening discuss-ing and deciding how the farming should be planned, what we should grow, what kind of animals we'd have and so on. We didn't get much sleep. There were a thousand and one things to be done in your so-called leisure time, after the truck-driving was over for the day. Sometimes it took half the night. But we were in our best years, I was only twenty-six.

The first year we brought in the hay harvest in the evenings and on Sundays. Our brothers-in-law and relatives helped us. During the fall I sometimes stayed at home all day long in order to get in the harvest. It turned out a good one and gave us a fine start financially.

In November Ann-Kristin was born. Kent was glad to have a little sister, and we were very happy too, of course.

1955 was a terrible year, the complete opposite of 1954. In April the weather seemed fine and I got ready to plant. Then it rained almost without let-up till the middle of May. When the rain finally stopped I was naturally eager to get on with things, and did the planting while the earth was set. It got as hard as brick. Everyone made the same mistake that year.

After that not a single drop of rain fell. The ground was like cement and hardly anything grew. Some fields yielded little more than the seed that had been sown that year. My salvation was the twelve acres of rich blacklands down towards Ångsjön which belong to the farm. Things always grow well there and best of all during years of drought.

By then I had quit driving a truck, as I had my hands full with work here at home. We dug deep-covered drains and filled in the open drainage ditches to make larger fields. Gun dug the first spadeful and I dug the second. The kids were out with us on the fallow field.

Because of the lean harvest I was forced to start logging in the forest at Gäddeholm in the winter to earn money. And I carried on with this in the winter for eight years. Gun tended the animals.

In 1955 I became a member of the Church Council. At first when I was asked, I didn't want to; I just told them the way it was that I couldn't manage that sort of thing. I wasn't interested and never went to church either. But the parish councillors told me that it had been the same with them, they didn't know how when they started either. They talked me into trying it out for two years and I thought what the heck, I could give it a try anyhow. I'm still on the council today. That's the way it goes sometimes.

Now I'm even a churchwarden, on probation. I wasn't particularly interested in that either. There's nobody I know who could possibly imagine me as a churchwarden, least of all myself. It's gotten around to all of my relatives, too, in spite of the fact that I've kept quiet about it myself.

'God damn,' they say, 'you – a churchwarden!' It's as if they've not quite got over the shock yet. On top of it all I've gone and got churchy as well. Well, they pressure you, you know.

Since Kärrbo became incorporated with Västerås in 1967, we're now paid both for the job as churchwarden as well as for each committee meeting of the Church Council. This latter pays forty-five kronor a time.

In 1957 I was chosen as parish delegate by the Rural District Council. The parish delegation is the board that controls all church property, church-owned forest, farms and dwellings. When the parishes out here were incorporated, the parish delegation disappeared and it was combined with the city too. Which let me out of that job.

I came on to the real-estate assessment board in 1959. It's not such a burden. Real estate is assessed only every sixth year. Then you *do* work three days a week for two months. The fee is seventy kronor a day and you get a mileage allowance for your driving.

People lie through their teeth about the value of their properties, especially where summer cottages are concerned. Of course, everyone wants to pay as little real-estate tax as possible. To take an example, they'll declare that their cottage consists of only one sleeping alcove and a small cooking-space, measuring altogether eight square metres, but when you drive out to take a look, it turns out that they have both a living room and an enclosed veranda and that the total floor space is about forty square metres.

Almost everyone whose taxes are increased contacts us; some write long epistles or letters of complaint. They ask us how we can know how large their shacks are. But it's uncommon for anyone to be caught for making a false declaration.

There is a small category of people who try bluffing in the opposite direction by jacking up the real-estate value unreasonably high. They're planning to sell and try to get a higher price using the high assessment as an argument.

About a quarter of them are honest and declare the correct real-estate value. In Kärrbo there are about 400 summer cottages.

In 1957 I was elected to represent Kärrbo in the co-operative slaughter-house. Normally we have only one board meeting a year. A person can bear that much, I guess. A month or so before the meeting of representatives, there's a general members' meeting. Then usually a couple of hundred farmers come to air their opinions to the board and to put them up against the wall.

There is always a contingent who shoot their mouths off

without meaning very much by it, people who have a need to be seen and heard a little. Then there are others who offer more meaningful contributions. And it's that sort who spark off discussions and cause investigations to be carried out and changes to be made.

Just now the freight rates are under discussion. Large scale producers of pork, for example, are demanding higher payments for themselves and justify it, pointing out that they deliver whole truckloads of pigs at one time. In this way the freight cost of each pig works out to be much cheaper than when the butcher's truck has to call around the farms, first a pig here, then a couple there, etc. But of course the original principle was that freight costs should be borne by everyone jointly, and that a small farmer off the beaten track shouldn't have to suffer because his location was poor.

What happens now is that the large scale producers are leaving the co-op slaughter-house and starting to sell to private firms, who pay a bit more because they don't have to bother about small deliveries. These tendencies apply not only to the slaughter-house movement but also to Arosbygden, the Milk Producers' Association and the Forest Owners' Association.

Now, as an example, the lumber market has been sluggish for quite a while. The farmers in the Forest Owners' Association have had trouble selling, prices have shown a downward tendency, and there has hardly been any lumbering at all in the small forests.

However, some of the biggest forest owners in these parts have formed something called the Society of Forestry. They've been cutting at full speed. They deliver to Korsnäs and have a five-year contract with fixed prices. That's how it is with the big guys, they know how to look after their interests.

For as long as I can remember I have heard it said, almost like an old saw, that the farmers' associations would be the farmers' downfall. The associations really did belong to the farmers in the beginning and have been very valuable to them. Nowadays the members have practically no say in matters. The organizations have become large apparatuses with no end of directors and executives, representatives and consultants, and the offices have grown into mighty construction complexes with hundreds of employees.

Before, I used to fatten up some of the animals for slaughtering, but not now. There's no point in it any longer. During recent years private people and companies have started so-called pork factories. Some of them have even received state loans to build these establishments, which is a slap in the face to the common farmer. They can produce more cheaply, so prices fall, there is over-production, and the small farmers get hit and are forced to close down because it's no longer profitable for them.

Since 1955 I've been on the National Farmers' Union Board here in Kärrbo. All farmers are in this organization, which is our labour union organization, you can say. It is not associated with political parties. You become a member more or less automatically. There's no point in any farmer trying to stay on the outside.

About four years ago I read about a farmer from Småland who had left the union. He was getting old and was going to give up farming and auction off his stuff, but not a soul came to the auction. He was boycotted, that's what. But then, that's the only example I know of when the damned farmers have held together and been united.

The union functions as a co-ordinating organization for all the various farming co-operative associations. If you've got a problem of any kind you apply to our union representative. The question of Kärrbovägen, for example, was taken up through the Farmers' Union. Actually the road is a district concern, but to my knowledge the district has never done anything about the matter. It was in a terrible state, completely messed up. Upkeep of roads is still, it seems, based on the

number of people registered for census purposes in the area,
But the summer cottage owners, who are ten times as many,
are mostly all registered in the city. Many more cars drove on
the highway than was shown by the assessments.

So we took this question up and then it went further to
higher places in the union. They brought pressure to bear on
the regional road administration and the outcome of it all was
that the road was repaired and covered with oil gravel, making
it like asphalt only easier to repair when it's damaged by frost.

It's the same with the National Farmers' Union as with
other organizations. They're just skeletons with no life in them.
The Board meets two or three times a year. The members
don't give a damn about what we do. They're not interested,
not even enough to go to the annual meeting. It makes no
difference whether the annual meeting is on a Saturday
evening, a Sunday evening, or an ordinary weekday evening.
We've tried all three alternatives without any result. At the
most three or four members turn up. In practice the board
functions on its own, like a balloon.

Membership fees are according to how big a man's farm is. I
pay 150 kronor a year. Out of this twenty-five kronor go to
group life insurance. You also receive the union newspaper
twice a month. It's good and gives information about all
current matters. So really I suppose the meetings aren't so
necessary after all.

Towards the end of the fifties farming was going quite well.
Wheat doesn't bring more now than it did then. However, all
prices, on the other hand, have skyrocketed. Cows were a less
profitable business because of all the work they entail, Sundays and weekdays. The price of milk then was thirty-five öre
per litre for unskimmed milk. Since then it's risen to fifty-five
öre. But we don't have cows any more here at Borgen.

Sows were a much better business than cows. We had eight
sows once and we fattened pigs for selling. It gave us a gross
profit of about 20,000 kronor a year. I can't say off-hand how

much feed and the work cost, but of course there were a lot of incidental expenses.

It's fun having pigs, they're easy to look after and pleasant animals. We were also lucky with the sows. They had twelve to fourteen pigs per litter. The gestation period is three months, three weeks and three days. We didn't give up raising pigs until 1967. Now we have hardly any animals at all, just a cat and a dog and some chickens.

In July 1960, Gun and I had our first vacation since we'd got married. It was just a pity that it rained so damned much the whole time. We took a trip over to Norway with the Larssons in Karelen, and arrived in Oslo on a Saturday. In the evening we sat in the tent drinking wine while the rain was splashing outside.

On Sunday we used the time to look at the royal palace and the town hall. We saw Crown Prince Harald in the palace park. In the town hall it was quite elegant. There were a lot of paintings done on the walls there. We also looked at an Arctic museum where we saw the skis that Andrée had used, and stuffed dogs and things.

It was my first time abroad, if you can call it that: everything is practically the same as it is here. We were there for only three days.

Five years later we went to Denmark for a couple of days. Gun and I and Kent and Ann-Kristin. Then we took a house-trailer. That's more like it. In it you've got heat from the bottled-gas stove and closets, and you don't have to roll up a soaking wet tent in the mornings.

We left the trailer and auto standing out by Råå embankments on the Swedish side the first day we went over to Elsinore on the ferry. It's a nice, attractive, little town, but what a jumble there was in the stores! You could buy overcoats and meat and *akvavit* all in the same store there. There were clothes hung on hangers everywhere, dangling in the wind on the sidewalks.

What surprised Gun most was how much beer they all drank. Truck and taxi drivers sat on their running boards with a bottle in their paws. We also looked at Kronborg Castle with its collections of war booty and all kinds of things they have captured. The castle is in a beautiful position out there looking out over Öresund.

The following day we took the car over and drove around a bit. The Danes seem to have rather small farms, at least where we were. They had a lot of pigs everywhere, rooting around in their pens.

In the summer of 1961, Gun's sister came to visit us with her Hungarian fiancé. He has coal-black, curly hair and his real first name is Zoltan, but he's usually called Jimmy. That's what he was called at home in Hungary too.

He introduced himself and spoke rapidly in broken Swedish. I couldn't make head or tail of what he said at first, though I could see that he was used to meeting people. I was a bit suspicious of him, and wondered what kind of a character he was. It turned out that he was a good guy, you couldn't meet a nicer fellow.

He came here to Sweden from Austria, where he had gone from Hungary after the 1956 uprising. He had been with the fighting in Budapest the whole time, but he doesn't like describing the battles. He and Maj-Lis were married in 1962. I was there at the wedding.

There were quite a lot of Hungarians here in the city; they stick together and have their own society. Sometimes they rent some big place and have parties à la Hungarian, with masses of heavily spiced food, and everybody drinks litres of sour white wine.

Maj-Lis told us about one of those Hungarian parties once. There's a difference in temperament, all right. They had their own orchestra of twelve or thirteen guys, and my God, how they played. A couple of hundred Hungarians were sitting at the tables and everyone joined in the singing the whole time.

They are a lively people. And then they danced half the night.

At first Jimmy used to sing when he walked down the street, Maj-Lis told us. But not any more. 'I've become Swedish now,' he says. 'There aren't any more reserved people than you Swedes. Although when you get drunk, you liven up, then you're almost worse than anybody else with your bellowing and bawling.'

I didn't like their sour wine to begin with. Now I do. They drink it all the time, litres of it. It's probably good for your health too, pure stuff.

In the summer of 1965 Jimmy went home to Hungary on a visit with Nisse and Britta, Gun's sister and brother-in-law. When they came to the border and saw the guards with their machine guns, Jimmy got all sweaty and wanted to turn back.

'No, you bastard,' said Nisse, 'now we've got this far, we're going on.' And so they did and nothing happened to them, they weren't even searched at the customs.

Then they drove to Jimmy's parents on the outskirts of Budapest. Nisse said afterwards that nothing can compare with Hungarian hospitality. The neighbours streamed in and everyone offered them food and wine; they stayed there for the whole of the vacation.

Hammarsten, my next-door neighbour here in Rönnbacken, gave up farming in 1960 and moved to the city. He was fifty years old and started as a construction worker. I was then renting half of Rönnbacken. I wanted all of it, but the agricultural board decided that Ture Hellström in Ekevi, the next neighbouring farm, should have the other half.

All leases expired that year and afterwards Ture and I got one-year leases. It was obvious here, though no one said anything, that the homes occupied by owners were going to be sold. You see, the shacks were beginning to be too primitive; they had no toilets, no hot water and no bathrooms.

Ture was able to continue as a tenant, but he didn't dare to

buy, he said, since he didn't think he would be able to manage
the interest and the mortgage payments. Later he became a
farm-worker instead.

I rode in and had a talk with the president of the agricultural
board and explained that I wanted to buy Borgen, Rönnbacken,
and Ekevi and make one farm out of all of them. He thought it
would be O.K. and promised me first refusal.

When it came down to it, all I was allowed to buy was Borgen
and that half of Rönnbacken which I was already renting. It
seemed I wasn't considered reliable enough to buy the whole
lot. The president didn't give any reason when I went in and
asked, and I was so mad that on my way out I slammed his
door so the whole office shook.

My brother-in-law down here in Rabo was the one who was
allowed to buy Ekevi and the other half of Rönnbacken. I gave
81,000 kronor for the fifty-four acres of farmland and about
seventy-two acres of forest that I was allowed to buy. I got a
loan from the Rural Credit Society to make the purchase with
and the agricultural board guaranteed the loan.

The mortgage loan is 40,000 kronor with no payments, and
has a rate of interest 1·5 per cent lower than ordinary bank
loans. On the other loan of 41,000 kronor, I pay off 2,000
kronor a year, plus normal bank rate of interest. It varies a
little upwards or downwards according to how the Bank of
Sweden changes the bank rate. The total cost for both loans
is usually around 7,000 kronor a year.

At the same time as I bought the land, I sold the cows. In
order for the whole thing to be more profitable, I was going to
have to be able to get hold of more land. The cost of machinery
sky-rockets all the time, and if you've got too little acreage,
then it's hell on your finances.

The question of more land was solved in 1962 when I got to
rent Olle's thirty-seven acres in Karelen, three kilometres
from here. He gave up farming then and went back to his old
profession as carpenter. At the same time I was able to rent the

land in Flitbo, fifteen acres of it. It's not quite so profitable because I've got to drive tractors and machinery seven kilometres there.

So now I have 105 acres of land, spread out in three places. If I'd been able to buy Ekevi and the other half of Rönnbacken I'd have had 109 acres all in one place.

It's sure strange how prices are on various things. I'll be damned if a harvester combine doesn't cost as much as a small farm with land, forest, buildings and all.

It's terrible how much money is shovelled into trading machinery. Almost half the price is an extra addition which is haggled over. I bought a new harvester combine three years ago, and the price was marked 35,000 kronor. But I paid only 11,000 kronor and for the rest they took my old bitch of a combine in exchange – first of all it was smaller than the new one, and it also needed repairs costing at least 3–4,000 kronor after four years' driving.

In 1963 Peter was born, and Anders came into the world the following year. It just happened and was almost a little puzzling. Though now we think it was a piece of luck, as otherwise we soon would have been sitting here alone, Mother and I.

Kent will soon be leaving, he's finished school and is planning to be an electrician. But it isn't so easy to get a place in a trade school, the one in Sala is the only one in the country that takes in pupils to study electronics, and it's not easy to get in. Ann-Kristin will also be going soon. She's already been confirmed. We're lucky to have the little boys, they help keep us young a bit longer.

If I were able to tone down our living standard and take things a little easier, I would stay at home and snooze away the winters like many other farmers do. But I'm not made that way: so I can't be at home if I'm not completely occupied. I've never been one to sit around reading, for example. I can't sit still, and I'm no wiser when I finish a book than when I began it.

'You just get nasty if you stay at home with not enough to do,' Mother says.

So instead of staying at home I started logging in Gädde-holm Forest in the winter. In 1964 I began doing a bit of hauling with a tractor, and the following year I bought a forest tractor for 47,000 kronor and got down to serious work. I'll be damned if I haven't been working in the forest from the very first time I started.

Now I drive in the forest almost the whole year round. I'm getting to be a so-called moonlight farmer, one who has other work in the daytime and does his farming by night. I drive for the Forest Society. The money is good.

If you crawl out of bed early enough in the morning you can carry away a hundred cubic metres of pulp wood a day from the forest. That yields a gross earning of 550 kronor. I have a hydraulic crane with a grab claw on the tractor. But it costs a lot. Interest and mortgages and fuel and spare parts take a lot of money.

Just the drag chains alone, made of special steel, cost 8,000 kronor a pair. The big tyres, cord reinforced by steel, cost 900 kronor each. A forest tractor with trailer gets worn out after three years. I need to buy new equipment now which would cost 85,000 kronor. Or 110,000 kronor, depending on the size. It's a risky business, buying such expensive machinery if you aren't sure of steady work. You have to keep it going all the time.

During recent years I've worked ten months out of twelve in the forest. Of course, it's nice as long as it lasts. God knows if farming up here in Central Sweden has really got a future at all.

More and more fields are being planted with trees. It sure does seem strange to have a policy like that when there's already a surplus of forest products, but there are a lot of strange things in this world.

We do have farming agreements and negotiations and the

idea is that we farmers will have guaranteed incomes like the industrial workers. In the future we'll probably be employed by the state and get our monthly pay-cheques through the mail.

The small farmers are being killed off. Apparently there aren't going to be any farms left. Everything's going to be concentrated on industry. Up in Norrland there are only old codgers left, and no young farmers are coming in their place.

The ones in Skåne make all the decisions. They're the guys who are the higher-ups in Stockholm, deciding how much we're to be paid for our products. The Danes can *have* Skåne.

To be fair, the country should be divided up into regions with different pricing systems for farm products – one region for Southern Sweden, one for Central Sweden, and one for Norrland. Down in Skåne for example, they have much bigger harvests and better drying weather. The policies for fixing prices are based too much on their conditions. They ought to be paid less and Norrlanders should get more per pound, and the Central Swedish farmers' payments should come somewhere in between.

We foresters up here should do what the French farmers did, we ought to take our tractors and combines and block the main highways up here. Then we could at least remind people that we exist before we're structure-rationalized away and completely disappear.

When I was a boy there were over forty farms in Kärrbo. Now there are only about a dozen left. The rest have been consolidated. Sweden has been rich for a long time, there has been money, the farmers have been able to buy more land and those who have been bought out have been able to find other jobs. But now unemployment is on the rise again.

I don't know what's going to happen. If it continues the way it is now, there will be only three or four farms left in Kärrbo in the end. Or maybe only two. The funny thing is that those farmers who are left here are quite young, about forty or under. Only Skämsta-Herbert is over sixty.

Now we've also got the first city farmer. David Harknäs has moved to an apartment in Västerås and drives twenty kilometres by auto to his farm down in Harkie in the morning. And back home to the city again in the evening. Who knows, yours truly may land up in the city one of these fine days too.

Sure, I've said many times that I was going to lay off farming. But anyhow, you stick to the land. I think I'd get heartsick in the springtime, when other folks start to plant, and in the fall when they're beginning to thresh, if I didn't have my farm.

Part Three

The Young Ones

Dream of Sun

Gunilla Rognestedt

Dad is from Kärrbo and Mom comes from around Enköping. I was born in 1947 here in Västerås. We lived in one room and a kitchen on Förstadsvägen. When I was between two and three years old I got a tricycle. Apparently I was awfully good at pedalling it out to Köpingsvägen. I don't actually remember this but Mom has told me about it many times.

Once Mom was with Ingmari's mother (Ingmari was the little girl I used to play with) down in the basement doing their washing, when a big ugly dog came dashing into the yard barking loudly. We were scared to death and started screaming. Our mothers came running out and chased him away. After that I was afraid of dogs until I was eighteen, when we got one ourselves.

We moved to Haga Parkgatan when I was about four years old. There we had one room, a kitchen and dining nook. Dad worked at the fire station and had to sleep there every other night when he was on duty.

In summertime we used to take the motorboat out onto the lake whenever he was off duty. Sometimes we would take the boat to Lindö pier in Kärrbo and call on Grandfather and Grandmother and my youngest uncle, Hasse. Or else we would go fishing or tie up at some little island or other and go sunbathing.

In the spring Dad would work on our boat, scraping and puttying and painting and varnishing. Mom and I often went down to the harbour to help him.

Once we were out fishing and had been sitting for a long while without any of us getting a bite, when suddenly I caught three big pike, one after another. Boy, was I proud then.

When I was six I went to kindergarten, half days. We used to sing a new song every day and one thing I can't do is sing. Though of course when I got home I had to sing for mom to show her how smart I'd been. I think practically everything I sang had the same melody.

Soon after this we moved to Runebergsgatan where we had a two-room apartment. We lived right across from Korsäng School where I started the following year. The first day we had to go with a teacher up to a classroom and draw a flagpole with a flag, and a house with a chimney and smoke. This was called the school readiness examination. The smoke was supposed to be blowing in the same direction as the flag: that was the point of the test.

A lot of the first year at school was just playing. The teacher was old and very sweet. She was the best one I've ever had all through my schooldays.

One day in April my grandmother died, and the next day my sister Ingrid was born. My mother was terribly upset about Grandma dying. I tried to console her by saying it was much more of a shame for Ingrid, who'd never seen Grandma.

I was very sad myself because I'd been with Grandma and Grandpa quite a lot. They lived by Vappa, on this side of Enköping. I don't remember Grandfather quite so well, other than that he and I used to go out picking rose-hips together sometimes.

My uncle (on Mom's side) also used to visit when I was staying with them in the summer. He was rather fat and I used to climb up on him and slide down his stomach.

I used to brag about my baby sister when I told my playmates about her. Dad and Mom wanted another baby very badly. They were very happy when Ingrid was born, in spite of being sad about Grandma.

I remember when they called home from the maternity wing of the hospital in the morning, and Dad telephoned all our relatives to tell them. Then I had to go down to my Uncle

Gösta and Aunt Mainy, who had an apartment in the same entryway as we, when Dad went to the hospital to see the baby.

It was fun to live on Runebergsgatan. I had lots of friends and we were always doing handstands and somersaults and cartwheels or balancing on the fence surrounding the school or climbing trees. My parents said that they saw me standing on my head more often than on my feet. We used to skip ropes until late in the evening.

Sometimes we biked to Väster Råby in Tortuna to visit Aunt Vera and Uncle Kalle and my cousins. They rented a place there. On the farm was a large barn where we were strictly forbidden to play. The farmer and our parents figured that we played with matches and maybe they were scared we'd fall from the rafters.

But we always made a bee-line for the barn, of course. We climbed up steep ladders and onto the crossbeams in the roof and jumped from them right into the straw bins, so our stomachs turned over. The owner of the farm also had three kids, who played with us in the forbidden barn.

We also used to go up in the hayloft. But when the cowman came we had to get out as fast as possible.

It wasn't so far to Tortuna, about twenty kilometres by bike. We rode our bikes a lot, sometimes all the way to Grandpa, Mom with Ingrid on the back of her bike and I on a smaller one which I'd been given.

It was thirty-five kilometres to Grandpa's. We'd pedal there in the morning, pick berries all day, and then home again. We also used to bike to Kärrbo quite often to pick blueberries, raspberries, and lingonberries. And in the fall we collected mushrooms in big baskets.

Hardly anybody rides a bicycle any more. Young people nowadays don't get any exercise at all.

We moved to Bellmansgatan on Skallberget when I was ten years old. There I got new playmates. We used to play sandlot baseball and I and two other girls played soccer. In the winter we skated and ski'd.

There was an athletics club there, which had a small hall with table-tennis and T.V. That was when television was something quite new. Nobody had T.V. at home. We had to take a written note from our parents saying how long we were allowed to stay there in the evenings.

The club members were all guys, before I and a gang of girls joined. The boys played bandy and football. We started nagging them to arrange something for us too. Eventually a girls' handball team was formed.

We practised in the gym at Emaus School. We were usually there without a captain. We often had to play without substitutions when we had games, since it was sometimes hard to get enough girls to make up a full team. We played our first game away from home in Fagersta and (Rah! Yay!) we won, six to one. After this we were in Västanfors and Arboga and Köping.

At first we were playing against rank amateurs, though fairly soon we shaped up and came up into the top league in Västerås. The same year I was chosen to take part in the city championships in skiing for the city's schools. The finals were to be held out in Rocklunda Forest. Those of us from the fourth grade had to ski 1·25 kilometres. Before the race began I was terribly nervous. One of my ski bindings kept giving me trouble, but luckily I managed to borrow a piece of cord from a friend who was a year older than me. We set off in pairs, and there was a huge number of entrants.

I didn't know anything about how to plan the race, I just poled along at top speed. In the afternoon they telephoned us at home and said I'd come in first among the grade fours in the whole city – I could hardly believe it was true.

Mom and Dad thought it was fun, of course. Then I had to go down to Herrgärde School where all the winners were lined up to have a picture taken. The winners were in our local newspaper, which I still have – my very first newspaper clipping. My parents had the clipping blown up and gave me the enlarged photo for my twelfth birthday in 1958.

The same year I started going in for track and field athletics. There was a poster on the bulletin board at school, so I signed up for the high jump and the sixty-metre dash. The contests took place at Arosvallen. I ran in my sweat suit; Dad and my little sister told me to take it off, but I was too shy to run in just my shorts and sweater. I won in spite of the sweat suit. I came second in the high jump. I got two cups as a prize.

Dad took a photograph of me when I stood on the victors' stand. I still have the photo. The next day my name was in the winner's column on the sports page. Naturally the victory gave me a taste for athletics.

Lessons in school went fairly well, too, but gym was the only thing I really enjoyed. Of course, I did do my homework and kept up.

In the fall I won the standing broad jump, the hop-skip-and-jump, and the high jump in the indoor school races at the Technical College. We competed in the gymnasium. After this I joined the Västerås Athletics Club and began with conditioning exercises. We had to run hundreds of laps around the gym and then continue with strenuous gymnastics. It was so tough that you were dead after one hour. The exercises were rounded off with a little handball or basketball.

I was the only girl athlete in my class. The other girls weren't interested in sports. I thought it was great and put in practice on Mondays, Thursdays, and Fridays, and sometimes I also played an extra game of handball in the evening.

That winter I came in third in standing broad jump in the district championships in Köping. The competition took place on a Sunday morning and we went by car – after the awards I had a quick shower and then we drove home again. In the afternoon my name was mentioned on the radio's sports news and that made me a little cocky, of course. I remember how I did a double-take in front of the radio: that was a funny feeling.

Then I was in Stockholm and took part in the Linnea Sports Club's national indoor races. I knew that my chances were not too good since I was the youngest, only twelve years old. I was shy too, since everyone else was older – I felt so small and didn't dare talk to them. I just ran around by myself limbering up.

It was a complete fiasco, I came in eighteenth out of nineteen competitors in standing broad jump. In the high jump I came in twenty-fourth. There were only twenty-six competing in this event.

But my name was in the local newspaper anyway, just because I was from Västerås. It was embarrassing. Newspapers are so darned patriotic about local folks.

It's the same at international meets, when they gloat, for instance, that the best Swede came in thirty-fourth. Why, it's excruciating for anybody who competed to have to advertise his poor showing just because of his nationality.

It's just as bad for somebody who's been presented as a favourite by the newspapers before a race and then doesn't make it. Journalists who write about sports ought to think about what they're doing.

I spent a lot of time on athletics during the rest of my time in school. One of the things I liked best was playing basketball, and I took part in various games at school. My handball game suffered, and I almost gave up playing it. My coach at the athletic club was a little put off at me because I practised different events at the same time, instead of concentrating on shot put. He thought that's where my greatest potential was. But I thought it more fun to try a little of everything.

In the sixth grade we had our first school dance. We'd kept after them for a long time to let us have one. One of the guys in my class who wanted to show how brave he was asked our teacher for a dance. He was much shorter than she was, but he managed quite well. She was really a swell teacher.

The teachers always had to be around watching over us. We weren't allowed to dance the whole time, but had to interrupt for motion picture shows and things like that. That's the way the rules were, and it didn't make any difference if we protested over it.

In seventh grade we also had some school dances, but it wasn't until the eighth, when we were fifteen, that it became a regular thing and we had a real orchestra instead of just a phonograph. The boys smuggled in bottles to show they were grown-up and drank *akvavit*. Now it seems to have gone so far that many schools have stopped having dances because of the drunkenness.

On Sundays after the dances we had to clean up. Once the boys' toilet was completely covered with vomit. We had a lot of fun while we were cleaning up – ran the films backwards and goofed around.

When I began eighth grade at Kristiansborg School, I made friends with a girl called Laila. She was as interested in athletics as I was, and we went around together a lot. The other girls were so afraid of physical exercise they didn't even want to take part in gym. They often came along with trumped-up excuses and tried to get out of it. Well, a lot of the exercises were pretty stupid.

My parents were always saying that it was a good thing I kept busy at athletics instead of gallivanting about town or hanging around with nothing to do. But that year Laila and I started going to a lot of dances in the city park and in the A-hall at the community centre, as well as in Folkets Park and at Sevalla rural centre.

Dad had sold the boat by then and bought an automobile instead. He and my mother used to drive Laila and me sometimes to Sevalla centre, and then go and visit my Uncle Harald and Aunt Ebon who lived nearby, during the evenings. When the dance was over we rode back home with them. Sometimes we did the same when there was a dance on at Tortuna rural community centre.

At first we just stood around together with all the girls, hanging back because we were shy. It was the same everywhere, the girls gathered on one side of the hall and the boys on the other. At each dance the boys came across the floor to see if there was any girl good enough to dance with.

Then of course there were girls who refused, who were a bit stuck-up and wouldn't dance with just anybody. The girls who were in demand sometimes stood farthest in against the wall, behind all the others, so the boys had to plough their way through the whole bunch in order to ask for a dance.

Neither Laila nor I were much good at dancing when we started going out in the evenings, but we soon learned. Dancing is the most enjoyable thing I know. Mainly you dance with the sort of people you already know. It seems as if boys are shy about asking girls they don't know for a dance. I like both modern and old-time dances.

When it was old-time dancing, Laila and I always used to dance together. We could do the waltz, polka and the schottische. But not the hambo. We tried to learn it at Laila's house, without music and all, but we couldn't get the hang of the steps.

So once at the Park, in The Barn where they have old-time dancing, Laila said, let's go up and have a try. I was hesitant. Well, anyway we went onto the floor. It went fine, and ever since then we've danced the hambo.

In the ninth grade we had a lot of fun at school. Two girls went through the ninth a second time, and they were always getting on the nerves of one of the teachers. Once one of them was talking and the teacher told her to go outside. She wouldn't budge. So then he got mad and shouted, but she still sat there. He got mad as a hornet and started to go towards her desk; she didn't dare go on sitting there, so she retreated to the door. But she refused to close it though he told her to, and when he was about to close it himself she pulled the other way, holding the handle from the outside.

She wasn't always fighting with him. She often made jokes and had a way of expressing herself which sounded hilarious.

During the last year at school I didn't think we were learning anything. We just sat around wishing we could get away. The teachers had their lesson plans to follow, and often told us we had to get through a certain piece that day in order to finish the course in time.

We had French, for example, in ninth grade, but we didn't learn anything. In German we had to review the conjugations we'd had in eighth grade, just because some people in the class didn't know them. But what they didn't learn in eighth they didn't learn in ninth either. I could speak English quite well, we began with it as early as fourth grade. A little German sank in too.

A lot of people who stopped going to school said they regretted that they hadn't gone on. Most of them from my class said the same when we finally finished, but I've never regretted that I stopped. It was much more fun to start working.

The summer before I started ninth grade I went to a training camp up in Boden, near the Arctic Circle. It took twenty-two hours to get there, sitting up in a train. The work-out was intensive and we were in marvellous shape after only two weeks. We also had a lot of training in technique. I improved my own record in shot put from 9·60 metres to 10·61 metres.

In the evenings we went bumming around Boden. It's a deadly boring place, with nothing but soldiers everywhere, and one single street plus some sideroads which merge into footpaths. My friend and I each bought ourselves a Lapp bonnet, and a tourist from Stockholm jumped out of his car and started filming us. There was a dance in the camp one evening, but the guys were too shy, they were all so young.

After school I became a clerk at Domus, the big co-op department store. It was terribly nerve-racking the first day. I didn't know what things were called and they only had time to show me once how the cash register worked before a customer came in I had to wait on. But it went O.K.

The people I worked with were nice and helpful and we really had a pretty good time. Though it was a bit monotonous just standing still waiting for customers and wiping off dust. One day a guy came in and asked me for a hedgehog. I kept a straight face and smiled, for I thought he was pulling my leg. But he explained that a hedgehog was one of these things with spikes in it that you put at the bottom of a vase to keep flowers in place.

Some of the customers tended to be a bit lah-di-dah, with a need to act stuck-up. But the majority of them were friendly and pleasant.

I didn't think we sold so awful much in the household utensils department where I was. You began at ten minutes to nine and the first job was to write down what you needed to get from the store-room. When the things came up, we set them out on the shelves at the same time as we were serving customers.

I used to stand longing for the coffee-break at about eleven, and then for the lunch-break between one thirty and three p.m., and then for closing time. We took turns going to eat. It was real nice to have a long break, and there was a little terrace up on the roof where you could sit in the sun. Sometimes I rode home and ate there during my break. A lot of people in Västerås still do this.

The pay was lousy. I got 425 kronor basic wages in the beginning, and the commission, which was based on how much the whole department sold, didn't give more that sixty or seventy kronor to the youngest of us. It was an unfair system; we young people had to work harder for our money than the older ones, who had a higher basic wage and often twice as high a share in the commission. But they didn't earn a very great deal either.

I got 150 kronor on the fifteenth and about 200 kronor at the end of the month. The rest went for taxes. At home I paid a hundred kronor for my room and board.

The turnover of staff was high, and nothing was done to make us comfortable in any way. Everything was so inflexible, it seemed impossible. For example, if you wanted to take a few hours off, there was a big fuss. We didn't get a discount on what we bought ourselves. (They did get this at other department stores.) Everything you bought had to be sent to the check-room. You picked up your stuff there when you went home.

At Easter 1964, Mom decided we could have a family vacation and go skiing but she couldn't get time off from work. So just Dad and I, my sister Ingrid, Aunt Gudrun, and her kids Sonja and Henrik went. A girl called Irma, who worked at the civil defence school where Dad had become a teacher some years previously, was also with us.

She and I lived in one of the two cottages we rented outside Lillhärdal, in the province of Härjedalen, and the others lived in the second, which was larger and had an open fireplace. It was just great up there and we ski'd for all we were worth.

Gudrun went to the hairdresser one day, and while she was away we drove around a bit to have a look; and as it happened, the back of our big Vauxhall skidded down into the ditch of a narrow road. Two guys in a Volkswagen offered to help us and then they skidded down too. Then we all helped each other getting the cars up.

On Easter Saturday we went dancing in Lillhärdal's community centre. We were already known there as the Västerås girls. Young as well as old people danced there, everybody knew everybody else and there was a very cozy atmosphere.

Laila and I decided to ride our bikes up there on vacation, so we started training in the spring and sometimes biked fifty kilometres in the evening. I asked my department manager at Domus if I could have my vacation in July when Laila had hers.

She worked in a factory and had to take her vacation when they closed down for the summer.

No, I couldn't, it was absolutely impossible for me to take off just then, even though I could arrange a stand-in myself. So the biking holiday was off and Laila went to Germany with her parents instead. Then I did get my vacation almost exactly the time I had asked for after all, because of some change in the schedule. Yeah, well . . .

Towards fall the trainer from the athletic club came to Domus one day to speak to me about applying for a job as telephone operator at the National Telecommunications Administration. He himself worked there as an engineer.

With my job as salesgirl, I hardly ever got time for any athletic contests. I didn't finish work until about six thirty p.m., and the competitions usually began at six or seven p.m. When our events were in Köping or Fagersta, for example, I didn't have a chance of going.

I wasn't able to do much training under such circumstances, either. However, if I were to start working at the telephone company, I'd have more time for both training and competing. But the people I worked with at Domus were great, and I wasn't too keen on quitting just then.

Well, I started in at the telephone exchange, anyway. That was in January 1965, and the first time I saw the experienced operators at the switchboards in the telephone hall, I thought I would never get the hang of it. They worked like lightning with all their wires. There wasn't a moment's hesitation.

There were four of us starting at the same time, and first we had to sit with a teacher in a room next door and learn the abbreviations of all the cities and areas with their own area code numbers. Many firms place calls through an operator, in spite of automation. They can check to see who's called and how long they've talked by the small cards which come with the telephone bill.

You also had to learn how to talk on the telephone, to speak distinctly and be courteous and friendly. The customer is always right, of course, just like in a store.

Our training lasted a month. We had to sit and listen at the switchboard, and the last week we started working ourselves with a fully-trained person beside us. It was quite a strain when you had to start by yourself, but soon it became routine, and after a while there was nothing to it.

Sometimes you got bawled out. Once I was in a great mood when I came down to start work on the afternoon shift, but I'd no sooner sat down and put on my headphones than a customer started fuming at me. I didn't even know what it was about. I had a good mind to tell him to go to hell, but of course we weren't allowed to. You have to keep smiling.

When there's a lot to do and you're getting tied up, you hear all kinds of sarcastic comments to the effect that you're drinking coffee or sitting there asleep. If they only knew how well-nigh impossible it is to leave the switchboard for a single moment. If you need to go to the toilet, you have to ask the supervisor for permission first. And it has to be quick. You get ten minutes at the most for a coffee break. And you have to write your name on a list beforehand.

Athletics got shunted aside at the telephone exchange too, since I worked in shifts and was on duty every third Sunday. But the work was more fun than at Domus and better paid. My friend Laila worked at a hat factory in those days, but I managed to talk her into starting at the telephone works instead, and we got to be on the same team of operators.

We often went out dancing. Neither she nor I went steady with any guy, except on rare occasions. We wanted to go out and enjoy ourselves, not dance with the same guy all evening.

I worked all summer and only had a week off, so I went to Revsand outside Kristinehamn, where my aunt Greta has a café and vacation cottages.

In September I took a vacation trip to Italy, which the athletic club arranged. There were about twenty-five of us. On the way down we competed in Borås one Saturday afternoon, and that Sunday we were going to continue on to Malmö. But I went along with three of the guys who drove down on Saturday evening.

We whizzed over to Copenhagen in a hydrofoil boat, but didn't have much time there before the last ferry left again for Malmö. In line there was a drunk who started pushing and shoving me, until I got mad and tackled him so he nearly fell over. Then he got furious and started after me. But the guards took charge of him, otherwise I would have been trounced.

The airplane flight to Rimini took three or four hours, and I felt sick the whole way. We landed and installed ourselves in Hotel Elba; and when we had changed and were ready to go out in the evening it began pouring rain. The whole gang of us went out anyway and spent the evening jiving and twisting. At the Embassy we learned how to dance the Zorba.

The fellows bought bottles of Muscato wine and sat on the beach in the daytime popping the corks. We were out of bed early in the morning. There was a meandering asphalt track nearby for go-carts, those things that look like dwarf automoiles. They were marvellous things to drive. You could borrow helmets and overalls. The minicars had no fenders, and you got all black in the face from the rubber, which sprayed up from the tyres.

It cost 1,000 lire, 8·50 kronor, for a turn around the track. We drove so much they gave us a discount. I'd recently taken my driver's test though it didn't make any difference there. Nobody asked you if you had a licence.

Between rides on the go-carts, we rented tandem bikes and a contraption of three bikes joined together horizontally with a parasol over them. The two on the outside pedalled and the one in the middle steered.

We checked out all the bars on the main street in Rimini. Giorgio's was biggest and best. We soon got to know Giorgio. Once, honking his horn, he came and picked us up in his Fiat

600 when we were at another place where they had a gambling den and bowling. Eight people in one little Fiat!

There weren't very many tourists in town, since it was the end of the season. Most of them were Swedes or Germans. We mostly kept together in our own gang, and were out every single evening until way past midnight.

One morning we went by bus to San Marino. The view is delightful there. They were selling gold cheaply in a bunch of stores along some narrow streets, and I bought a ring for myself, a bracelet for my mother and earrings for my sister. For Dad I bought about 100 kronor worth of postage stamps. He has a large collection. I also bought some miniature bottles of liquor, ones that are only seven or eight centimetres high.

The flight plus full-board at the hotel for the week we spent there cost 490 kronor, but the club paid for some of the costs, in proportion to how well you had done in various competitions. A couple of people who were on the international team and had got an 'elite badge' got to travel free. You had to provide your own pocket-money. I'd been careful to save beforehand, and spent over a thousand kronor.

When I got home I sat around completely shot for a couple of days at work. I almost fell asleep. God, was I tired. The week after our homecoming we had a club match and I set a record in discus throwing, though not much to write home about, only a little over thirty metres.

Otherwise things went their usual way. Work was pure routine. Then came the Christmas rush, when everyone calls up their relatives. We worked in shifts over holidays.

At the end of February 1966, Laila and I went to the Canary Islands. We flew, but God, what a long time it took, almost nine hours. We flew in a slow old propeller plane. At Bromma airport it was cold, and there was a lot of snow when we left. In Las Palmas there were summer breezes blowing.

You could go out in a thin summer dress in the evenings. We

paid 1,250 kronor for the trip. The hotel was marvellous and had a bathroom and a big roof terrace which Laila and I had all to ourselves.

In the daytime we sunbathed and went to the hairdresser. The hairdressing salons were dirty, miserable places with rusty hair clips and rollers that were not cleaned properly. When we sat under the dryer, the hairdressers didn't bother about us one bit, but just sat reading detective stories. That would never happen in Sweden. But of course everything was much cheaper down there. I went to the hairdresser six times and Laila went seven times during the two weeks we were there.

The first place we went to was called El Pirata. It was two places with a dance floor between, and there we drank Cuba Libre, which is rum and Coke. We also went to the Astoria several times. We met two Swedish guys there. They kept trying to get us to come to another night-club.

Eventually we gave in and we really didn't regret it. The place they took us to was unbelievably plush with waiters in white tuxedos and the women in mink capes. I've never been to a fancier place, either before or since.

The guests were mostly middle-aged and rich. We got loads of delicious food and used silver cutlery. The boys who took us there were obviously well-off. I believe one of them owned a farm in Southern Sweden somewhere. They were due to go back the following day. We danced on the roof terrace, then had drinks in the bar. Late in the evening there was a show by a Spanish couple who danced flamenco with castanets in their hands.

Laila and I would never have dared go to such a grand place on our own. Another night-club we went to was called Aloha, a magnificent place below ground level, which had palm trees and flowers and fountains. It felt as if we'd come to Hawaii. Someone ought to open a neat place like that in Västerås.

One day we flew to Africa on an old Spanish plane. We landed in Spanish Sahara. Some taxis stood waiting in a row at the airport. Laila and I ran straight to the smartest looking one, a fairly new Opel Kapitän.

The autos drove together straight out into the desert. There was such a wind that the sand was blowing around and it was so hot you could hardly breathe. We came to a small oasis where just one family lived. They offered us tea out of dirty glasses and then we went out into the desert and visited some Bedouins in their tents. There we were given mint tea again and camel meat on skewers.

The meat looked disgusting. Nobody tasted it. There were about forty of us tourists in the group, Yanks and Germans and several other nationalities. The ladies sang for us and danced; one of them with no front teeth had an unbelievably shrill voice. Afterwards the old Bedouin guy danced with Laila. She said that he smelled something awful. They never wash. There's a shortage of water there, you know.

After this we were allowed to ride on a camel, those who wanted to. Just a little ways. It swayed and rocked so, you'd have been seasick if you'd ridden any farther. The camel looked really nasty – the actual expression on its face, that is.

The programme ended with dinner at the officers' mess in El Aiun. The place was thick with flies and filthy dirty with bits of left-over food everywhere: disgusting. I didn't taste the soup. We flew back to Las Palmas the same day. Shortly before, a guy in military uniform came up and asked Laila and me if we collected stamps. I gave him my address. Later he and Dad swapped stamps by letter for a time.

Back in Sweden there was a snowstorm when we arrived at Bromma. We'd bought a lot of liquor and I was stopped in customs and had to pay thirty-three kronor for one bottle which exceeded the allowed amount. But nobody asked how old we were. If they'd checked it, we would have had to give up everything, since neither of us was twenty-one. What a democracy, huh?

After that we had to get down to work again for a month

before Easter. Then we went on a skiing vacation to Kaxås outside Östersund for two weeks – Mom and Dad, Ingrid and I and our dog Fluff. We went with another family, in two cars.

We were lucky with the weather. We ski'd and dug holes in the snow, laid pine branches at the bottom and sunbathed on reindeer hides and furs. A couple of evenings we went down to the village to play bingo and we won some coffee and boxes of chocolates. It was much cheaper to play there than it is in Västerås.

I'd worked overtime beforehand in order to get that long a vacation all in one stretch. Afterwards I worked through the whole summer without a vacation. Sometimes in the evenings I biked out to Tortuna, where we rented a summer cottage at Väster Råby.

Towards the fall I met one of the guys in the athletic club when I was at the Park dancing one evening. He had been on the trip to Italy the year before, and told me that you could go down a week earlier this time and have two weeks there instead of one.

I liked the idea right off, and the next day I began swapping shifts and arranging overtime so as to be able to get away for the trip. Some of the shifts I had to sell to one of the temporary staff.

We went by train to Malmö. It was the first time I'd been in a sleeping car, and I woke up every time the train stopped. From Malmö we flew in a plane that was so cramped that you were squeezed up tight between seats. We wound clothes around our heads because there was a draught from somewhere all the time.

What a beautiful feeling it was to land again in Rimini. But this time we were staying in the neighbouring town of Riccione. It's only one kilometre between the cities on a perfectly straight highway.

Besides us there were a lot of other Swedes at the hotel, and we all had great times together when we went out in a big gang in the evenings. At a fish restaurant there was a man in the band who played an accordion, and he could play both Swedish and German tunes, so we took turns singing in unison, we and a group of Germans sitting at another table. We danced the *jenka* and drank beer out of big tankards. The guys had a competition to see who could drink most.

In Bologna one evening we had what resembled a club meet in field athletics. The Italians were picked from several clubs, but, together, we managed to win. I was second in shot put. Another girl from the Västerås athletic club won.

Afterwards they invited us to dinner in a big club-house with a swimming pool, and we danced a bit. We'd won a big cup as a club prize, and they filled it with wine and passed it around.

When I got back to Västerås there was a letter waiting for me that said I'd been accepted for a six-months' course at the Telecommunications Administration in Stockholm as a foreign telephone operator. We'd often talked about how well paid the foreign telephone operators were, and that's why I'd applied for the course.

They weren't able to arrange an apartment for me, but at last they promised to try. To begin with, I got a room to share for two weeks with another apprentice, out in the suburb of Fruängen. After this I lived for two weeks in Hökarängen with friends of friends. Then Dad and Mom bought a house in Katrineholm and I was able to swap their apartment in Västerås for one in Stockholm. In the apartments-for-trading ads. in *Dagens Nyheter*, I received just one answer, but it worked, and I traded to a two-room place in an apartment building at Danviks Cliff.

The first day at the telephone office in Stockholm I just about turned around and went home again. Those old babes there were incredibly sarcastic towards us beginners. Later I figured out that it's part of the Stockholm style to be sarcastic a lot of the time.

We got full pay and a subsistence allowance during our

apprenticeship, since it was the office in Stockholm which had applied for people from the countryside. During the first week I put through calls within Sweden in the domestic department. Then we moved down to the information office and looked up numbers in directories for a while.

The next step in our training was to be in the Nordic department. The Danish telephone operators were the most difficult to understand, and they were hard to hear besides. We had a little listing with Danish numbers – *halvtreds* (fifty), *tres* (sixty), *halvfjerds* (seventy), *firs* (eighty), etc. – but you never had time to look things up in it. (The Danish number system is different from the Swedish, more like the French – that is, it's based on twenty, and written as multiples or fractions of twenty.)

After a month in Nordic we were put in the foreign department. First the German-speaking countries, which included West Germany, East Germany, Austria, Switzerland, Yugoslavia, Hungary, and Albania. I never had to put any calls through to the last-mentioned country.

The Soviet Union, Czechoslovakia, Poland, France, Italy, Spain, and Portugal belonged to the French-speaking countries in the telephone world. England, Ireland, Holland and Overseas – that is, the United States of America, Mexico, Canada, and the Bahamas – belonged to the English-speaking ones. The telephone operators who serve the rest of the world have to be fluent in German, English, and French.

We had to sit and practise listening quite a lot, and we had lessons in which we practised various phrases, numbers, days of the week, the most common stations, the alphabet and so on. It was exciting work but also very tiring. It was a real relief when the six-month training course was over.

When you started on the foreign telephone exchange your wages went up. I earned 1,544 kronor a month. People make more calls than you might imagine. The calls came streaming in and customers would often have to wait in turn for several hours. You certainly earned your money.

There was a control room where they could listen in to all the stations unnoticed, and check to see that you were doing your job properly and weren't sitting eavesdropping. For that matter, there's no chance of doing this, there isn't time and anyway you don't dare.

The reason for the control is not just to keep a check on the operators to make sure they don't have private conversations or talk unnecessarily to operators in other countries, it's also to check the number of calls and to determine whether any of the girls need more training or other assistance.

When the supervisor had listened in and made a note of your mistakes, she called you in and explained them to you. A report of proceedings was drawn up that you had to sign. They also had tape recorders, so there was no point denying what they said.

I was lucky and got through O.K. The first time I was called in to control I was pretty jittery. There was no need to be, because I was praised profusely. She happened to listen in to me once when everything was going smoothly – fast and friendly. One girl was fired for having private conversations, but then she must have also done other things earlier.

A pal of mine from Uddevalla named Maud was in the course at the same time I was. At first she rented a room from an old lady, and later she moved in with me in my apartment. The rent was cheap by Stockholm standards, 245 kronor a month for us to divide.

Stockholm is a rather dismal city. It's too big, too. The daily routine was the same all the time. Up in the morning, catch the bus and then subway to work. The same in the evening. Sometimes in rush hour the bus might get stuck in the same place for a quarter of an hour. In gas fumes and traffic jams folks get cross and angry. I feel sorry for people who live in Stockholm.

In the evenings we were exhausted and managed to get down just a little tea and sandwiches. We were hungry but just didn't get around to cooking food. We lay on our beds at home reading magazines or did nothing. Sometimes when the spirit moved us, we'd run down to the movies. If you stopped a moment to look in a store window, some greasy middle-aged bastard would immediately take you for a whore. No, give me Västerås any day. Here folks are normal.

Just like kids, Maud and I and another pal called Marianne went around Gröna Lund, the city's amusement park, one evening. We screamed with delight on the ghost train, but the more we screamed the scarier it got. We behaved like little kids. Another evening we went to the opera. I'd never been to any place like that before, it was certainly much better than I'd expected it to be.

We saw *Die Fledermaus*. It was amusing. I hadn't thought it would be. I imagined that everything would be boring and long-drawn-out and dead serious with a snobbish, older audience, the upper-crust people. But there was a crowd of youngsters there and they weren't very dressed-up, either.

In fact, we talked about going again but we didn't. I was at a theatre once when I was small, but I don't remember what play it was they did.

Of course, we went out dancing sometimes. A couple of times we went to school dances. Marianne had friends who were at school and used to tell her when and where there would be a school dance on. People could get in easily – even outsiders – they didn't check on you.

Some students are a bit stuck-up and overbearing, though not all of them. They don't just come from the upper class any longer, but they sure do live in their world of school. I believe a lot of them stay at school to get out of working or because they think it's the thing to do if you're well bred.

There was more action at the ordinary dance places. I didn't think it was much fun there, actually, there were too many people and too few who knew each other. You become so anonymous at places like that.

Actually I soon discovered that I wanted to move home to Västerås. Everything takes such a long time in Stockholm and there's often an unfriendly atmosphere – people push each other around and are bad-tempered. If anything happens there doesn't seem to be anyone prepared to help his fellow-man.

I applied for a re-transfer to the Telecommunications Administration in Västerås. But there were no vacancies. After various complications I got a job at the hospital as an operator at the ambulance station, and moved back to Västerås. Before that I was down in Italy again, for a week of fun and games in Rimini. Great!

There was no trick to trading an apartment in Stockholm for one in Vasterås. I put an ad. in the local newspaper and got fifty-three answers. The person I swapped with was very pleased with his luck of exchanging his two-room apartment for one in Stockholm. He worked there and had been commuting for a whole year, 240 kilometres a day. That's ridiculous.

The apartment I have is modern and lovely. I've picked up various exotic objects, like a monkey skin, a matador poster in silk, Arabian leather ottomans to sit on, Negro sculptures, a great big sun-hat from Nicaragua, a Japanese lantern with red tassels, and a stuffed alligator. I bought this for 125 kronor from a guy who had been at sea. And various other things. I dig this kind of stuff. Though sometimes I wonder who it is I take after, actually.

I'm happy here. I don't know what's so special about Västerås. Perhaps the reason you feel so at home here is because it's easy to find your way around and you have a lot of relatives and acquaintances. You can also get out into the countryside in a flash here, by bike if no other way. You can go in the water by Björnö or out in Kärrbo, row a boat and swim. But I never want to swim out very far. I have respect for the water.

My athletics came to a halt the year I lived in Stockholm.

When I came home again I started training regularly for a while, pure grind. My record in shot put is now 11·32 metres.

The work is good, though we have shifts of course, seven a.m. to three p.m., or three p.m. to eleven p.m. There are two of us working full-time plus a relief worker who does part-time. Sometimes you have to work on Sundays, too. On the average I have two and a half days free a week. The basic wage is 1,483 kronor and with a supplement for awkward working hours, that brings me up to about 2,000 kronor a month.

But I've never had so little money as now. I'm out a lot, racing around having a good time. For a while I went dancing several evenings a week at the restaurant Klippan. They had a marvellous Hungarian orchestra at that time, and I was booked for every dance. Sometimes I only slept a couple of hours before I started work.

It was a bit dead for a while when they had a Swedish orchestra which attracted an older audience, and it didn't start really swinging until they got a southern band there again. There's no entrance fee, it's included in the first drink or juice you have. This costs between fifteen and eighteen kronor, and the next one costs the normal price. If you come late and can sit at a friend's table in the bar, then you can stay there for free.

The ambulance guys at work are all great. I love it there, it's an independent job. During the evening shift you get time to see a bit of T.V. sometimes or sit outside and talk, in summer at least. Of course it can happen that there are a lot of accidents all at once, and then you have to be on the alert. And there's other driving too, patients who have to be moved from one place to another and so on. My present job is the best I've had.

I don't know if I'll get married, not for a while yet, in any case. They say live while you're young, and I don't want to tie myself down now. But a fortune-teller has told me that I was going to have three kids.

Dark men are the most handsome in my opinion – brown or black, with blue-black hair. I'd like to go to South America or the West Indies on a vacation. Or to the South Seas. There must be some place, some island that's untouched and not just full of tourists.

Though of course it's difficult to take off work for so long. You also have to have a good friend with you as a travelling companion. I ought to be able to save up the money it would cost. It's easier to save up for a trip than for anything else.

I'd leave here and set off around the world if I were a guy. If I were, I could sign up to work on board a ship.

Not So Much Fun All the Time

Eva Söderman

Myself, I'm from here in Västerås, but my mother comes from Kärrbo and Dad is from up in the province of Jämtland. He was born in Lapland, and then they moved south to Strömsund, where Yngve Gamlin, the artist, is from.

Mom came to the city when she was sixteen. Mom's sister also lives in town. Her brother still lives in Kärrbo. Grandma moved to the city in 1963, although she still has the cottage on the slope behind Vretbo and lives there through the summer.

I was born in 1954. We lived on Svärdsliljegatan. We moved to Kumlagatan in Skiljebo when I was two and a half years old, but I can remember what it looked like on Svärdsliljegatan.

There was one room and a tiny little cooking nook, with no place for a table; instead they had to sit in the room and eat, but I used to eat in there sitting on a high-chair. We had a lion-coloured armchair with white stripes. I used to stand on it and wave to Dad through the window when he pedalled to work.

A neighbourhood girl named Rigmor who was ten or eleven used to look after me sometimes when Mom wasn't home. That girl is lame now and sitting in a wheel-chair.

On Kumlagatan we had two rooms and a kitchen with enough space for a table, chairs and a sofa. Mom started going out to work three days a week, and she took me on the bus to my aunt Gullan in the mornings. Dad picked me up in the car in the evenings. At my aunt's I used to play with my cousin Maggan. She's two years older than me.

I was given a tricycle when we lived on Kumlagatan, and I used to ride around on it indoors – once I banged into the cupboard door so the mudguards scraped against it and made a

large mark there. Afterwards I wasn't allowed to ride inside the
apartment any more.

My playmates there were named Kristina – she was a year
older – and Kicki who lived above us – she was a year younger
than me. She had two younger sisters. There was a parking
space behind the house and a park in the middle with a bicycle
path and walks for pedestrians. And a sandpit and swings and
grass.

Kicki had got a two-wheeler. We rode it a lot and we ran
away from her little sisters 'cause we didn't want to stick
around them. In the winter we built snowmen and rode on our
sleds. Sometimes if there were quite a number of us we would
play *Bro, bro, breja*, a Swedish version of *London Bridge Is
Falling Down*. Two kids hold hands to form an arch for all the
others to go through. They walk in a long line and everybody
sings:

> *Bro, bro, breja,*
> *the blocks and the rocks,*
> *all good reindeer,*
> *nobody gets by here,*
> *by here,*
> *till he says his sweetheart's name!*

And then one kid from the line is captured by the two holding hands. They rock the one who's caught and sing:

> *Who's taken the pastor's shoe,*
> *the pastor's shoe,*
> *the pastor's shoe*

– and then repeat it once more. Then the person says yes or no.
But he can also say sun or moon, stone or mountain, white
flower or blue flower, or something like that instead, as long
as it's two alternatives.

The two who stand making the arch or tunnel have already
agreed privately that one of them is 'yes' and the other 'no'.
The one who is caught whispers, for example, 'yes', and has to

stand behind the keeper who is yes. When everyone in the line has been caught and said yes or no, two rows are formed and everyone puts his hands around the waist of the one in front, and the two who have made the arch take each other's hands and then there's a tug of war to see which side is best, the yeses or the noes.

We played games like this when we were between four and six years old.

When I was five I went to a kindergarten where we lived. Mom didn't have a job then, she stayed at home, but I wanted to go anyway because all the kids I knew went.

For the first hour each day we used to sit in a circle around our nursery-school teacher and she would tell us stories or play the piano and sing, and we used to sing with her. Afterwards we were allowed to play with what we liked.

The boys had great big building blocks which they built cabins and little houses with. We girls were never allowed to have the blocks. If we tried, the boys used to hit us.

There was modelling clay to play with and dolls and old clothes and hats to dress up with. That's what I did mostly. We could be there from noon to four p.m. Another group was there in the morning. I went for a year.

In the summer we went out to Kärrbo over Saturdays and Sundays, but on vacation we used to take a trip up to Dad's parents in Strömsund. Granny (on my mother's side) has also been up there with us several times.

Grandpa in Strömsund is a tailor, and they live in a two-storey house. Downstairs he has his workshop with its own entrance. We usually live in my aunt's and uncle's summer cottage a kilometre away, since Dad's brothers and sisters and my cousins live at Grandfather's. We usually take turns eating meals at each other's places.

There's a lake there called Flåsjön which you can swim in. The water is colder than in Lake Mälar, but not so cold you can't swim.

When I was six we were in Norway. We travelled through the province of Värmland up to Trondheim and a bit north. The roads wound around and around in several places. We camped in tents, it was nice there, with beautiful, steep mountain peaks.

The elementary school I started at was in a building next-door to where we lived. There were over twenty in the class. I was excited about beginning school, though I already knew how to read. Mom had bought an ABC book and helped me. I was the only one in the class who could read when we started, and I could also *write* my name (not just print it). It's only three letters, after all.

I couldn't count. We had Christian religion but no hymn books, so we had to learn some psalms by heart. We sang other songs too, ones we knew.

At recess time we girls skipped rope and played 'twist' with a length of elastic. The boys didn't jump rope. Usually all they did was fight and make a lot of noise. We were never left in peace. When we were skipping they used to stick their hands in the rope so we couldn't continue, and we had to start all over again. We thought they were absolutely ridiculous.

We used to swap pictures of film stars and actresses and singers and that kind of thing. You could buy ten coloured photos for thirty-five öre.

Our class went on an outing to Strömsholm once by coach, and we looked around the castle a bit, then went to look at the riding tracks, but there was nobody out riding just then so we never got to see any horses. We drank juice and ate rolls that we had taken with us, and then we travelled home.

Our parents were allowed to come and watch when we had examinations. That's not the way it is anymore; now they have visiting days for them instead.

Dad and Mom were out one evening and I was asleep at home alone. Then I woke up and telephoned to where they were spending the evening and asked them if they were going to come home soon. Later I woke up again and called up a second time and the man was horrified – he thought something must have happened. It was three o'clock in the morning. I didn't know it was so late.

But then it occurred to him that Mom and Dad had probably come home without my having noticed. He told me to go and look, and there they were, sound asleep. I was almost afraid then but he wasn't mad at me for calling and waking him up.

Second grade was almost the same as the first year at school. Our teacher was Inga-Lisa Olsson. She was young, and we had the same classroom.

At that time Grandma was living with us for a couple of months. Dad was working at Asea, he still does. Mom had a part-time job. In third grade Mom had started working full-time, so I was given a key to the apartment and had to stay there alone until they came home from work. I had a pal I used to go around with, and sometimes we were at her place.

Grandma had moved into town then, after Grandpa died, and sometimes I used to take the bus after school to visit her. She didn't live so terribly far away. It was fun to be at her place, she had a black cat with a white nose and with white on his tummy and front paws. The cat was called Peewee.

I've never had any animals myself. I'd love to have a dog but Mom and Dad think that it's almost cruelty to animals to have one, since it would have to be alone all day long and couldn't go out and get any exercise.

In the third grade we went on a school trip around Lake Mälar. It rained cats and dogs. At Gripsholm Castle there was a guide who told us a whole lot about the castle and that was fun. There are a lot of rooms and halls and big pictures. We didn't ride as far as Stockholm but drove home by way of Strängnäs and Hjulsta.

I did go to Stockholm on a school outing when I was in sixth grade, though I had been there once before with Mom and Dad when I was on a winter-sports vacation from school.

Our class and another one had to take turns using a regular class-room and a smaller one when I was in third grade. Afterwards we moved over to Stentorp School when they finished building it, and that was a much better place. There we had our own classroom and our own assembly-room too.

The teacher divided us into groups and each group had its own assignment: to look up things in reference books, read and write about a specific animal, for example. Then you had to report to the whole class and tell what the group had written. You were allowed to look at your notes when you gave your talk. If there were four people in a group, they each had to give a quarter of the report.

Or else we had to find out what a certain book was about. Later, in the seventh grade, we also had group work. Then we were supposed to read a book each and report on it to the class. But there was never time.

I started playing the mandolin in the afternoons when I was in second grade. I'd really intended to learn to play the guitar, but in a brochure we got at school it said you should start with a mandolin, since your fingers were too small for all the different positions on a guitar.

The Västerås music school arranged the lessons, and a music teacher came once a week. You could rent an instrument for a year and then buy it; you could even buy it after a few months if you wanted to.

First we learned to read music and then to play. When we were a little better we played in parts, first, second, and third. Several kids got fed-up and stopped, because it wasn't very much fun to practise.

Sometimes we gave performances at different places. That was fun. We used to stand on the stage in the auditorium in Skiljebo School or in the cafeteria at Malmaberg School, and a whole lot of parents, relatives, and friends came to listen to us. There used to be other groups too, who played the recorder, violin or piano.

When we learned to play better we performed at Monday gatherings in Folkets Park in the afternoon and at pensioners' and old folks' homes and out on the recreation area at Lövudden.

The audiences were generous with their applause. We used to play Swedish folk tunes and English pieces. Our teacher looked after the money which we got for our performances, and in the spring or early summer when school finished, we got fifteen kronor each. I took part in about twenty performances during three years. After that I started to play the piano.

In mandolin we always played the lesson in a group and if you didn't really know it or you made mistakes, it wouldn't necessarily be noticed. But with the piano you have to play the lesson by yourself, and the teacher notices immediately if you don't know it.

In mandolin you only had to practise a little the day before the lesson. Piano you have to practise every day. I usually practise a little in the afternoon, sometimes half an hour or three-quarters. When you know the pieces, then it's fun to play.

We have to pay seventy-five kronor a semester for my piano lessons. My pal Monika and I go together to play once a week, and we each have to play for twenty minutes. First of all you play what you have for a lesson and if you play it well, then you get a new piece to learn. Otherwise you have to practise the old piece again and a new lesson too. Our piano teacher comes from Germany, but she speaks good Swedish. She's very demanding. It's fun to play and not so terribly rough to learn.

In the fourth grade I had to change schools and go to Gryta, which was surrounded by fields and things like that. It was a couple of kilometres to bike there. The school was old and the teachers' desks were on raised platforms. In modern schools the teachers don't sit any higher than the pupils.

I thought it fun out there – there were just two grades so it wasn't so noisy. In a big school there's always a terrible racket

during the breaks. Naturally there were some boys who were
rowdy in Gryta too. We had the same teacher for all subjects,
except sloid, gym and English.

We had to go to Skiljebo School right in the neighbourhood
for our sloid and gym lessons. It was only girls who did
needlework. In fifth grade I had needlework half the time and
carpentry the other half. You have gym together until seventh
grade and then girls and boys are split up.

I only went to Gryta for a while for then Dad and Mom
changed to a three-room apartment on Skjutbanegatan, so I
started going to Malmaberg School. You weren't allowed to
talk in the cafeteria. There were women especially employed
to watch us, and anybody who spoke had to go out of the room
and wait until all the others had finished eating. After that
they had to go in and eat, and if they didn't come in by themselves, the ones on duty went out to bring them back. When we
came over to Haga School in seventh grade, it was strange to
be able to talk while we ate; you were allowed to there.

The summer before I was due to start fifth grade we went
to Öland on vacation. Mom and Pop had rented a cottage in
Böda by the shore of the Baltic. There were so many tourists
there that the supply of bread ran out and they had to ration it.
You were only allowed to buy a little at a time. I think sugar
was also rationed, but I'm not sure about that.

We got very tan there, but I didn't have any friends. We
lived so far away from things. Kärrbo is a lot better than
Öland, because there I know so many people. My cousin
Margareta, called Maggan, and I usually live with Grandma
during the summer vacation in her cottage or in the trailer
there.

One summer an old man drowned off Aggarö. The police
came with a little square motor pump, and they found him
the same day. We weren't allowed to go down to the pier,
so instead we stood on a rock and watched what went on.
Then we crept down to the shore and hid behind two trees

when a hearse came, but we didn't get to see very much anyway.

In seventh grade we had different teachers in different subjects – eleven different ones. I like English and Swedish best. I don't care for maths or French at all. English is more fun because you've been at it for a longer time and understand more. I don't think drawing is much fun either.

I've always liked gym a lot, and in fourth grade I was in a group which practised in the evenings once a week. Unfortunately so many people came that practically all we did was to mess around and there was no real order. When I was twelve I joined another group which was much better organized. We practised twice a week. We did it for pleasure.

Now I belong to the Västerås Gymnastics' Association and practise three hours a night on Monday, Wednesday and Friday, and on Saturday from two to five. On Thursday I have my piano lessons after seven o'clock, so I'm home only on Tuesday evenings.

There are nine of us in the gymnastics group, plus Yvonne Pernhall and Marie Lundqvist. Marie is a Swedish gym champion and Yvonne is also well-known. They practise mainly by themselves, but sometimes they join us. We have the same leaders – there are several.

In the spring of 1968 I was supposed to take part in the School City Championship and District Championship for juniors. I couldn't because I had a pain in my arm. I fell from the bar during a practice. It hurt terribly and we thought the bone was cracked; I had to go to the hospital to have an X-ray. They said that my arm had been dislocated at the shoulder and then gone back into place. When the School District Championships were held I was O.K. again, so I was able to take part, and I came in third.

I usually play records when I come home from school in the afternoon, mostly rock. But I have no special favourites. Well, anyway I don't like Elvis. The Beatles are neat. Nearly everyone collects records, but they're too expensive. I get a monthly allowance. Sometimes fifteen kronor, sometimes twenty kronor.

I don't go to all the school dances because it's not much fun. Guys have sometimes invited me to go. Girls sometimes pay for guys who are broke.

I read quite a bit, novels as well as detective stories – and books about horses, of course. One book I remember especially was called *Child No. 312* – it was about a refugee child.

I don't know how long I'll stay in school. See, it all depends on what kind of grades you get, and things like that.

Being and Becoming

Rolf Mälberg

I was sick a lot when I was little. I was born with asthma. It was usually at night that I had attacks and then I'd have to fight for breath. I would automatically sit upright, as you can't breathe right if you're lying down.

You don't get scared, but it's nice to have a grown-up around. When I sat up and relaxed I would get relief after about half an hour. When I had an attack I woke Dad with my wheezing and coughing.

He and I lay on the kitchen sofa in our place on Metallgatan. Mom slept in the parlour with my brother Peter, who is five years younger than me. It must have been rough on my parents, getting wakened at night so often.

In those days there wasn't any medicine you could take to relieve the attacks. Nowadays there are sprays that help you get over it in half a minute. I had trouble getting back to sleep again when I was woken by an attack.

Children's illnesses hit me harder than other kids because of my asthma. When I was six years old I nearly died from whooping cough.

You had to control yourself and take things easy. You breathe in the whole time when you have an attack of asthma. It takes so much effort to inhale, you get tired from it. You don't do anything besides breathe.

Everybody told me that the asthma would go away as I grew older, and it did too, gradually. Now it's almost disappeared, though I'm not absolutely dead sure of that. The worst time was before I entered school.

The year before I began school I spent half the day in a nursery school. It was just across the street from where I lived.

There were loads of toys there to play with, and we did some painting too. That's something I still do now and then. We used to like modelling with clay. Sometimes we all went out on walks in a flock. It was fun there.

Most Saturdays and Sundays we would go visit Grandpa and Grandma in Ekeby. Dad and Mom and my little brother still go to see them once a week. Grandpa was a farm-worker in Kärrbo before he became a carpenter at Ekeby, which comes under Skultuna Works. He's retired now.

Dad grew up in Kärrbo and then he worked in a peat-bog and a lumber mill and some other places before he came to Västerås and began work at Asea. Before long he went over to construction work and became a bricklayer. That's what he still is.

My mother comes from the district of Nyland in Finland. They speak Swedish there. She moved to Helsinki before she was twenty, and trained as a children's nurse. Then she came to Täby and Kärrbo, where there was a home for Finnish children. It was at that time that she met Dad.

I thought it fun to begin school and to make new pals. I had been a bit isolated because of my asthma, since I often had to be indoors and was frequently sick. Of course I did have some playmates. It was just that I couldn't be with them as often as they could be with each other.

At school we had an old schoolteacher who would draw flowers in our books if we read well. She drew them in lead pencil. If she drew a whole bouquet, that meant very good. I knew how to read before I started school, because they all tried to teach me a bit at home. My Aunt Vera gave me picture books which had belonged to my cousins. They're a bit older than me.

Korsäng School where I went had two school-yards, one for grades one to five and one for grades six to nine. We all had recess at the same time. The playgrounds were packed with kids, several hundred of us. We had to line up two by two, before we went in again.

The food in the school cafeteria wasn't up to much, just soups and thick, doughy, oven-baked pancakes, for example. They took off pancakes when they found out that they aren't very nutritious. Teachers and kitchen staff stood watching to make sure that we sat there till we ate up all our food.

At the door we boys had to bow and the girls curtsy towards the teachers' table as a *tack för maten* ('thanks for the food'). If someone tried to get out of doing this, there was always a teacher who would dash out after the sinner and lead him or her back in again. It was mostly the older ones who tried to slip by, to show that they dared. Sometimes they were successful.

When I had finished in the first grade, we moved to this one-family house on Ramnäsgatan. It has three rooms and a kitchen, dining room, garage and store-room. At first it was an open garage without a door, but then we laid a floor, put in a door, made the storage-place winter-proof, brought in electricity, and converted it into a carpentry room with a carpenter's bench and things. It's a really neat place to be in.

Here on Ramnäsgatan I made new pals. John, who lives in the house at the end of the street, and I went around together all through school, and we still do. They have a summer cottage on Nybynäs out in Kärrbo.

In second grade I went to a temporary schoolroom in the cellar of a high-rise apartment building. Now it's been turned into a laundry room. Once I and three other boys made some fire-crackers. We screwed a nut onto a bolt and turned it a couple of times, then we put some detonating powder in the nut and then we screwed another bolt onto the other end of the nut until it touched the powder. It went off nice and loud when we threw it in the corridor.

Someone who lived upstairs in the house complained to our

teacher, so we had to stay after school an hour in the afternoon as a punishment. That's the only incident I remember from that year.

In the third grade I went to Malmaberg School. It consists of two buildings which we called the 'sugar box' and the 'banana'. One house is built in the form of an arch and looks like a banana. The third and fourth grades went there. Five and six went in the 'sugar box'. The advanced grades went to Skiljebo School, but there were still about five hundred kids in Malmaberg School.

The teacher in the third grade was named Birgitta Fahlström, and then we had Margit Lundström in fourth, fifth and sixth. We started learning English in fifth grade. The following year they began with it in the fourth grade. We had a special teacher for languages and thought it was a nice change to have a man teacher.

It was fun to learn a foreign language. In those days nobody knew a single word of English; now everybody knows a little bit even before they start school. They learn it from the lyrics of rock tunes and through cowboy films on T.V.

At home we got a T.V. when I was in fourth grade in 1961. There weren't very many foreign programmes to begin with, they were mainly Swedish. Now I only look at T.V. occasionally, but before, I always used to be lolling around in front of the set. Neighbours of ours who didn't have T.V. would come in to look at films on ours sometimes.

Almost every summer we took a trip to Finland to visit Grandma and Grandpa and my cousins. Before the automobile ferries started running we used to have to take the auto on a cargo-ship. They lifted it on board by crane, then we followed by passenger boat to Helsinki, and from there we went on by auto to Nyby outside Borgå, where Grandpa was a teacher. Grandma taught needlework.

Both of Mom's sisters and my four cousins lived there the whole summer every year. The kitchen was gigantic and it needed to be, since there were fourteen of us when we were all assembled.

On rainy days we kids were allowed to stay in and play in the gymnasium and the handicraft studio. Otherwise we were outside. You could swim in a lake a few kilometres away. There was also a stream nearby where we caught a whole bucket of crayfish, which we cooked and ate one year when we were there in late summer.

At Nyby there's quite a lot of forest and peat around and we used to pick a lot of blueberries. Sometimes we drove with Grandpa in the surrounding countryside or to Borgå to shop. It's a rather small town.

In the sixth grade I was made a school patrol. All those whose parents gave them permission to be school patrols wrote their names on pieces of paper. Then they were drawn from a hat. The police went around visiting the schools and arranged the whole thing.

The main reason for being in on this was that you felt big and important when you stood at a crosswalk letting the younger ones cross the street morning and afternoon. In the winter we got sandwiches and milk chocolate in the cafeteria after the morning shift, and the best part of it was that you got out of morning assembly, which was deadly boring.

I was a member of the Police Youth Club. Our meeting place was in one of the wooden houses by the main square, where there was also a café. There were all sorts of games there. But we mostly sat and read magazines which were lying in a large pile there, since we didn't have anything else to do. We messed around some, of course.

There was seldom a policeman there, only a man called Urbi. He came to check up on us and see if we needed anything, now and again. The only organized activity was a study circle in mechanics. I didn't enjoy it much, even though I was interested in automobiles and engines. When I'd finished sixth grade I wasn't a member of the Youth Club any more.

At school I managed to scrape through somehow. The best marks I had were for drawing and woodwork. I've been drawing ever since I was small and occasionally I still do.

When I was in first grade the local newspaper had a contest – there was a picture on the back page which you had to colour. I won first prize and got a story book named *Klas Kälttermus*. Konsum (the co-op organization) had a contest when I was twelve years old. On the lid of their coffee cans there were three different guys symbolizing three sorts of coffee, a Red Indian, a Mexican, and a third, but I don't remember what he looked like.

You were supposed to draw something that had to do with one of the figures, and I drew the Indian when he was picking red coffee berries off a bush. I received a diploma for the drawing.

I went to grades seven, eight and nine in Skiljebo School. We didn't have any permanent classrooms there – we each had a locker for our books. We had special teachers and different classrooms for each subject.

I like sloid, drawing and biology best. And Swedish. In sloid, we were allowed to choose ourselves what we wanted to make, and in the first year, when we had wood-working, I made lamps and wooden figures. In eighth grade I made a tea-cart.

We had a lathe, a band-saw, a drill and a power plane. But we weren't allowed to use that unless it was something large we were making. Then our teacher would help us. Otherwise we planed by hand.

In biology in seventh grade we learned about birds and insects, and I started collecting beetles and butterflies. You catch them with hoop-nets and kill them with some ether which you have on a bit of cotton wool in a jar. A buddy of mine and I used to catch moths up on the ridge at Hälla, where the street lamps outside the cottages are mercury lights.

They're so stupid that they fly right up at the light and get stunned a bit and come spinning down in a spiral, land on the ground and lie there for a few seconds. It was fun to watch the motorists and to see their curiosity about what we were doing there with our nets.

I used to go looking for beetles in the forest under rocks and in old trees. Once when we were up in Dalarna over a weekend in the summer I found a big, beautiful larva which I took home with me.

I thought it would die in my jar, but it transformed into a pupa. In the middle of winter, when there was snow out, a big yellow butterfly crept out of the pupa. It's called a Makaoni and it's quite rare. I let it out in our big room and it fluttered around among the flowers in the window for some days.

That was the start of my butterfly collection. Now I have about eighty, but the first one is the rarest. I gave away my beetle collection to a girl I've known since I was a kid.

I collect postage stamps too. I guess everyone who collects butterflies collects stamps as well. Nowadays I only collect Swedish and Finnish stamps. Mom used to collect the Finnish ones, so I took over her collection. I have seven or eight hundred. To begin with I collected other countries as well, and I have about two or three thousand of these. I didn't collect them systematically, I just went by the various motifs. There are lots of fine, colourful pictures on stamps.

But it's more fun to concentrate on complete series. The Finnish ones always have four sided serrations; Swedish ones vary; they can be two-sided, pairs, and three-sided serrations. Stamp collections are worth money and usually their value rises later.

The catalogues of stamp valuations are quite expensive, eighteen to twenty kronor. My collections are probably worth about 2,000 kronor. I also have about sixty first-day covers. You can order them through a postal account from the Post Office Philately Department in Stockholm and the corresponding organization in Helsinki.

Another hobby of mine is building model boats and airplanes. I began when I was only seven years old, when I got a plastic boat-building kit. When I was twelve I got a wooden model of a fishing vessel to build. It isn't finished yet. I've been working on it now and then since Christmas 1963.

Some parts were pre-cut and others were drawn on plywood sections, which you had to saw out yourself. The frames came ready-made. The outside planking was difficult. You had to measure up and saw off the ribs, and then steam one at a time until it was soft enough to withstand the transverse curve at the stern. The glue had to be daubed on at the same time.

That kind of a job takes patience. It requires precision and it won't do to get irritated. The same thing applies when you're building a sailplane. I joined a club which built airplanes at Skiljebo Municipal Youth Centre when I was twelve.

One whole winter I worked on a plane which had a wing span of two metres. Dad and I rode out to Johannisberg to test it when it was finished. The plane went straight up at first and then it came spinning right down on to the ground. The wings were broken. I had forgotten to put lead shot in the nose in front, in order to make it balance properly.

But I had a smaller plane that did work. Dad had paid for the kit for me. I had weekly pocket money and sometimes I used to get extra money to buy larger things.

When I was thirteen I earned the money I needed myself by selling *Dagens Nyheter* on Sunday mornings. I got about fifteen kronor for the forty copies I sold, though most of it was tips, of course. What I made on the papers alone was not very much, only four öre a copy. I kept it up for three years and then my kid brother took over my route.

When I was fifteen I got a motor-bike. Many of my buddies also had them. We used to whiz along the streets and ride scramble in the forest, on paths and in the mud.

One day I saw on a poster that Hammarby Motor Club arranged trail races in which anybody was welcome to take part. The contest was split up into seven rounds on seven consecutive Saturdays in the forest, by Malma track. That's a scramble track which the club had prepared.

There were about fifteen of us the first time. On Saturdays in bad weather there were fewer. I won on the first Saturday, and came in fifth in the whole contest and was awarded a little cup as a prize. It didn't cost anything to be in the club. The club had arranged the race in order to get new members. But I never joined.

In the gang on our street there were just guys. On the neighbouring street their gang had both guys and girls. We went to the same school and knew them a little. When we were about fourteen we used to go over and get acquainted a little better. Then we became a gang of six guys and four girls.

Mostly we used to go around to each other's houses and play the phonograph or tape-recorder, or read magazines or just talk. We talked mainly about school, naturally, and about our teachers and classmates. Occasionally we'd go for walks in the forest or along the road as far as Badelunda, and walk around there, ten kilometres. Or else we'd hang around on our bikes up on Malmaberg.

We were never down in the city, since there was nothing that interested us there. You only went down if there was something you needed to buy. In the summer we used to bike out to Björnö and swim during the daytime. This was at the end of the summer after everyone had been on vacation. Before this it was almost too cold to swim.

If we went to someone's home, the cottage would be jam-packed. Since those days the gang has grown so big that sometimes as many as eighteen to twenty people can come visiting. On Saturday evenings sometimes the whole band would go to someone's house to see T.V. or to play cards. But we never played for money. The person we visited gave us coffee.

Most kids are confirmed, not because they're Christians but because it's a tradition. I've been confirmed too. In my class there were only three or four who weren't. I don't think that any of those confirmed were believers. It's largely because of the parents and the fact that you're already baptized.

In eighth grade on Monday mornings we had two free periods, so then we went to confirmation classes. They began midway through the fall term and went on until the spring. Nobody took it too seriously. We had a small book which we read, and we sometimes had to do homework but nobody bothered about it, unless the minister said he was going to test us afterwards. There were about twenty in the group.

We also had to go to church at least fifteen times. The minister checked us off in a little book to record that we had been. I only went fourteen times but was confirmed anyway, in spite of this. We rode out to Badelunda Chuch in a special bus and took part in a special service, which was shorter than the regular worship service. We all thought it was long-drawn-out and boring anyway, and I don't think anyone listened to a word. You just sat waiting for it to get over with.

I got presents from my parents and my relatives in Finland and from my cousins when I was confirmed. Mom and Dad and Grandpa and Grandma were there in the church.

We started with Pracvo (practical vocational orientation) when I was in eighth grade, and I practised one and a half weeks in the fall as a decorator at Gulin's and the same amount of time in the spring as a draughtsman at Bygg-Paul.

At Gulin's I had to print and stamp letters on the show cards in the window, and help the window-dressers to hold things. There was variety to it and it was fun. The studio had four employees, two men for Gulin's and one man and one woman for Pepita.

The department I was in at the draughting room at Paul's had two draughtsmen and a desk man. I had my own drawing table and sat tracing over a draught in order to learn how to draw lines. The copying was done in a photocopy machine. The people in the office were kind and told me a lot about things and explained this and that when I asked questions.

Nearly all the girls were out practice-teaching to be elementary school teachers. Sometimes they got a class to work with by themselves. The guys practised a lot of different things. Some were in building firms, learning carpentry, and others were in automobile shops.

We were getting quite grown-up in our last years at grade school, and there was a whole lot of talk about sex. For the most part it was the girls who suggested they'd had a lot of experience, in our class at least. But it was mostly only talk and boasting really. Everybody was pretty romantic actually, the guys as well as the girls.

In ninth grade we had a teacher who gave us vocational guidance. He told us which schools we could continue in after grade school and what kind of education you got there and what you could be afterwards. Which schools you can apply to depends on how your grades are. He also had an office you could go to and chat with him in private and get advice.

They handed around a whole lot of brochures in school to read at home with your parents. I applied to five different schools, Asea's Industrial School, the Vocational School – where I applied for two different lines, partly as draughtsman and partly as window-dresser – Kolbäck's Trade School and Zimmerman Technical School.

The vocational-guidance teacher helped us with our applications. You had to send a copy of your certificate with each application. The answers came some time in the summer. I was accepted by all five schools I had applied to, and chose Zimmerman's. Though it may not be so easy to get a job when you've become a fully qualified engineer, the way things are on the labour market just now. But I hope things will change for the better.

It was a lovely feeling to finish grade school in 1967. In his farewell speech the principal urged us to continue with our studies, but there were quite a few in the class who wouldn't be found dead sitting at a school-desk again.

They wanted to be out earning money. Some started to work even before they'd finished school, as errand-boys in the afternoons. Some of the girls worked at the counters in the cafeterias at the Youth Centres or waitressed or washed dishes. They got used to having money and wanted to earn more as soon as possible. This meant that they didn't have too much time left for studies during the last years, and their school records showed it. But they didn't give a damn. Money was what they thought about most. I guess they didn't think about the future.

What they looked forward to was getting a driver's licence and an automobile. If you go on in school you can't afford that sort of thing. It's also a question of independence. A student is dependent on his parents.

Most kids go on living at home even when they have got a job, it's cheaper that way. Renting a room isn't a solution either because you're even more dependent there than you are at home. I've heard about one or two lucky dogs who've managed to get hold of their own apartment, some old one-room place. But I've never met one of them.

I worked at Vargbo truck-garden for a while when I'd finished grade school. I did this for a month or so, and afterwards we went to Finland on vacation. I had worked there before, on the Christmas vacation and at Easter. My job consisted of delivering flowers. I had my own motor-bike and I got the job by answering an ad.

People telephone to order flowers for friends and relatives for holidays, weddings, and birthdays. The deliveries were paid by the job, one krona per delivery, regardless of distance. It wasn't much. Other places pay 1·50 kronor. The best thing is if someone has a birthday, as then there are usually a lot of flowers ordered to the same place, and payment is one krona per order.

In between deliveries I had to dust the floor and do odd jobs, but I wasn't paid any extra for this. Though I used to earn between thirty to forty kronor a day even when things were bad. One day at Christmas I earned 150 kronor. I usually get tips too, enough to buy gasoline.

Naturally a job like that is a bit monotonous. And it's tiring to run up and down stairs. When I was making deliveries at Christmas it was —20°C. and snowing. You had to bundle yourself up in lots of clothes so as not to freeze to death on the motor-bike. No grown person would accept such a job.

During our vacation in Finland I went to see my cousins in Helsinki and stayed over with them one night. We went to Borgbacken fairground. It's bigger than Gröna Lund in Stockholm and even more expensive, although now it must have become somewhat cheaper after devaluation. Everyone in the booths spoke Finnish, there was no one speaking Swedish anywhere.

In the fall of 1967 we had to begin a week earlier than usual at Zimmerman's because of the switch-over to right-hand traffic, which was introduced at that time. The teachers had a lot of informative material which they were to go through with pupils. Some of them didn't bother because they thought the stuff was stupid.

After the traffic switch-over we had to stand by the street crossings and tell people if they were looking the wrong way. This was the most common mistake. One or two got mad when you told them to look the right way, but nobody was rude. Here and there an automobile was driving around on the wrong side of the traffic circles on the first day. But these were exceptions. On the whole it went smooth as silk.

I'm studying mechanics. In every way, the teachers are harder at Zimmerman's than the ones we had in grade school, at both teaching and discipline. I don't know how many go to Zimmerman's, several hundred probably. There are many technical-school classes and special classes.

We had one girl in a class of twenty the first year I was there. In all of Tech. School, there are only a dozen girls, at the most. I had physics, chemistry, mathematics, including draughting and calculations of materials' resistance; production, that is, the science of engineering and building materials: metals, plastics, and so on; Swedish, oral and written, English, etc.

The written Swedish consists, among other things, of writing reports and learning to write orders to various companies for nuts and screws and so on. As well as compositions. You were required to read books and report on them either orally or in writing. Some of the books I read were Steinbeck's *Cannery Row* and Orwell's *Animal Farm*.

In oral Swedish lessons we sometimes had discussions about politics and world affairs – for example, the war in Vietnam. Personally, I don't know too much about it. I usually skip those pages of the paper where they print things of that kind.

During the discussion periods some people speak for and some against, but that's mainly to get a debate going. When we discussed the American deserters, there were several who wondered why they're allowed to stay in this country while other people who come here from way down in Europe looking for jobs are turned back at the border. Is that fair?

Not all the pupils are young at Zimmerman's (or the Upper Technical School, as it's also called). Some of them are between thirty and forty years old, people who have worked before and who have cars and everything. Eventually they've realized that they ought to get themselves some education. Their wives work and support them during the time they're studying, and they also get scholarships.

There's better discipline in the class with older students. The younger ones stop playing around so they don't make fools of themselves in front of the older people. The old ones have more experience and manage maths and Swedish better than we younger ones. They have a harder time getting through

English, and in general they have more difficulty keeping up in the other subjects, but they study harder in the evenings.

By and large the teachers are good – still some of them have trouble presenting different things so that you understand what it's all about. These types are not popular, because you have to try to grapple with the subject yourself by cramming at home at night. It's pretty difficult. Some points you just can't figure out by yourself, and this leaves holes in your learning. We do have the right to complain to the principal, but nobody does.

On the last Saturday in April 1968, I went along as map-reader on a cross-country rally. My buddy Affe entered his car in the competition. We'd decided upon it before he bought it. He's studying to be an electrician at Zimmerman's, and during the apprentice year he earned such good money that he could buy a car. Now he's back studying for a year again and after this he'll do his military service, so perhaps he'll have to de-register his car until further notice.

Eighty automobiles started in the race, and out of those, seventy were beginners like us. The track followed gravel roads only, and there were time-checks and a lot of signs on the sides of the roads with numbers, which the driver had to make note of and tell the map-reader to fill in on a special card. The one who reads the map never has a chance to look at the road himself.

Affe drove past a board he didn't have time to see the number on. He put on the brakes and backed up the auto. It was pitch dark and the car had no back light, there was a bend in the road, and Affe landed in the ditch. Four other competing autos stopped and the guys in them lifted our jalopy out of the ditch.

We got so many minus points that we were out of it, but it wasn't just because of the loss of time in the ditch. Quite a lot of the others were also disqualified. The stretch we drove was ninety kilometres. The entry fee was twenty-five kronor and the contest licence was five kronor per auto. Even though we got wiped out, it was fun anyway.

Now, during the second year of my training as engineer, I'm practising at Asea. I've been looking forward to my practice year, since I've never worked at a real job before. And it's nice to earn a bit of money.

The minimum wage is twenty kronor a day the first month, and then at least thirty kronor after that. But on piecework one can earn more, and I make about fifty kronor a day.

Last summer I also earned some change on a job delivering newspapers, which I took over from a pal when he was away on vacation for two weeks. I delivered the local paper in the summer cottage section on Fullerö.

It was pretty difficult since many of them don't have a number on their shacks, and in several places the road signs are missing. A few of them don't even have a mailbox. The newspapers arrive out there at around three a.m. and are supposed to be delivered before six a.m. I left home at around three-thirty a.m. to be there in good time. It took twenty minutes to get there on the motor-bike.

They dropped off the pile of newspapers outside the store. The pay was twenty-five kronor per morning for the deliveries or 150 kronor a week. The local paper doesn't come out on Sundays. When it rains it's no fun at all on that job.

Before this I'd tried to get hold of a somewhat more permanent job, but it was hopeless. There were practically *no* summer jobs for students. I tried at the post office. Nix. The park administration because I'd like to have driven a power lawn-mover. Nope. They only took five people.

I had trouble with my motor-bike too, and it cost a lot of money. The day before I finished school, a piston ring cracked and damaged the cylinder. A new cylinder cost 105 kronor and the piston twenty kronor. But a bit had fallen down into the crankcase, so the new piston cracked and had to be changed again. Luckily the cylinder was O.K. The whole business cost

145 kronor. I repaired it myself, otherwise it would have been much more expensive.

Shortly before this I had changed tyres, both back and front and a tube. This cost sixty kronor. The tax is ten kronor a year, and the insurance went up from twenty-seven kronor to forty-nine kronor in a year. This was because so many motor-bikes are stolen and there are so many insurance swindles that the insurance companies were obliged to raise the premiums. So it's expensive to own a motor-bike, all right.

I spend most of my time with the gang on our block here and some of it with other buddies who live here and there around the city. We usually just sit and talk. Sometimes I go to dances on Saturdays, though not often. In the summer there's only the Park to go to and it's not up to much there. But naturally you go to a dance when there's some special occasion, like the first of May and Midsummer.

When I've finished my year of practice I'll go back to Zimmerman's for another year to finish. They've started with a five-day week there, like all the other schools. I think it's stupid. You have to stay longer on the other days instead, to make up for the hours on Saturday. The school day was already long and tiring enough before, and now it's even longer.

After that I have my year of military service to do. And then it remains to be seen whether there'll be any jobs. The type of engineering I'm studying is relatively new and untried. The first-year class graduated in 1967.

I hope I'll get fixed up with a job all right. The profession is a good one and you get pretty high pay after you've been work-ing a few years. I'd prefer to stay here in Västerås, but I may have changed my mind by the time I've finished military service.

We Didn't Call Ourselves Anything

Viola Nehrén

Hardly anybody calls me Viola, they usually just say Lola. I was born at Lindö in Kärrbo where Dad was a farm-worker at that time.

There are four of us, all girls. My eldest sister was born in 1940. I'm the youngest and was born in 1949. The others are all married. One lives in Hälsingborg, one in Märsta and the next youngest out in Råby here in Västerås.

Mom comes from Solbacken in Kärrbo and Dad from Romfartuna, but he grew up at Vallatorp in Kärrbo.

At Lindö we lived in the shack located between the road to Springsta and the one leading to the lake. There was a hall when you came in and then a large kitchen and a parlour and upstairs there were two rooms – it was a fine place.

Dad and Mom slept in one of the upstairs rooms and we kids in the other, all four of us. Though Birgit, who is the eldest among us, left home before I started school, when she was only fourteen.

I stayed outside playing all day long, mostly with boys. There weren't any little girls out there in those days, so I hung around with three guys, Bosse, Brage, and Bjarne. Kent from Nyby was often with us, he used to bike over Gammelgårds-backen.

We were real terrors, according to my parents, making a lot of mischief and doing things we weren't allowed to do. We were forbidden to be in the barn and on top of the wagon shed, but that's where we used to be mainly. Often we used to get chased away.

The reason we weren't allowed to be there was because there was a whole lot of machinery and things we could easily have hurt ourselves on. Another reason was that my eldest sister and some kids the same age had played with matches and candles once behind a haystack outside the barn. The stack caught fire and burned down. Luckily the barn was all right. If that had caught fire too, then the cowshed would also have burned down, since it was attached to the barn.

Dad tried to frighten us by saying that there were lynxes down there, but we didn't believe him.

We had built a hut in the straw. One day we heard a terrible caterwauling: Uuuu-u-u-uhu-uuu! then a heavy thud like some big animal jumping from under the roof and down into the straw-bin.

We were so afraid then that we started crying and ran away from that place so fast everything went hazy before your eyes. After that we were so scared of the barn that we didn't even dare go near it. Not until a long time afterwards did Dad tell us he was the one who had frightened us.

I remember once when we chased the pig. He was in a little pen and we beat him with birch branches and then we poured cold water over him. The pig shrieked so that you could hear it from miles around, mostly because he was scared, I guess.

Another thing I remember is coming in one day and having to pee. We didn't have an outside john, there was an inside toilet, and one of my sisters was already sitting there so it was occupied. I went out into the kitchen and did a trickle on each chair. I did it out of sheer defiance, just to be mean. Mom got so angry that she beat me seven times. First she spanked me out in the kitchen and afterwards she carried me out into the hall where I got another dusting, and so it went on up the stairs.

On holidays we always had a lot of visitors, every single Christmas and every Easter, Whitsun and Midsummer. My Uncle Börje and my aunt from Stockholm and my Cousin Maggan, who was my age, came every Eastertime. Other relatives and acquaintances came too. The ones from Västerås used to visit on ordinary Saturdays and Sundays.

We were always pleased to have visitors. They used to bring a lot of goodies with them for us, and your parents were much nicer and didn't say anything when you made a lot of noise. On summer Sundays they took us with them down to the lake and swam and rowed out in the old boat that Dad owned.

We never used to go away ourselves. I don't remember ever visiting anybody, other than when we went by bus to the city some Saturdays to shop. It was always the other people who came to us.

Mom used to go to the Ral's at the big house at Lindö to clean for them one day a week to earn a little extra. She used to sew most of our clothes herself. It was too expensive buying ready-made ones. Since I was the youngest I nearly always used to have old dresses and shoes handed down from my sisters. I sulked sometimes, but I didn't care to protest openly by refusing to put on made-over clothes.

If I did do that Mom got angry, she had quite a hot temper. Dad was kinder, but I was the youngest, too, and his favourite. Many times it was an advantage to be the littlest, though it could be irritating too, for example in the evenings when the others were allowed to stay out and *I* had to go to bed.

Sometimes Dad let us come with him while he worked. Lindö is a big farm, the biggest in Kärrbo. The farmland there must come to around 420 acres. Ral had a truck that Dad drove.

Sometimes we rode along with him, on the back on the way out and on top of the load on the way back. We could sit in the cab too if we wanted, but it was more exciting to ride on the back. Now and then we got to ride into town with Dad when he drove grain to Arosbygden. And then we had to sit in the cab.

In wintertime Dad took care of the horses and then I went with him and Solveig, who is three years older than me, to the stall in the evening when he fed and watered them and put clean straw under them for the night. There were only two horses and one of them was called Julle. Now they have no draught horses at all at Lindö and nowhere else in all of Kärrbo either, only tractors. There are only one or two horses for pleasure.

I started school when I was six years old. I don't know why I was supposed to begin a year earlier than other kids – it was probably my parents' idea.

One spring day I was sent to Orresta School to be tested to see whether or not I was ready for school. I went along with Anita Bergström who was in the upper grades at Kungsåra then. First we rode on the school bus to Irsta and from there we took another school bus to Kungsåra, and then I had to ride alone on another Volkswagen bus to Orresta. The driver showed me which bus went there.

There were several six-year-olds who were going to be tested. We were given printed papers which had a house and a chimney with smoke coming out of it and a flagpole. We had to draw a flag onto this and they told us to think about drawing it in the right direction. I managed that O.K. I've forgotten what else we had to do.

In the fall I started with Miss Kant in the elementary school by Kärrbo Church. It's been closed down now. There were only two of us in the first grade and four in the second, so Miss Kant had only six pupils to teach. I liked her, she was so nice.

I had trouble learning to read and then to spell when it came to writing. My teacher used to sit with me and go through things over and over; I think she got quite fed-up with me because she couldn't get anything into my head. Maybe she thought that I didn't do my homework, but I did. I used to sit and study every evening at home, but it didn't help.

When I had to read aloud in class I was petrified and felt ashamed in front of the others because I couldn't read. I didn't want to but I didn't dare refuse either, so I sat there struggling with the words.

After a bit Kanty realized that it wasn't because I was lazy or stubborn that it went badly. She started sitting with me in the classroom during recess a few times and then it went more easily, when the others weren't there to listen.

Arithmetic, on the other hand, was easy as anything, I thought it was the most fun, even better than drawing. Every Saturday we had an enjoyable hour when she read us stories. There was always a piece of candy lying inside our desks then. See if the chicken has laid anything in your desk, she'd say.

In the winter my classmate Mona Vidlund used to board with us. Her dad was a fisherman on Aggarö and she couldn't get home when the lake had frozen over. I went to visit her once in the summer. It was beautiful out there on the island – their cottage was on top of a hill and there was a path leading down to the pier.

If there was snow we would go by sled to school, otherwise we rode our bikes. We ate in the school cafeteria up in the community centre, both seniors and juniors. At Christmas we all had to buy a present for about a krona; we put them all in a pile and then exchanged.

At home we had a real Christmas celebration. There was always a very special feeling at Christmases. One year I got a pair of skis as a present and another time it was skates, expensive things you were awfully glad to get. We also used to get presents from relatives who came to see us and from neighbours' kids.

A Christmas brownie always came to distribute presents after we'd finished eating and washing the dishes. I believed in the Christmas brownie. Sometimes several of them came, and I was almost scared out of my wits. Our neighbours were always playing pranks on Christmas Eve, and they would send a brownie over with a sugar-cake or something else good to eat.

The stork, on the other hand, was never mentioned in our

house. We knew all about how things worked. (Say, I saw a joke in a magazine about a boy who said yes when his teacher asked him if he believed in the stork. 'Why?' she asked. 'Well, Pa's been in jail for five years and I've had three more brothers and sisters during that time.')

In second grade things were more or less the same as in the first, and when I started third grade, we moved to the city. Dad and Mom had talked about it beforehand, and I thought it would be quite fun. But when we were about to set off I started crying and didn't want to move away from Lindö for the whole world.

One evening before we moved we were invited down to the Ral's, all of us. Solveig and I and Kerstin were given hot chocolate with whipped cream and rolls, and the grown-ups drank coffee and talked.

Yngve, whom my eldest sister was engaged to then, borrowed a truck from his job and helped us move. He and Birgit got engaged when she was only fifteen and she had Tord when she was sixteen. That's pretty rough, and it didn't last either. Yngve was a bit older, eighteen or nineteen.

I remember when she came home with Tord and showed him to us. I thought how grown-up she was, though I don't think Mom and Dad did. They weren't very pleased about it. Birgit and Yngve lived in a one-room apartment on Allégatan, and stayed together for several years and had another son, Tony, before they separated.

Birgit managed Tord and Tony on her own after that. She's not the type that gives in. She's married to a guy now who neither smokes nor drinks.

Our first apartment in the city was on Allégatan. Dad was janitor there. It was because Dad took this job that we got the apartment. It was semi-modernized, with an indoor toilet and two rooms and a kitchen. We were the only ones in the whole block who had an indoor toilet.

Dad worked at Asea for five weeks, but he didn't like it so he quit. There were too many foreigners there, he said. I don't get on with Italians and Spaniards and that sort either. When you're out dancing, they're always hanging around you like leeches. If it's got to be, then let it be a Swede or a Norwegian. They're not so greasy.

A lot of kids who were curious stood and watched us when we were moving in. Then in the evening they stood and waited for us to come and play, me and Solveig. We were extremely popular to begin with. They were curious to see what we were like and what kind of things we played, since we were straight from the country.

We knew Bertil Ullberg, a guy who lived next door. They rented a summer place at Gryta in Kärrbo.

Soon after we had moved to the city I was swinging with a boy one day and I swung too high. The swing turned over the top and I knocked out my front teeth on a post. I started to lisp because of that and had to go to a speech therapist for an hour every week.

The school in town was great fun. You made a lot of friends. There were about thirty of us in my class (third grade). But I was still as bad at reading and spelling there as I was in Kärrbo.

When Dad quit at Asea he began a job at the Power Administration's warehouse. He's still there and doesn't want to change. When he had been there a while he bought a second-hand auto. The registration number, I remember, was U 30508. So we often used to drive to Lindö and visit on Sundays. It was fun to see our old chums again. Of course we were probably a bit stuck-up too, coming from the city.

When I was in fourth grade I surprised my sister Kerstin once when she was smoking in secret. So I wouldn't tell on her, she got me to smoke too. She was fifteen and I was nine years old. Then we went on smoking, and there were several kids there in our backyard smoking in secret.

If you'd begged or been given a twenty-five öre to buy candy with, you bought two cigarettes instead. If Dad had only known!

In his opinion I shouldn't have started smoking before I was sixteen.

Almost everybody smoked at school. It was forbidden, of course, we had to do it outside the schoolyard. At lunch break there was always a gang of us guys and girls who went with a girl named Sonja to her basement just across the street and stood there smoking.

There were certainly some teachers who knew about our smoking in secret, but nobody ever said anything.

I preferred gym to all other subjects. I qualified in several school contests and often took part in running, swimming, and handball.

When I was in ninth grade there were only a few of the girls who took part in gym. There was a gang of us who went around together. The others were weedy, 'anaemic' types who gave all sorts of excuses to get out of gym, like they had a period or a stomach-ache or a headache. But the real reason was that they didn't want to get sweaty or get their hair tousled.

The year after we moved to town we changed to this apartment in the Haga district. But there was no room for me in the school up here, so I had to stay in Herrgärde School in fourth and fifth and sixth grades, and I had to commute by bus.

The summer I was twelve I went to a summer family home for children in the province of Blekinge. You could apply for this through school, and I applied for a place with the grandparents of my girl friend Vivan. They'd had vacation kids during previous summers as well. The school paid people who took kids from the city over the summer. The parents had to contribute a part of the costs to the school authorities, the rest was paid by municipal authorities.

Vivan and I travelled down alone together. It took the whole day and we had to change trains three times. Her grandparents lived a little way outside Karlshamn and had big strawberry fields.

We helped pick strawberries all the time. You had to start at seven in the morning. We got fifteen öre per litre for what we picked. When they went in to the market-place to sell strawberries, we killed a lot of time, of course. But anyway we picked enough to earn 300 kronor each that summer.

When we weren't picking strawberries we were weeding. We were on our hands and knees all day long in the fields. We got awfully tan, at least. Grandma was strict, but nice too. We got good food. I called them Grandma and Grandpa just like Vivan did. In the evenings we always used to go down to a little lake nearby and fish. There were a whole lot of tench fish there in the lake which Grandma fixed to eat. Grandpa was swell. He was crippled and couldn't bend down easily, so he couldn't pick any strawberries himself.

When we had been there half the summer I got a letter from my sister Solveig saying that Mom and Dad were going to separate. I started howling as I sat up in my room reading the letter.

Grandma came up, but I didn't tell her why I was crying. Then Grandpa came up and I told him about it. He said I could stay there with them if I wanted. A bit later Dad wrote and said he wanted me to come home.

Mom had moved away by then and rented a room on Knutsgatan. Solveig lived with her. She's three years older than me. Kerstin, who is six years older, lived with Dad and me, but she got married the next year and moved away from home.

They split up the furniture and linens and the household things. Mom got the refrigerator and the kitchen furniture; we kept the parlour furniture. They had a lawyer too. Dad didn't have to pay any support. After all, he was looking after me. Mom worked at the hospital where she'd been for several years.

Before Kerstin got married she was housewife and did the cooking and cleaning for us. *I* went to school, but I didn't like it too much there. I've never liked school really. I wanted to start working and earn some money. Afterwards, you regret that you didn't go on studying after grade school.

I went to see Mom now and again. She didn't say much and didn't ever talk about the divorce. And I never asked, either Dad or her. Naturally I was upset and got depressed and thought it would have been better if Dad and Mom had stayed together, but there was absolutely nothing I could do or say that would help matters, so I kept my mouth shut.

I started going out in the evening, not because of the divorce but because I was at that age. Dad and I have always got on well together. I had to be home by nine to nine-thirty p.m. and I was, too, for the most part. If I was late I got bawled out a little and then things would be fine again.

You told guys you were sixteen, you always add on a couple of years when you're that age. Often you rode along with guys on the back of their motor-cycles.

A gang of us used to meet down here by the Cross, which was the pedestrian underpass underneath the railway through to Emaus School. There were about fifty guys and girls. They didn't all have motor-cycles. They wrote in the newspaper that there were a hundred of us.

Sometimes the police used to come. Folks complained about the noise we made with motor-cycles and motor-bikes. Some times we swiped apples in the gardens of the houses. Some people chased after us like crazy or called the cops. I managed never to get caught or have my name taken.

In the local newspaper they called us the Haga Gang; we didn't call ourselves anything. Sometimes some of us would camp out on Johannisberg. The camping place out there on Joberg was called Lövudden. Lasse, who I went around with, had a big motor-cycle. He was eighteen. When he found out I was only thirteen, we broke up. Though we did go on seeing each other for a while after that.

He got hold of a car in the fall and went around with some other guys downtown. I wasn't allowed to be out that late at night. When we went together we mostly used to drive out to Hökasen for a bite and a cup of coffee or we went to Joberg.

Sometimes we went around to a guy who had his own apartment, one room and a cooking alcove. His parents lived upstairs.

I didn't sleep with Lasse. I was a virgin until I was seventeen. That way you could trust guys, if you told them to lay off, they respected that. They weren't the sort who would just walk right over you.

The other girls in the smaller gang were young as I was, except for one who was fifteen. She slept around a bit. My pal Jannicka's Mom was strict and kept a tight hold on her. She was eighteen before she slept with somebody for the first time. Her dad is Russian. He went back to Russia and the family was supposed to have followed after, but it didn't work out. She'll become a Swedish citizen when she's twenty-one.

When Lasse and I were at this guy's place, the one with the apartment – his name was Janne – we used to eat and drink and play records, mainly Elvis. He and Cliff are still my idols.

I was thirteen when I was at my first movie 'for mature audiences only'. It was called *Mother-of-Pearl*, a Swedish film with Sigge Fürst. I don't remember who else was in it. It was a risqué film – sexy. . . . It was about a poor chick and a rich guy who couldn't get together because of the guy's parents. 'Course they did anyway.

The guy's parents owned the property, and when he was away they evicted the chick and her family from their apartment. So they never saw each other again.

The scenes where they were in bed weren't really so daring. Though I must say it was a bit exciting, and a little ridiculous too. When we came out of the theatre I walked along sniggering because I was a little embarrassed.

'That's nothing to laugh about is it?' Lasse hissed at me. He took the movie seriously. It was a bit tragic and all. Lasse had been in an accident with his car and his right leg was in a cast at the time.

He and I did some petting, of course, but he was the nicest guy in the world. I didn't want to go all the way, I didn't dare either. He's still unmarried and we meet now and then. He's got a kid now by a chick, and he pays for the kid. They're not together, though.

In the big gang all that went on was petting, kissing, and hugging. Roughly half of them went steady with each other, the others switched around. Near The Cross there was a grove of trees with a clearing in the middle. We used to carry wooden benches from the playground nearby, put them in a circle and sit on them and pet a little and so on.

We never took the seats back when we'd finished. Of course we trampled down a lot of the flower beds. The lawn got shot to hell. The guys drove in on their motor-bikes and motor-cycles. Anyway, we didn't have any transistor radios, but of course it was noisy all the same.

The cops came several times. We could usually see their cars because of the searchlights, and then we took off. But once four or five cops crept up on us from different directions and blocked the pathways which led into the grove, and took as many kids as they could and wrote down their names and addresses. The majority managed to get away. I did too. We went there again the next night anyway.

The reason we congregated there was because we didn't have anywhere else to be. Here at home we were never allowed to be in the corridors or in the backyards of the apartment building. Down there we had a little more privacy from the buildings.

Later on we changed to another place here, behind a hill on the slope up to the railway. We weren't allowed to be there either. The police drove us away. Folks who rode their bikes took a detour and were scared to death of us. We didn't think we were hurting anybody. And we didn't, either.

The nearest meeting place that there was to go to then was Gideonsberg centre. It is a youth centre. It was quite a way away from here. But they never wrote anything about *that* in the local paper. All they said was that we destroyed grass and made a lot of noise.

There was also another gang which had slightly older guys around twenty to twenty-one. They were called the Haga League. They called us the Haga Gang. They did some house-breaking and things like that. We never did. We never went around with them.

We really didn't do much in our gang, we just hung around together. Everyone was welcome, nobody got pushed out. We didn't want to stick around home. It was no fun to sit indoors in the evenings when it was summer.

The gang stayed together all through the autumn, up to the time they dressed the store windows for Christmas. Then we walked all the way downtown together, forty-eight of us. We counted ourselves.

People backed off when we came along, and crossed over to the other side of the street.

Among ourselves we laughed at them and made a ruckus. But we never accosted a single person, not old people, either, not then or earlier. It's disgusting when gangs are cruel to old people.

Everybody in our gang was poor. What money we had went for cigarettes. I didn't have any steady pocket money but I got some when I dared to ask for it – then I usually got enough for a packet of ten cigarettes. I guess Dad knew that I smoked.

Jannicka was allowed to start at home. Her Mom discovered that her fingertips were yellowed, so she decided that it was better she be allowed to smoke indoors rather than run around the streets doing it there – it looked so shabby, in her opinion.

When it got cold in the winter, they disappeared, one by one, and soon the whole gang had broken up. In January I was fourteen. I was sick of school, like most of them. I wasn't in the academic curriculum at school, I was in the vocational one – we called it the practical programme, P-programme. In eighth and ninth grade we had more practical subjects than academic ones. In seventh grade we had academic subjects plus cooking and sloid.

We had cooking on Monday, Tuesday, and Wednesday mornings in ninth grade. There were only girls. The guys had metal-craft and mechanics and that kind of thing. We made food from things we brought from home and we baked and cooked and took what we made home. The teacher checked to see that we did things the right way.

There were four ovens there and we were divided into four groups; each group represented a household. Everyone had various jobs to do within the group each time. For example, we were supposed to bring dirty washing from home to wash by hand or in a machine and mangle and iron it.

Some girls didn't want to drag along a whole lot of filthy clothing from home, so they said they didn't have anything to wash. They had to do washing for the school instead. We had to wash the school teachers' clothes and their men's shirts as well.

On Wednesday afternoons we had home economics. In it we learned about vitamins and calories, nutritious and non-nutritious food, and we also had to calculate how much a meal would cost per head.

We learned to be little housewives. It was a great help to me in looking after everything at home. Though Dad has really been tops and helped me with the work and things at home, I had to do most of it because I got home earlier than he did in the evenings. He always wrote a list of the things we needed and I said what I wanted. We always discussed what we were going to buy.

On Thursday and Friday mornings we had ordinary academic subjects, history, geography, maths, Swedish, biology and chemistry. It was the same on Saturdays. Then we had Christianity too. I studied English only in fifth, sixth, and seventh grades. In eighth we could drop English if we wanted, and I did, because I hated it at school. It was the same with Swedish, I had so much trouble with it.

In the afternoon on Thursday we had child-care. We had a

doll that we had to bathe and dress and weigh and we learned how to pick it up and how to lay a baby down and all kinds of things. That was fun. On Friday afternoon we had weaving.

The guys had the same class hours as we had. When they had practical lessons they went to a special workshop school. None of the girls went to the guys' courses, but my sister Solveig did, actually. She was the only girl among a whole crew of guys. Of course, she became a housewife afterwards anyway. In a parallel class in our school, there was one guy who took cooking with all the girls.

At home I always got up when Dad went to work. I didn't dare go back to sleep, because I turned off the alarm clock in my sleep. Dad always gets up terribly early, sometimes as early as around four. Then he sits down and reads the local paper before he goes to work. He usually goes to bed around nine p.m.

If he's away any time I wake myself up quite early, maybe a couple of hours too early. That's because I get tense and don't dare go back to sleep either.

Dad used to make some tea and set the table. All I had to do was sit down and eat when he had gone. So I certainly had it pretty good. Then I would go and comb my hair and put on my make-up right up until it was time to go to school.

I hardly had time to do a thing at home in the mornings. So when I got home in the afternoon I cleared up and got things out of the way, washed the dishes, ironed and so on. Sis took care of the big wash. She lived in an apartment without modern conveniences, so she came to us, to our laundry room in the cellar to wash her things, and did ours at the same time.

In August 1964, I started at a hat factory as an apprentice milliner. It was a course that the trade school had set up. We got 2.50 kronor per hour plus piecework, though that was rare. We got mostly just hourly pay.

The factory is situated right opposite the Power Administration's warehouse where Dad works, so I was able to ride with him every morning. We both started at seven. He finished at four-thirty, and I finished at quarter to five, so he used to wait a quarter hour for me. On the way home we did our shopping.

I liked my job, but not the department supervisor, who was our teacher as well, an old maid. She was strict. We weren't allowed to talk when we worked, and she kept her eye on the clock when you went to the toilet.

Nobody liked her. She drove one girl out after only three hours because she talked back. One girl had to leave after a day and a half because she couldn't sew a trimming onto a hat.

'You're incompetent as a milliner – you'll never learn if you can't do something as simple as sewing a trimming on a hat,' the old bag told her.

There were seventeen of us who began the course. One after another quit because she was so horrible towards us. When the course was over after twenty-three weeks, there were only three girls left.

In the mornings we had a quarter-of-an-hour coffee-break and then a half hour for lunch. You could order individual portions of ready-cooked food from the meat co-op. The food cost three kronor and came in aluminium containers that could be warmed up in the oven. I used to take food with me from home. You brought your coffee in a thermos.

There were a lot of people working at the hat factory. On the bottom floor there was a training workshop for invalids, but they didn't have anything to do with us. The cap factory upstairs belonged to the hat factory, and there they sewed leather caps and sport caps with bills and so on.

We made felt hats. In the course we were busy mostly with trimmings, but we also learned to make ladies' hats from start to finish. They look like a funnel in the beginning. Then, using steam, you pull them down into form on blocks and shape them. If there was a brim on them, you had to pin it on before the hat was put into a drying cupboard.

It's fun doing things like that. After the course was over in the winter, I stayed on until the July vacation. Then there was a fuss about vacation pay for the period we three had been in the course, but we were members of the labour union, so they saw to it that we got what we should have.

I've belonged to a labour union all the time; so has Dad. Nearly everyone does. As soon as we'd begun at the hat factory, a woman who worked there came to talk with us and we all signed up. She was on the union board.

I didn't go to any union meeting, either then or later. I never get around to it. You just pay your dues, and that's all, as long as there isn't any trouble, but there seldom is any.

After the course was finished, I earned 885 kronor a month. Less than five kronor per hour.

Towards summer we used to drive out to Kärrbo quite often and stay with Granny in Valla, in the shack beside the store. It's closed now. Granny lives out there in the summertime. She lives in the city in the wintertime. My girl friend Jannicka always came with us.

We drove down to Lindö Pier to swim and sunbathe. On Saturday evenings we used to hitch to town and then back at night or on Sunday morning. We'd go to the Park or Björnö for a dance, or to Joberg where a lot of our buddies had tents. What a life we led sometimes, hooting and hollering, kicking up a storm and having a lot of fun.

I don't remember which guys I was going around with then, there was nobody special. Some of them had automobiles and we'd drive out toward Fullerö or Irsta. In those days the girls didn't help pay for the gasoline like they do nowadays.

If I've got into an automobile and the guy asks me if I want to go to such or such a place, and then asks me if I've got 'some money for juice' on me, I just wouldn't dream of going along. In that case you just get out again. It's something else again if you've agreed beforehand to drive somewhere together, then you can share the costs.

When it comes to admission tickets, each person pays his own way these days. It's rare to find the guys offering to pay for you. You can't go out stone-broke and expect to be treated. That's only fair: the guys haven't got any more to get along on than the girls have, really.

After my vacation in 1965, I started in the grocery store nearby where we used to do our shopping. The owner had heard a rumour that I wasn't too happy at the hat factory. So he asked me one day when I was in buying something if I would be interested in working in a store.

'I'll think about it,' I said. They don't have Saturdays off in a store, but I thought to myself that those hours would soon pass – though I've bitterly regretted that afterwards.

It was before vacation time, and I said that I wouldn't start unless I'd had a vacation first. I also demanded the same wages I had been getting at the hat factory. He told me that was over the standard contract, but anyway he eventually agreed to my demand. I gave notice to quit only three days before the vacation, but I was allowed to finish at the hat factory in spite of everything and didn't have to go back after the vacation. Two weeks' notice was required, according to the standard agreement.

My new job was nice and close to home. One soon got the hang of things in a store. It's not too difficult. I didn't feel embarrassed, since most of the customers knew me and knew that I was a beginner. It would have been harder in a completely strange place. I didn't even have to learn the customers' names here, since I already knew most of them.

It was not entirely a good thing that my job was so close. Many of the customers who lived around here began poking their noses into my private affairs; 'So you came home at such and such a time, in an automobile, such and such a model, with fellows who looked thus and so, and you were wearing that and that!'

There was always somebody who'd seen me, no matter what time of night it was I'd come home. And you couldn't tell them to go to hell either, when they started in with their little digs. You just can't do that when you work in a store.

Some of them are so curious they make you want to scream. If they think they're being youthful and are trying to get on my good side by keeping check on all I do, then they're mistaken.

I would never have dreamed of telling the world about this or that customer's financial problems. But they think they can do whatever they like to a *young* person.

There were some folks who had to ask you to put things on the cuff before every payday. Although most of them were very reliable and paid up as soon as they got their money, one or two moved away without paying what they owed the store. But it was only about a hundred kronor at the most we lost.

It sometimes happened that you made a mistake on the cash register, however, more often than not it turned out to be the customer who was at fault. One woman called up once, for example, and said that I'd rung up two cartons of cream too many. A couple of days later she called again to say that she'd found her cream in the broom closet. Her grandchildren had helped her unpack her groceries, and they were the ones who had put the cream in the closet.

Another person called down and claimed that a package of crispbread had been put on the bill without her having got the package. The next day she found it in the refrigerator. The worst thing was when they called up and complained, but didn't call back to say when they'd found their things. In those cases it was the people at the cash registers who got hell for it.

There were five of us in the store when I started. There was me and Evy, who started the same time as me, and a woman called Johansson who worked extra on Saturdays, and Sven and Gudrun – they owned the store. They were always there themselves the whole day.

Then a guy called Christer came. He worked as an extra on the meat counter on Saturdays. He had first worked there before

I started, and then he became a travelling salesman for half a year. After that he came back to the store and worked full-time for several months, and then he got a job driving one of the Dala-Baker's bread trucks.

I used to get up at six-thirty a.m. when Dad went to work. When I was at the hat factory I got up at about five or four-thirty a.m. The store was closed for lunch from twelve-thirty to two p.m., and then I used to go home to eat and read newspapers. I often used to borrow some of the weeklies we sold at the store, had a look at them and then took them back again. It didn't matter so long as you didn't mark or stain them in any way. I usually took home a whole pile with me over the weekend.

During that fall, I started going to gym classes in Korsäng School. The leader worked us hard. At the start I had such terrible muscular pains and was so stiff that I couldn't get out of bed the usual way – I had to roll myself out in the mornings. You got such a pain in the midriff that you didn't dare cough or laugh.

When you were fully conditioned, then it was nice. We had both free-standing gymnastics and workouts on exercise equipment. I think the equipment is much more fun. There were older women there who had been doing gymnastics for many years, they were terribly good at it. I had to rush like mad in order to get there on time. Gym began at seven-thirty p.m. on Tuesdays and Thursdays and I didn't finish work until six-thirty, and then I had to eat and get ready.

Jannicka and my eldest sister went along too, but they gave up after less than a semester. I kept up with it until I was eighteen, when it was time to take my driving test. Then I had to give it up since I had theory lessons in the evening, and I didn't get around to starting again. The fees for gym were only twenty kronor a semester.

The preceding fall, when I was seventeen, I used to go with a friend of mine sometimes to the 'Profile House', which is an apartment building owned by the Metal Works for single girls and guys to live in. Everyone has a room with a cooking-cabinet, toilet and bathroom.

I met a guy there whom I hadn't known very long. One evening it happened. I was wild about him to begin with. I don't know whether he was in love with me. Afterwards I detested him and didn't want to have anything to do with him.

Six months later I met another guy. He came from Östersund. It was quite different with him. Why, I don't know. I guess I must have liked him better.

We went steady for eight or nine months. I just don't know how we got by. Neither of us used any protection.

Nowadays most girls use the Pill. That's what they usually say, I've been to the doctor to get a supply of pills. The guys seldom take precautions, they don't care about what happens. They must figure it's up to the girl to bear the consequences.

Several girls I know have had abortions. Some of the girls downtown sleep with just anybody and it's their own fault if they get knocked up.

One of the girls went around saying that a certain guy – she gave his name – was father to the kid she was expecting. Another guy told me that she really couldn't say that, because he'd been with her the evening after.

The funny thing is that those girls who've run around with just about any and everybody get hold of the best guys, the ones who are studying or who have permanent jobs. It's something Jannicka and I have often discussed, that the girls who have been worst get hold of the best guys.

I didn't get any percentage on food or other things when I worked at the store. On the other hand, I got a discount on bigger articles down at the Hakon Company. The first thing I bought was a tape-recorder for 443 kronor. In the radio stores it cost 600 kronor. The next thing I bought was a sewing machine. And a refrigerator, but Dad paid for that.

Then I went on a buying binge for a while. First a whole lot of linens. That's handy to have. My hope chest is so full of things now that I can't get another thing into it. I bought an iron, a stew-pan, knives, forks, and spoons, cups and table-clothes, towels and all sorts of things. I spent all my money.

I haven't been buying all these things with marriage in mind. I'll need them for when I move away from home. You can't live at home all your life. But it's almost impossible to get hold of your own little place. It's expensive too, if you have to pay for your own food as well as the rent.

However, not all my money has gone for clothes and pleasures. Towards the end of the three years I worked at the store I was earning 1,055 kronor a month. Out of that 300 kronor went to taxes. The union dues were twenty-four a month.

I paid Dad a hundred kronor a month for food and rent, until I started taking driving lessons a couple of years back. Each driving lesson of forty-five minutes cost twenty-four kronor. Together with theory and all, doctor's examination and so on, my licence cost almost 800 kronor.

Dad then said that I could live at home free of charge, since I helped a lot in the house. But I pay for the gasoline when I borrow his car.

Jannicka and I borrow it quite a lot in the evenings and drive out to the café on Björnö or the gas station in Irsta to get a bite to eat and chat with the guys.

In summer we usually drive to Kärrbo and swim by Lindö Pier. I never swim anywhere else. The water isn't muddy and sickening like it is at Björnö. I haven't been swimming there for several years. The city has now made a fine place for swimming down by Lögarängen, but it's always so crowded with people.

In September 1968 I started at Asea. I guess everybody here in Västerås has worked there at least once in their lives. I don't know how many thousands there are who work out there, but certainly a third of all Västerås must make a living out of Asea. So it's Asea who has the say in this city.

I sit at a machine and assemble fine wires. They're called conductors. You get to learn a job like this the first day you're there. It pays well. I make seven to eight kronor on average and up to 8·90 kronor on piece-work. That's much more than I earned as a clerk in a store. I nearly had a heart attack when I got my first pay envelope, it was so much. When taxes are deducted I get about 375 kronor on the fifteenth and about 500 kronor on the last of every month.

However, there's no future in it. You don't want to keep on doing a job like that all your life. We may soon go on shift-work too, which is no fun.

My God, I really regret that I didn't go on to junior high after grade school. That is to say, if I had got in – it's not certain I would have been accepted even if I'd applied.

My vocational guidance teacher told me to go on studying, otherwise I'd regret it later. 'No-o-oo, I won't,' I said. You got so fed-up with school. It ought to be set up so that you can work a few years and then start studying again later on.

I've applied several times to the School of Practical Nursing to become a nurse's assistant at the hospital. The first time I applied there was in the fall of 1967. They told me they were full up. The other times I've been notified that I'm on their waiting list.

There are so many who apply there. At the present there's a great shortage of jobs, and it's worse for the young people. It's worst of all for the young girls. I know a lot of young kids who go bumming around town all day without anything to do.

If you look at the ads. in the paper, you'll see that there are only cleaning jobs available. A pal of mine went to the employment office to see what they had. There were long lists of job openings, but only for cleaning women and maids.

I was up at the hospital in March or April 1968, thinking that at least I could get a temporary job there. But the line in the waiting-room was so long that it took nearly two hours before I got into the employment office. And there was nothing doing there – they had loads of applications for every single job.

But woe to the one who gives up. I want to get in somewhere in the nursing business. It's much more interesting than standing in a store or sitting at a machine. Perseverance wins the day, I'll make it in the end.

The first guy I was really serious with was named Affe. The second was named Uffe. He and I went on vacation in his car to Norway. I was going to driving school when I met him, and he said if I passed my test, he'd buy a car. He did too, a big second-hand Studebaker.

We drove together with his parents first to Östersund, where they had lived before they came to Västerås. and then over to Norway to do some fishing. I dig fishing, all four of us did.

The first few nights we camped – family style, so to speak – in two tents. Then it started to rain like hell so we rented a cottage. We drove from Östersund up to Gäddede and over in that direction to Namsos and Namskoga.

We spent one and a half weeks in Norway. We also went to see Uffe's aunt and uncle and cousins. They lived just outside a small village.

God, how beautiful it was up there with the snow on the mountain tops and the greenery down below in the valleys. We camped near the snow up on Stenfjället but, damn it, it was cold, only 2° C in the morning. Anyway, we didn't have mosquitoes. They froze to death.

The people there were swell, much simpler than here, easier to come into contact with and talk to. Here in Västerås you can meet folks every single day without them ever speaking or saying hi or anything. They just put their noses in the air and walk on by.

Uffe and I always pooled our money. There were a lot of really neat clothes up there and I wanted to buy a lot, but he kept saying that that one and that one and that one was too expensive, which was just as well, actually, for otherwise I'd

have spent a great deal of money. The auto used a lot of gas, which we had to save up for.

When we came home Uffe and his parents moved to Stockholm and got jobs there. He used to come here Saturday and Sunday to see me. His sister lives nearby here. He came by train since he didn't have a licence.

I had the car weekdays, and Jannicka and I used to be out in it evenings. She worked as a maid then, and the family she was with had a summer cottage down in Harkie in Kärrbo. I used to pick her up there and I drove her home again when we'd go out driving. A lot of money went for gas, of course, it's twenty kilometres from here to Harkie.

When Uffe used to come to visit me here, we were hardly ever alone for a single evening. His pals always had to be in the car. It was packed with people and I had to do the driving. I got sick of that.

One Saturday we had a fight. I told him he could come home and pick up his clothes and get out. He just said, 'Oh,' and wondered what the matter was. So I told him I wanted to be free.

A few evenings later he came here and wanted to make up. But I wouldn't. If it weren't for that old car, it might have lasted longer. That's what spoiled it all.

More about Penguins and Pelicans

Penguinews, which appears every month, contains details of all the new books issued by Penguins as they are published. From time to time it is supplemented by *Penguins in Print*, which is a complete list of all available books published by Penguins. (There are well over three thousand of these.)

A specimen copy of *Penguinews* will be sent to you free on request, and you can become a subscriber for the price of the postage. For a year's issues (including the complete lists) please send 30p if you live in the United Kingdom, or 60p if you live elsewhere. Just write to Dept EP, Penguin Books Ltd, Harmondsworth, Middlesex, enclosing a cheque or postal order, and your name will be added to the mailing list.

Note: *Penguinews* and *Penguins in Print* are not available in the U.S.A. or Canada